REVIVAL AND REFORM IN ISLAM

Related titles published by Oneworld

City of Wrong, Kamel Hussein, ISBN 1–85168–072–1
Common Prayer, A Muslim–Christian Spiritual Anthology, Cragg (ed.), ISBN 1–85168–181–7
Companion to the Qur'an, Watt, ISBN 1–85168–036–5
Defenders of Reason in Islam: Mu'tazilism from Medieval School to Modern Symbol, Martin, Woodward and Atmaja, ISBN 1–85168–147–7
The Event of the Qur'an: Islam in its Scripture, Cragg, ISBN 1–85168–067–5
The Faith and Practice of Al-Ghazálí, Watt, ISBN 1–85168–062–4
The Formative Period of Islamic Thought, Watt, ISBN 1–85168–152–3
The Heritage of Sufism, ed. Lewisohn et al, Volume I, *Classical Persian Sufism from its Origins to Rumi (700–1300)*, ISBN 1–85168–188–4; Volume II, *The Legacy of Medieval Persian Sufism (1150–1500)*, ISBN 1–85168–189–2; Volume III, *Late Classical Persianate Sufism (1501–1750)*, ISBN 1–85168–193–0
Islam: A Short History, Watt, ISBN 1–85168–205–8
Islam and the West, Daniel, ISBN 1–85168–129–9
Jesus and the Muslim, Cragg, ISBN 1–85168–180–9
Jesus in the Qur'an, Parrinder, ISBN 1–85168–094–2
Muhammad: A Short Biography, Forward, ISBN 1–85168–131–0
Muhammad and the Christian, Cragg, ISBN 1–85168–179–5
Muslims and Christians Face to Face, Zebiri, ISBN 1–85168–133–7
Muslim Devotions, Padwick, ISBN 1–85168–115–9
On Being a Muslim, Esack, ISBN 1–85168–146–9
The Qur'an and its Exegesis, Gätje, ISBN 1–85168–118–3
Qur'an, Liberation and Pluralism, Esack, ISBN 1–85168–121–3
Rabi'a, Smith, ISBN 1–85168–085–3
Revival and Reform in Islam: A Study of Islamic Fundamentalism, Rahman, ISBN 1–85168–204–X
Rumi: Past and Present, East and West, Lewis, ISBN 1–85168–167–1
Rumi: Poet and Mystic, Nicholson, ISBN 1–85168–096–9
A Short Introduction to Islamic Philosophy, Theology and Mysticism, Fakhry, ISBN 1–85168–134–5
Tales of Mystic Meaning, Nicholson, ISBN 1–85168–097–7
What Muslims Believe, Bowker, ISBN 1–85168–169–8

REVIVAL AND REFORM IN ISLAM

A Study of Islamic Fundamentalism

FAZLUR RAHMAN

Edited and with an Introduction by

EBRAHIM MOOSA

ONEWORLD
OXFORD

In memory of my late husband Fazlur Rahman.
Fondly remembered by Bilqis Rahman and the children.

REVIVAL AND REFORM IN ISLAM

Oneworld Publications
(Sales and Editorial)
185 Banbury Road
Oxford OX2 7AR
England
http://www.oneworld-publications.com

Oneworld Publications
(US Marketing Office)
160 N. Washington St.
4th floor, Boston
MA 02114
USA

A CIP record for this title is available
from the British Library

ISBN 1–85168–204–X

Cover design by Design Deluxe
Typeset by LaserScript, Mitcham, UK
Printed and bound in England by Clays Ltd, St Ives plc

CONTENTS

EDITOR'S NOTE

Posthumous publishing is always a hazardous task, and thus editors of such published work must be prepared to take the risks involved. At the time of his death the Pakistani scholar Fazlur Rahman (1919–1988) had partly completed a draft of a book entitled "Revival and Reform: A Study in Islamic Fundamentalism." The author got as far as five chapters that covered the early history of Islam and some of the major epoch-making figures in the history of Islamic revival. Life did not permit him to complete his commentary on the section dealing with modern fundamentalism as he wished. Some critics may argue that it may have been best if the incomplete book was never published. Others may appreciate Fazlur Rahman's last thoughts. Despite my hesitation, I was encouraged by the fact that several of the late author's friends and students were eager to see this volume published. In particular Fazlur Rahman's wife, Mrs Bilqis Rahman, was supportive of the idea of publication. After her husband died, she placed this manuscript in the custody of Professor John Woods, director of the Center for Middle Eastern Studies and a colleague of Fazlur Rahman at the University of Chicago.

Although I was not a student of Fazlur Rahman in the formal sense, I consider myself among those who benefited tremendously from his writings and ideas. Thus, when as a visiting South African fellow at the University of Chicago in 1990, Professor Woods showed me this manuscript, I immediately expressed an interest in examining it. For anyone familiar with Fazlur Rahman's major and important works such as *Avicenna's Psychology*, *Islam*, *Islamic Methodology in History*, *Major Themes of the*

Qur'an, and *Islam and Modernity* it was exciting to read the materials that now constitute this book. The already published works of the late author shaped his oeuvre and constituted the main template for his interpretation of developments within Islamic thought. Revival and reform was a theme Fazlur Rahman ceaselessly pursued and it defined his later intellectual project. Therefore, students of Fazlur Rahman's thought will find that in this volume he revisits some of those figures and ideas in detail that he otherwise briefly treated in his many scholarly essays and books.

The manuscript itself appeared to be a first draft. Fazlur Rahman was afflicted with arthritis in his hands, which made writing difficult. The author's son transcribed the recorded manuscript. One of the main issues this editor had to contend with was the fact that the sentences in the text were long and speech-style. At times a single sentence constituted a paragraph. For this reason editing was necessary in places. With the exception of a few sources cited in the text, none of the citations had references. All the citations were laboriously traced and checked to ensure that the translations and sources were accurate. While this was at times extremely frustrating and time consuming, in the end it was also rewarding to pore over the sources that this extraordinary thinker marshaled in his research.

ACKNOWLEDGMENTS

At various stages of this project many people have encouraged and assisted me. My thanks go to Professor John Woods and Mrs Rahman who were gracious in entrusting me with the editorship of this manuscript. At the University of Cape Town, I would like to thank my research assistants Abdirashid Mohamed, Abdelkader Riyadi, and Tahir Sitoto; Ms Asia Brey, the departmental assistant at the time, provided selfless support and assistance. At Stanford University, Sayema Hameed and Hamed Saeed also provided some help. Professor Wan Mohamed Nur Wan Daud and Dr Muhammad Zainiy Uthman at the International Institute of Islamic Thought and Civilization (ISTAC), and Professor Mercia Hermansen of the University of Layola (Chicago) all provided some clues in tracing a few references. Professor Amina Wadud provided helpful comments on the introduction and genuine support. Mary Starkey's incisive and highly professional editorial skills saved me from several infelicities. Special words of thanks to all of my friends whose encouragement and support over the years cannot go unacknowledged: Abdurrashid Omar, Abdulkader Tayob, Chuck Wanamaker, Shamiel Jeppie, Sa^{c}diyya Shaikh, Farid Esack, Muhammad Saeed Kajie, Ashraf Mohamed, Abdul Aleem Somers, Richard Martin, Bruce Lawrence, Abdulaziz Sachedina, Muneer Fareed, Ahmad Manjra, Ismail Manjra, Shuaib Manjra, Faizel Dawjee, and Mahmood Mamdani.

I have special thanks for a person to whom I have grown close in friendship over the years. Robert C. Gregg, Teresa Hihn Moore Professor in Religious Studies and former dean of Stanford Memorial Church, was instrumental in making my first and subsequent visits to Stanford University possible. Arnie Eisen, Chair of Religious Studies and his colleagues at Stanford were supportive during my year as visiting professor in 1998–1999 during which most of this editorial work took place. Richard Roberts at Stanford history department was always at hand to offer advice and explore avenues for which I am grateful. Finally, my appreciation to my extended family: my parents, Isḥāq and Ḥūrī; my brothers and sisters Suleiman, Aisha, Nazeema, Faizel, and Zaiboenisa; my in-laws Goolam and Farida Pandit; my wife Fahimoenisa (Nisa) and our children Lamyā and Shibli; my uncle Mohammad and his wife Zayboenisa for all their care over the years; to all of them I want to acknowledge my gratitude for their love and care and for making my life meaningful. I am very much in debt to all of them.

Ebrahim Moosa
Stanford, 1999

INTRODUCTION

Ebrahim Moosa

Biography of Fazlur Rahman[1]

Fazlur Rahman was born on September 21, 1919 to the Malak family in the Hazara district in pre-partition India, now part of Pakistan. He died on July 26, 1988 in Chicago, Illinois. His family's religious roots can be traced to the teachings of the Deoband seminary that has broad influence on the Indian Subcontinent.[2] His father, Mawlānā Shihāb al-Dīn, was a graduate from the famous Indian seminary Dār al-ᶜUlūm Deoband. At Deoband, Shihāb al-Dīn studied with some of the great luminaries of that seminary. Among them were Mawlānā Maḥmūd ul-Ḥasan (d. 1920), better known as "Shaykh al-Hind" and the renowned jurist (*faqīh*) and Ṣūfī mentor Mawlānā Rashīd Aḥmad Gangohī (d. 1905). Although Fazlur Rahman did not study at a traditional *dār al-ᶜulūm*, he mastered the dars-e-Niẓāmī curriculum offered in such institutions in private studies with his father. This provided him with a background in traditional Islamic knowledge with a special emphasis on law (*fiqh*), dialectical theology (*ᶜilm al-kalām*), prophetic traditions (*ḥadīth*), Qurᵓān exegesis (*tafsīr*), logic (*manṭiq*), and philosophy (*falsafa*). After these initial studies he attended Punjab University in Lahore where he graduated with distinction in Arabic and later also acquired an M.A. degree. In 1946, he went to Oxford where he prepared a dissertation on Ibn Sīnā's psychology under the

1. I will use the name Fazlur Rahman in full without diacritics. Fazlur Rahman was his first name. The late author did not use his family name, which is Malak, since it was not customary to do so in the Indo-Pakistan Subcontinent. In the West the second part of his first name, Rahman, became the equivalent of his family name. In the bibliography, he is listed under Rahman.
2. See Metcalf, *Islamic Revival*.

supervision of Professor Simon van den Bergh. The dissertation was a translation, critical edition, and commentary on a section of the *Kitāb al-Najāt* of the famous eleventh-century Muslim philosopher.[3] After Oxford he taught Persian and Islamic philosophy at Durham University from 1950 to 1958. He left England to become associate professor in Islamic Studies at the Institute of Islamic Studies at Canada's McGill University in Montreal.

After three years in Canada, Fazlur Rahman embarked on one of his life's most ambitious projects, which also was an experience that would later become a turning-point in his career. Pakistan under General Ayyub Khan embarked on a renewed effort at state formation. In Khan's view one of the elements for the revival of the country's national spirit was to initiate political and legal reforms. The reforms were intended to bring the country closer to its *raison d'être*, as a state with an Islamic vision and ideals. Fazlur Rahman's own enthusiasm for this project can be judged from the fact that he left a secure and comfortable academic career in Canada for the challenges of Pakistan. At the newly formed Central Institute of Islamic Research, he first became a visiting professor and later director over a seven-year period from 1961 to 1968. As director of the Institute he also served on the Advisory Council of Islamic Ideology, a supreme policy-making body. While these important positions gave him an opportunity to observe the running of government and the machinations of power from a very close proximity, it also turned out to be the most tumultuous period in his life. In this vital position he had to play the role of a philosopher-king. He came face to face with the hard realities and complex intellectual and political problems affecting religion and society in Pakistan. Together with the resources of the Institute of Islamic Research he had to propose policies to the Advisory Council for implementation by government.

The policy side of his job was open to public scrutiny and this meant that his ideas and proposals often became entangled with power and politics. Thus, Fazlur Rahman's intellectual labor in the service of social reform was drawn into the messy political fray of Pakistan in the 1960's. Like Ibn Sīnā, his intellectual soul-mate, Fazlur Rahman had to contend with the constant threat of politics and power affecting his intellectual work. Although eager to reform society, political patrons such as Ayyub Khan invariably had to

3. Fazlur Rahman, *Avicenna's Psychology*.

balance their ideals with a good dose of political discretion. Political parties and religious groups that were opposed to Ayyub Khan's government knew that one way to frustrate the government's reformist orientation was to target the main ideological architect of reform, Fazlur Rahman, as the object of criticism and demonization. Very soon Khan's opponents turned every controversial issue proposed by the government into a charged political debate with a focus on the director of the Institute.[4] Some of the critical legal and religious issues Fazlur Rahman became involved in included the status of bank interest, *zakāt* (the compulsory religious tax), mechanical slaughter of animals, family law and family planning, the authority of prophetic reports (*ḥadīth*) and prophetic practice (*Sunna*), and the nature of revelation. After a turbulent period that adversely affected his health and his leadership role at the Institute and in the Advisory Council, Fazlur Rahman resigned.[5] After a short spell as visiting professor at the University of California, Los Angeles, he was, in the spring of 1969, appointed as professor of Islamic thought at the University of Chicago in the fall of 1969. In 1986 he was named Harold H. Swift Distinguished Service Professor at Chicago, a title he held until his death in 1988.

His Legacy

Few people will hesitate to include Fazlur Rahman among the leading scholars of Islam in the latter part of the twentieth century. He will be remembered for his sharp and incisive mind, prodigious memory, and unique ability to synthesize complex issues into a coherent narrative. In addition, he was also courageous and outspoken in his views, unable to suppress his convictions given his principled commitment to the "truth." "At the level of intellectual discussion," he said, "I did not, and do not believe in compromises extraneously motivated, such as is the case with

4. Fazlur Rahman, "Some Issues," pp. 284–302.
5. The controversies reached a high point after sections of Fazlur Rahman's book *Islam* were translated into Urdu. After such publications charges that he denied the uncreated and divine nature of the Qur᾽ān were leveled at him. This was after he asserted that the issue of the nature of revelation was a more complex issue than the version commonly stated by Muslim dogmatists. Following the public outcry against him, he tried in a joint press conference with the Law Minister of Pakistan, Mr. S. M. Ẓafar, to explain the folly of the charges leveled at him. So charged was the situation that while the Minister categorically stated his support for Fazlur Rahman and that he found "nothing objectionable" during the press conference, afterwards he instructed pressmen "to remove the 'no objection' sentence from his statement." For the politicians it was clearly a clash of interests: politics vs. principles. The cumulative effect of these controversies resulted in Fazlur Rahman being exposed to bear the brunt of vicious verbal attacks orchestrated by reckless and petty-minded conservative elements in Pakistan. See Fazlur Rahman, "Some Issues," p. 300.

many intellectuals in Pakistan."[6] In pursuit of freedom he sought out the humanist aspects of Islam. He tirelessly tried to find the proper balance between reason and revelation. And, if there was a price to be paid for his cherished ideals, then he was ready to face such hardships. "In the face of the heavily obscurantist and hypocritical atmosphere in almost all sectors of public life [in Pakistan], an intellectually radical position gave me greater satisfaction as time went on, because it did the work of shock treatment... The results may be uncertain. It may jerk some members of the large segment of educated and committed Muslims into active Islamic re-thinking."[7] As a person who held strong convictions and the author of provocative ideas, Fazlur Rahman was maligned and castigated by the Muslim clerical establishment, neo-revivalist political activists, and political conservatives in Pakistan and wherever their influence extended. Demagogues, of both religious and political stripes, orchestrated campaigns of mass hysteria and protests against him on the pretext that they ostensibly found some of his views and interpretations offensive. The threats against him escalated to the point that there were genuine concerns for his safety and the real possibility of physical harm. In the end, he chose a self-imposed exile for the last nineteen years of his life in the United States. It was in the United States that he found an environment conducive to further his scholarship and to formulate some of his landmark ideas in interpreting modern Islam. As a researcher, he was prolific. As a teacher he is remembered for being kind and caring. The effects of his legacy can be seen in the work of his students and his impact on scholarship in Islamic studies is highly valued. There can be no better tribute to Fazlur Rahman than the words of Wilfred Cantwell Smith, the doyen of Western Islamicists, who said: "He was a person of integrity; a religious man with a brilliant mind using it as part of his religion. He was a moral person; a serious Muslim motivated by deep concern for his culture and his people."[8]

Islamic Modernism

One of the major questions that exercised the mind of Fazlur Rahman, as well as many other twentieth-century Muslim scholars, was: how does Islam as a religious, cultural, political, and ethical heritage deal with a modernizing and rapidly changing world? Modernity was conceived in the

6. Ibid., p. 298.
7. Ibid.
8. Cited in Jesse, "A Modern Muslim Intellectual," p. 15.

Muslim world as a Janus-faced phenomenon. It certainly brought the benefits of technology and science to Muslim societies, but with far-reaching consequences for culture and values. Some societies adopted modernity in a pragmatic manner that resulted in certain unforeseen discontinuities with the historical intellectual tradition. Despite a wide ideological spectrum among modernist Muslim scholars in the nineteenth and twentieth centuries, most shared a common desire to fuse the present with the past in different ways, in order to retain some continuity.

During the first phase of his intellectual career Fazlur Rahman's interest was in Muslim philosophy. Soon he found the philosophers to be clever and excellent in their subtlety of argument, "but their God remained a bloodless principle – a mere intellectual construct, lacking both power and compassion."[9] Thereafter he focused much attention on theology, especially on religious figures that combined their expertise and interests in law with theology and Islamic thought in general, such as al-Ghazālī, Ibn Taymiyya, and Shāh Walī Allāh. Although he thought the theologians less skillful than the philosophers, they were nevertheless instinctively aware that the "God of religion was a full-blooded, living reality who responded to prayers, guided men individually and collectively, and intervened in history."[10]

> Convinced that the Muslim philosophers were headed in the wrong direction, I was "reborn" with a new impulse to understand Islam. But where was that Islam? ... I then realized that although Muslims claim their beliefs, law, and spirituality are "based upon the Qurʾān," the scripture embodying the revelation of the Prophet Muḥammad [570–632], the Qurʾān was never taught by itself in any seat of traditional learning, but always with the aid of commentaries. A study of the Qurʾān itself, together with the life of the Prophet, enabled me to gain fresh insight into its meaning and purpose, making it possible for me to reevaluate my tradition.[11]

In the study of the Qurʾān it was ethics that interested him most. Al-Fārābī (d. 950), Ibn Sīnā (d. 1037), al-Ghazālī (d. 1111), Ibn Taymiyya (d. 1328), Aḥmad Sirhindī (d. 1624), and Shāh Walī Allāh (d. 1762) were his favorite paradigmatic figures. He frequently cited their core ideas in constructing

9. Berman, Fazlur Rahman, "Belief-in-Action," p. 155.
10. Ibid.
11. Ibid.

his own reformist interpretations. Among the modern scholars, he identified with the nineteenth-century reformers such as the itinerant reformer and revolutionary Jamāl al-Dīn al-Afghānī (d. 1897) and his Egyptian disciple and interpreter, Muḥammad Abduh (d. 1905). Indian thinkers with whom he shared an intellectual affinity included Sir Sayyid Aḥmad Khan (d. 1898), the founder of Aligarh Muslim University; Muḥammad Shiblī Nuᶜmānī (d. 1914), a traditionalist-cum-modernist thinker and one of the co-founders of the Nadwatul ᶜUlamāᵓ in Lucknow; and Muḥammad Iqbāl (d. 1938) the renowned poet-philosopher of the Subcontinent. Among the Turkish thinkers he frequently cited Ziya Gökalp (d. 1924) and Nāmik Kemāl (d. 1888).

As director of the Central Institute of Islamic Research, Fazlur Rahman gained crucial insights about the magnitude and challenges that religious and social change posed. From then on this experience would inform and drive his intellectual agenda to find solutions for some of the intractable problems experienced not only in Pakistan, but also elsewhere in the Muslim world. His intellectual quest addressed real-life issues such as economic and political welfare in newly independent Muslim societies. These included in particular the redistribution of wealth and the promotion of education. He was concerned that an education system bereft of a progressive Islamic spirit could run the risk of turning into an atheistic system that "destroys the sanctity and universality (transcendence) of all moral values."[12] In order to avert such grotesque consequences, he embarked on a project to reconstruct the intellectual foundations of Islam in the modern age.

Revival and Reform

Revival and reform was therefore a central theme in Fazlur Rahman's scheme of thought. The categories of *tajdīd* (renewal) and *ijtihād* (independent thinking) would qualify as the key elements under the rubric of re-thinking Islam.[13] His primary concern was to prepare the ground for such re-thinking that would gradually be realized by means of education. One of the most neglected areas of educational reform, in his view, was the traditionalist–conservative educational system of the ᶜulamāᵓ. This sector of Muslim society resisted the changes brought about by cultural and

12. Fazlur Rahman, *Islam and Modernity*, p. 15.
13. See Mūsā, "al-Ḥadātha wa ᵓl-Tajdīd," pp. 109–114.

intellectual modernity. Fazlur Rahman and others thought that such resistance was at the expense of Muslim societies at large because it resulted in the Muslim world lagging behind other contemporary societies that were advancing in economic, political, and scientific spheres. Religious leaders (ʿulamāʾ) produced by the traditional educational systems, especially in the Sunnī world, but also possibly true of the Shīʿī world, could neither fulfill socially relevant functions nor give guidance to the modern educated sector. Fazlur Rahman admired and respected the sophisticated intellectual tradition that the ʿulamāʾ inherited. His complaint however was that the ʿulamāʾ themselves had by and large abandoned important aspects of that legacy, especially critical thought and innovation. This intellectual tradition in its twentieth-century guise was now devoid of its erstwhile depth, diversity, and critical apertures. What remained was an atrophied and skeletal tradition that only contributed to stagnation. In fact, he charged the ʿulamāʾ with having abandoned the most effective aspect of their intellectual legacy: to engage in reform and creatively address new challenges.[14] For this reason he hardly strayed from the fundamental building-blocks of the traditional Islamic intellectual legacy. It could be revived, renewed, and updated, he believed, with the aid of serious scholarship, even though he would appear to be radical in his critique of the selfsame system. If reformed this renewed intellectual tradition could become the basis for Islamic revival which would inform those social movements in the Muslim world that had an ethical and activist agenda. Where he differed from figures such as Abū ʾl-Aʿlā Mawdūdī of Pakistan or the Ayatullāh Rūḥullāh Khumaynī of Iran, of whom he was very critical, was that their social movements were based on rage and anger.

A precondition for any social activism was that "patient and complex intellectual labor, which must produce the necessary Islamic vision," must accompany it.[15] He had in mind the project of someone such as Shāh Walī Allāh whose intellectual legacy provided Muslim India with an impressive, dynamic, and variegated intellectual movement for nearly two centuries. Genuine leaders of the Muslim community, Fazlur Rahman believed, would be identifiable by their vision. An intellectual and ethico-spiritual leaven must of necessity temper this vision. This he found in figures such

14. Fazlur Rahman, "Modern Thought in Islam," pp. 91–92.
15. Fazlur Rahman, "Roots," p. 25.

as al-Ghazālī in the twelfth-century and Ibn Taymiyya in the fourteenth-century. What appealed to him was the intellectual renaissance, rather than the specific ideas, pioneered by such intellectuals and the consequent impact this had on social change. Primary and tertiary educational institutions had to foster such a vision and provide the maximum opportunity for intellectual growth and nourishment. A prerequisite was that education should be unencumbered by the concerns of dogma and imaginary fears about change. In this regard the role of science, the social sciences, and the humanities were all indispensable aspects to such envisaged intellectual reform. He identified the main problem in education as a "lack of creative synthesis and of an organic relationship between the traditional-religious and the modern-secular. The institutions of traditional and modern learning are for the most part brutally juxtaposed, and produce two types of people who can hardly communicate with each other."[16]

The existing educational system that reproduced the ᶜulamāᵓ was, in his view, in need of radical surgery. Therefore, he urged the ᶜulamāᵓ not to resist change by equating their self-interest of power and control with the intellectual traditions of Islam. He felt that such an approach was a vulgarization of a respectable intellectual tradition that was second to none. For this reason he urged various societies, from Indonesia to Turkey, with whom he had contact, to redirect their energies in rehabilitating the ᶜulamāᵓ tradition by proposing changes to their syllabi at the various training institutions. He thought that if such educational adjustments were realized, it might well be that future generations of Muslims could become active agents in the modern world.

It was in the context of revival and reform that Fazlur Rahman encountered the phenomenon called "Islamic fundamentalism." While many writers hesitated to use this media-coined term, he was not averse to employing it. For him this was an opportunity to explore and revisit the intersection of theology and politics in the formative and post-formative periods of Islam. This book, *Revival and Reform*, is one such effort. Time denied its author the opportunity to comment on modern Islamic fundamentalism. At first it may not be clear how in this book the author intends to employ the historical narrative that he sketches. His primary goal, in my view, was to demonstrate that at various intervals in history, the disciplines of law and political philosophy lost their connection with the

16. Ibid., p. 30.

ethics of the Qurʾān. The ethical imperative of the Qurʾān during the formative and post-formative periods of Islam was subjugated to several other overriding concerns such as power, the creation of a community (*umma*), and the maintenance of an Islamic political order. The loss of ethics in political philosophy and law was only partially restored by the discourses of Ṣūfism. The restoration of ethics occurred when some jurists, such as al-Ghazālī and ᶜIzz al-Dīn Ibn ᶜAbd al-Salām, took recourse to Ṣūfī piety. In such instances also it only partially affects change. Most jurists in practice maintained a boundary between personal piety and their profession of law. His most damning charge in the book presented to the reader is directed at Ashᶜarī–Sunnī thought. Despite its influence in the Muslim world, right until the present, Fazlur Rahman believed that Ashᶜarism succumbed to the twin evils of a theology of predestination and a suspension of ethical judgment (*irjāʾ*). He repeatedly highlights the negative effects of *irjāʾ* in Muslim theory and practice.

Qurʾān and Hermeneutics

One thing that puzzled Fazlur Rahman, to a point nearing incredulity, was why past Muslim thinkers did not make the Qurʾān the primary source for ethics in Islam. If so, this would have provided the legal, political, and other crucial discourses with a sense of consistency. "One cannot point to a single work of ethics squarely based upon the Qurʾān, although there are numerous works based upon Greek philosophy, Persian tradition and Ṣūfī piety," he claimed.[17] Given this vacuum there was a need to "elaborate an ethics on the basis of the Qurʾān, for without an explicitly formulated ethical system, one can never do justice to Islamic law ... Law has to be worked out *from* the ethical systematization of the teaching of the Qurʾān and the *uswa* (*sunna*) of the Prophet, with due regard to the situation currently obtaining."[18] Thus in his *Major Themes of the Qurʾān* and *Islam and Modernity* as well as dozens of essays dealing with diverse topics ranging from contemporary Muslim politics to medicine, Fazlur Rahman ceaselessly explicated a Qurʾān-centered ethics. He later construed this as a proposal towards formulating a Qurʾānic hermeneutic. In *Islamic Methodology in History* he demonstrated with great skill and insight the absence of a Qurʾān-based ethics in Muslim thought. There he showed how

17. Fazlur Rahman, *Islam*, p. 257.
18. Ibid., p. 256.

revealed authority – the Qurʾān and Sunna – were mediated by preexisting historical and cultural realities in those societies in which Islam spread. This interaction between society and the new revelation bolstered Fazlur Rahman's claim that revelation was always mediated by the prevailing historical conditions. The dialogic of hermeneutics (interpretation of revelation) and history (social context) was a very complex and intricate relationship. This strategy was also both his shield and sword. On the one hand it showed how revelation was open to history. On the other hand, he would use the Qurʾān as the normative standard to exclude those local traditions and parochial values and practices that impeded or conflicted with the norms derived from the Qurʾān and the Sunna. Practices that did not advance the vision of Muslim society became an obstacle to human progress. For this reason he argued that "while traditions are valuable for living religions in that they provide matrices for the creative activity of great minds and spirits, they are also entities that *ipso facto* isolate that tradition from the rest of humanity. Consequently, I am of the belief that all religious traditions need constant revitalization and reform."[19] In this respect he was very much a modernist who believed in the universality of values and who would not bow to relativity. The effect of Fazlur Rahman's hermeneutic serves to legitimize and delegitimize certain aspects of the past and present by presenting the totality of the Qurʾān-centered hermeneutic as the privileged source of Islamic teachings. Broadly speaking his approach was no different from that of Ibn Taymiyya, Muḥammad b. ʿAlī al- Shawkānī (d. 1834) of Yemen, and Shāh Walī Allāh, who also emphasized the centrality of the Qurʾān.

He was inspired by, if not enamored of, those pre-modern social-reform movements that attempted to revive the meaning and relevance of Qurʾān-centered norms in every age. These were the "fundamentalist–traditionalist–conservative" pre-modern groups that revolted against an interpretation of the Qurʾān that was driven by parochial traditions, as opposed to an interpretation that relied primarily on an inter-textual Qurʾānic hermeneutic.[20] In his vocabulary, a genuine "fundamentalist" was a person who was committed to a project of reconstruction or re-thinking. Such a person must recognize that one lived in a "new age" and with honesty, as well as with both intellect and faith, encounter the message of the Qurʾān through

19. Ibid.
20. Fazlur Rahman, "Roots," p. 32.

the mirror of that historical moment. Even though he showed great admiration for al-Ghazālī at an earlier stage of his life, later on he tended to agree with Ibn Taymiyya that al-Ghazālī lacked the requisite depth of knowledge of the Qurʾān and the prophetic tradition.[21] While Ibn Taymiyya is known for his exaggerated claims and judgments, it is even more surprising to find Fazlur Rahman unconditionally endorsing his verdict on al-Ghazālī. This possibly explains Fazlur Rahman's own enthusiasm, if not zealousness, to retrieve the Qurʾān. Therefore this book, *Revival and Reform*, must be seen as a continuation of the author's project of developing a Qurʾānic hermeneutic.

Fazlur Rahman's Qurʾān-centered hermeneutic is based on two pillars: firstly, a theory of prophecy and the nature of revelation, and secondly, an understanding of history. Both components constitute his general hermeneutic of the Qurʾān. While the notion of revelation is not very explicit, it is a fundamental assumption in his hermeneutic, and ignoring it can result in misreading his contribution to modern Qurʾān studies. It is also a radical departure from the unsatisfactory Sunnī orthodox explanation of revelation. In brief, the traditional orthodox theory stated that the Prophet Muḥammad received revelation via the agency of the archangel Gabriel on every occasion. This was accompanied by a belief that such revelation was totally and absolutely from God. In a bid to retain the objectivity of the revelation, doctrinal correctness required that a view be projected that the Qurʾān was exclusively from the "other" (God). The Prophet's own role as recipient of the revelation, namely his subjectivity, therefore was not accounted for in the orthodox theory. Dogma said the Qurʾān was not only the very word of God, the *ipsissima verba*, but it was also the "uncreated" and eternal word of God stemming from His eternal attribute of knowledge. In the ninth century, this doctrine was challenged on the grounds of dialectical theology (*ʿilm al-kalām*) by the rationalist–pietist group called the Muʿtazilīs who believed that the Qurʾān was created. They believed that only God's essence was eternal and none of his attributes enjoyed this status of eternity. For the Muʿtazilīs it was impossible for the Qurʾān to be the uncreated word of God. Such an assertion, in their view, implied that the Qurʾān was co-eternal with God, a notion that was an anathema to their monotheistic sensibilities. Aḥmad b. Ḥanbal (d. 241/855) and his followers, the Ḥanbalīs, as well as Abū ʾl-Ḥasan

21. Fazlur Rahman, "Islamization," p. 9.

al-Ashʿarī (d. 324/935–6) and the Ashʿarīs who followed him, opposed the Muʿtazilī view. This conflict over an "uncreated" Qurʾān turned into a schismatic division, with the Ḥanbalīs and Ashʿarīs opposed to the Muʿtazilīs. Later Ashʿarīs desperately defended this doctrine with hairsplitting theological arguments. They suggested that the eternal Qurʾān was not so much the physical text in the form of a script, but rather an "inner speech" (*al-kalam al-nafsī*), an indivisible mental act of God. They conceded that the physical Qurʾān on ink and paper and in the Arabic language was created. The socio-political implications of this rather "strange" theological contest, to use the words of Gibb, and its impact on Qurʾān interpretation in the formative period of Islamic thought, requires further exploration.[22]

The Ashʿarī defence of a very crude Ḥanbalī position produced a doctrine of an eternal and uncreated divine speech that was "similar" (*tashbīh*) to the material Qurʾān. The Muʿtazilīs in turn, insisted that the divine attributes, and therefore the Qurʾān, were incomparable (*tanzīh*) in human terms. This polemic prefigures elements of two theological tendencies: Ashʿarī theocentrism and Muʿtazilī humanism. Ashʿarī dialectical theology tended towards certain forms of fideism. The latter had implications for the role of history and by inference on the place and role of revelation. Muʿtazilī humanism, in turn, did not have a sense of history although it did acknowledge a form of evolutionism. To the modern scholar of the Qurʾān the significance of this debate may not be self-evident. It discloses very different, and possibly antithetical, sets of metaphysical assumptions. Muʿtazilī doctrine understood that the Qurʾān was the truth from God. However, in the absence of revelation the truth in itself was still accessible via reason, extra-Qurʾānically. Primary moral values were essentially extra-Qurʾānic. Nevertheless, the Qurʾān confirmed and reinforced primary values by means of second-order rules that were contained in the revelation, such as the broad range of ordinances affecting human transactions. Thus rules regarding marriage, trade, war, inheritance, and a plethora of other teachings in the Qurʾān were practices that underscored the primary values such as justice, fairness, and avoidance of wrongdoing among other things.

In the eyes of the Ashʿarīs this proposition was inconceivable. The Qurʾānic values could not be mediated by reason. On the contrary, the

22. See Moosa, "Law as Simulacrum," pp. 1–24 .

injunctions of the Qurʾān were premised on a command theory of values, the Ashʿarīs argued. The only interpretation permitted was an intra-textual one by which the entire revelation acquired coherence and consistency. In theory at least, no extra-Qurʾānic referents other than authentic prophetic reports were admitted. If this debate appears to be "strange" then it is precisely because the partisans to this schismatic polemic suppressed the tension inherent within the Muslim notions of revelation, by only emphasizing one dimension. The tension lies in the fact that revelation emanated from a divine and transcendent source but occurs within history and is understood by the human mind. The ferocity of medieval theological conflict neglected this tension between revelation and history.

For modern thinkers such as Fazlur Rahman it was vital to make sense of revelation in historical terms. If history was to make any impact in understanding a transcendent revelation, then it was necessary to explore the interface of revelation with the world. An insistence on the complete "otherness" of the Qurʾān, as orthodoxy required in order to minimize the Prophet's involvement in the revelatory process, was not only historically inaccurate in his view, but also contrary to the Qurʾān itself. Historically, it was difficult to ignore the fact that revelation itself commented on matters that affected the prophet's personal behavior and travails. For instance, the Qurʾān mildly reproaches the Prophet for frowning when one of his Companions, a blind man, arrived unannounced while he was engaged in talks with important Makkan guests (80:1–3). The Qurʾān also tells us that at times the Prophet's interactions with his wives were a cause of his personal unhappiness (33:28). Similarly, he was very anxious that the Makkans, especially members of his own clan, convert to Islam. In one such an instance when he agonizes about the lack of Makkan receptivity to the divine message, revelation informs him that guidance is the prerogative of God. On other occasions he anticipates revelation, such as on the occasion of changing the prayer direction (*qibla*) from Jerusalem to Makka (2:144). These concrete manifestations do suggest that without understanding the Prophet's personal history and his historical context, many sections of the revelation will remain unclear. The Qurʾān explicitly states that Muḥammad's speech was revelation (*waḥī*) that descended on his heart. Revelation was entirely from God and at the same time the locus of revelation was the "heart" of the Prophet where it is vouchsafed in historical time.

Drawing on the early intellectual heritage of Islam, Fazlur Rahman attempted to provide a complex theory of revelation that linked philosophical and psychological arguments with a sociology and anthropology of history. This most critical task must surely remain one of his most ambitious intellectual attempts. His arguments were at times characteristically brief, defensive, and polemical. Indian scholars such as Sirhindī and Shāh Walī Allāh provided him with some insights on which he could build a case for a theory of revelation that went beyond the standard dogmatic account. Sirhindī provided an explanation that added to the standard Ashᶜarī notion of "inner speech" (*al-kalām al-nafsī*).[23] In the eyes of God, Sirhindī said, "the Word of God, is, in truth, one single [mental act]."[24] In its essential and non-manifest perspective, revelation is the unfathomable identity of the Creator. At the manifest level, revelation as a divine mental act appeared in the diverse forms. From the latter perspective the Torah, the New Testatment, and the Qurᵓān are part of the same essence. Shāh Walī Allāh stated that "verbal revelation occurs in the mold of words, idioms and style which are already existent in the mind of Prophet."[25] In another place, Walī Allāh wrote that God

> subdued the mind of the Prophet in such a way, that He sent down the Book of God in the "pure heart" (*ḥajar baḥt*) of the Prophet in a nebulous and undifferentiated manner (*ijmālan*). In the pure heart of the Prophet, the divine speech becomes apparent in the identical form in which it appears in the Supernal Plenum (*ḥazīra-t al-quds*). The Prophet thus comes to know by conviction that this is the Word of God. Subsequently, as the need arises, well-strung speech is brought out of the rational faculties of the Prophet through the agency of the angel.[26]

Influences of the mystic from Muslim Spain Muḥyī al-Dīn Ibn ᶜArabī (d. 638/1240) are apparent in the respective formulations of the various Indian thinkers on the concept of revelation.

Relying on these explanations, Fazlur Rahman argued that revelation was a unique form of cognition in the form of the idea-words that are part of a creative divine act. Past authorities admitted that the Prophet's mind already possessed the words, style, and idioms of revelation. The obvious

23. Fazlur Rahman, "Divine Revelation," p. 66.
24. Ibid.
25. Ibid., p. 67; Shāh Walī Allāh, *Fuyūḍ*, p. 89.
26. Shāh Walī Allāh, *Saṭaᶜāt*, pp. 30-32; also see Fazlur Rahman, "Divine Revelation," p. 67.

conundrum was that the theologians claimed that such revealed words were uncreated, divine, and eternal. The medieval Muslim thinkers, Fazlur Rahman argued, did not rise to the occasion. They failed to suggest succinctly in one comprehensive theory that the Qur᾿ān was a combination of divinely revealed idea-words, which were conveyed to humanity in the Prophet's sound-words. In his words: "Indeed, all medieval thought lacked the necessary intellectual tools to combine in its formulation of the dogma the otherness and verbal character of the Revelation on the one hand, and its intimate connection with the work and the religious personality of the Prophet on the other, i.e. it lacked the intellectual capacity to say both that the Qur᾿ān is entirely the word of God and, in an ordinary sense, also entirely the word of Muhammad."[27] In making the latter claim, Fazlur Rahman surprised the ᶜulamā᾿ of the Indian Subcontinent, especially those in Pakistan, with a new reading of an intellectual tradition to which they claimed affinity but failed to appreciate. They in turn mobilized large-scale public demonstrations and protests against his allegedly heretical views. To his own detriment, Fazlur Rahman did not make the detailed argument derived from Sirhindī and Shāh Walī Allāh in his book *Islam*, where he gave the argument in summary form. This summary statement was taken out of context and no amount of contextualizing or citation of authorities could quell the mood of the demagogues.

This complex, albeit embryonic, notion of revelation becomes the backdrop of his theory of Qur᾿ān interpretation, called the "double movement" theory.[28] The interaction between divine revelation and history remains a central theme. The question can be put differently. How do the norms and values of revelation have an enduring relevance to religious communities without becoming anachronistic? The first movement of this double-movement theory is to study both the micro and macro context in which the Qur᾿ān was first revealed. This would establish the original meaning of revelation within the moral–social context of the prophetic society as well as the broader picture of the world at large at that time. Such an investigation must then yield a coherent Qur᾿ānic narrative of the general and systematic principles and values underlying the various normative injunctions. Here the concepts of occasions of revelation (*asbāb al-nuzūl*) and abrogation (*naskh*) among other well-known exegetical

27. Fazlur Rahman, *Islam*, p. 31.
28. Fazlur Rahman, *Islam and Modernity*, pp. 5–7.

techniques come into effect. The second movement entails an attempt to apply those general and systematic values and principles to the context of the contemporary reader of the Qurʾān. Making sense of the second movement, namely the application of retrieved historical values in the present, required a very sophisticated analysis. Fazlur Rahman did not elaborate on the social and intellectual coordinates of this analysis and how it takes place. It does appear that he endorsed the modern social sciences and humanities as being sufficient as tools for this function which can make a contribution by providing a good understanding of history. He certainly did not believe in setting up artificial boundaries between various kinds of knowledge. He opposed the idea of the "Islamization" of knowledge. The latter, in brief, meant that all human and natural science should be studied in such a manner that it does not fail to disclose some revealed metaphysical principle or must by necessity lead to a theomorphic understanding of the self and the universe. Instead, Fazlur Rahman advocated unfettered intellectual exploration free from dogma and cultural limitations. Not unaware of the fact that Muslims are in a confrontation with the West, he asked rhetorically: "Can we confront the West and declare what knowledge is good and what is bad and what is appropriate and what is not appropriate without knowing ourselves?"[29] The main task of intellectual endeavor was to produce "creative knowledge" that would only come about once one had internalized the ethical attitude of the Qurʾān on matters of creativity and had generated new knowledge. Evaluating and judging the production of knowledge through critique are not the goals, but only the first steps toward the discovery of new knowledge, he argued.[30] In the end it is the individual Muslim scholar and the Muslim community, he said, that will decide what constitutes an acceptable analysis in the light of their faith. Again, he did not address the process of consensus-building, scholarship, and communities in any detail. He did nevertheless advocate the adoption of a general democratic culture, parliamentary democracy, and modern educational institutions. The Qurʾānic imperatives must find efficacy and application in the new context in which Muslims live.

Fazlur Rahman's construction of a Qurʾānic hermeneutic is a response to the dominant "atomistic" and piecemeal approach of medieval and even

29. Fazlur Rahman, "Islamization," p. 8.
30. Ibid., p. 11.

contemporary traditional exegesis. This approach ignores the coherence and underlying unity of the revelatory message and prevents the generation of a Qurʾānic *Weltanschauung* entirely on its own terms. The high point of the atomistic approach was a dry legalism, but one in which the legal function did not foster an energetic and dynamic legal culture. In the domain of law and ethics the exegetes placed the emphasis on isolated verses that addressed very specific instances. Little attention was given to the general principle underlying several individual verses or themes that were scattered in different parts of the Qurʾān. Without grasping the worldview of the Qurʾān, modern interpreters would not be able to differentiate the past social contexts, mores, and customs that were grafted onto the interpretation of the original revelation. Notwithstanding this idealism, Fazlur Rahman's hermeneutic was concerned with a cognition of the historical facts of revelation and its values. Chief among these concerns was his desire to arrive at a theory for the interpretation of values. "All values," he said, "that are properly moral – and it is these with which we shall be concerned – have also an extra-historical, 'transcendental' being, and their location at a point in history does not exhaust their practical impact or, one might even say, their meaning."[31] The need to anchor revelation in the context of the prophetic society was thus of paramount importance.

In trying to explain the manner in which an intellectual tradition unfolded in history Fazlur Rahman shared the general concerns of Gadamer.[32] The relationship between tradition (in this case a revealed truth) and history remains a challenge to our understanding of intellectual traditions. There is a need to show the movement of tradition, the kinesis at work in it and its dynamic components. Fazlur Rahman is explicit in expressing the need to develop and refine our knowledge of the history of the Islamic disciplines such as law, theology, philosophy, and Ṣūfism. Such studies have no other purpose but to disclose the continuities and discontinuities of tradition. Historical studies allow us to grasp how ideas originated and what role they played in the making of the intellectual tradition. In stating his agenda, Fazlur Rahman wished to show that as a religious tradition, Islam was constructed. For this reason he strongly decried those Muslims who "defend the past as though it were our God"

31. Fazlur Rahman, *Islam and Modernity*, p. 5.
32. See Gadamer, *Truth and Method*.

and criticized those who claimed that the scholars of the past were unsurpassable.[33] His major strength was in explicating the "what" of tradition. To the "how" and "process" of tradition he gave insufficient attention.

Against Gadamer he preferred the views of the Italian jurist-philosopher Emilio Betti (d. 1968), whose hermeneutic theory he explicitly endorsed as being preferable to that of Gadamer. Fazlur Rahman did not engage Betti's ideas and theories. A close examination shows the influence of the Italian scholar on Fazlur Rahman's double-movement theory. Like Betti, and before him Dilthey, Fazlur Rahman accepted the Kantian notion that knowledge is not a passive mirror of reality; its objects are determined by the way we comprehend them. It is well known however, that the "autonomy of reason" as a category has always been under attack from two sides: firstly, from the side of psychologism and sensualism, starting with Hume. On the second side, the existentialists collapse the distinction between phenomenal and ideal objectivity and as a consequence also do not distinguish between intellectual and ethical values. What made Fazlur Rahman prefer Betti was that he recognized that "ethical and aesthetic values belong to a second dimension of objectivity which is neither phenomenal nor any less different from the subjectivity of consciousness than the others ... Spiritual values represent an ideal objectivity that unerringly follows its own lawfulness."[34]

Both Betti and Fazlur Rahman shared the Diltheyan notion of mental objectification. Betti identified interpretation as a triadic process in which the interpreter (subject) apprehends the object. When the interpreter apprehends the meaningful form as an objectification of the mind, it is achieved in such a way that it reproduces the original creative activity of the author. Betti then developed four canons that guide the interpreter in objectively reproducing the original meaning. The first is the canon of the hermeneutical autonomy of the object. This means those meaningful forms "have to be understood in accordance with their own logic of development, their intended connections and in their necessity, coherence and conclusiveness."[35] Meaningful forms, he adds, "should be judged in relation to the standards immanent in the original intention: the intention, that is, which the created forms should correspond to from the point of view

33. Fazlur Rahman, *Islam and Modernity*, p. 147; "Islamization," p. 10.
34. Bleicher, *Contemporary Hermeneutics*, citing Betti, p. 28.
35. Betti, "Die Hermeneutik," p. 58.

of the author and his formative impulse in the course of the creative process."[36] The second canon is the principle of totality, also called the principle of the coherence of meaning. This canon proceeds on the presupposition "that the totality of speech issues from a unitary mind and gravitates towards a unitary mind and meaning ... and on the basis of the correspondence of the processes of creation and interpretation."[37] From this he concluded that "the meaning of the whole has to be derived from its individual elements, and an individual element has to be understood by reference to the comprehensive, penetrating whole of which it is part."[38] The third is the canon of the actuality of understanding. It is here that the interpreter retraces the creative process and reconstructs within herself a part of the past as an "event" into the actuality of her own life. The idea is to integrate such knowledge into one's own "intellectual horizon within the framework of one's own experiences by means of a kind of transformation on the basis of the same kind of synthesis which enabled the recognition and reconstruction of that thought."[39] Betti's fourth canon is called the hermeneutical correspondence of meaning or harmonization where the interpreter deals with subjectivity. In terms of this view the interpreter brings his or her own "actuality into the closest harmony with the stimulation that he [she] receives from the object in such a way that the one and other resonate in a harmonious way."[40]

Given Fazlur Rahman's own predilection for objectivity it is not surprising that he favored Betti instead of Gadamer. His double-movement theory for interpreting the Qurʾān is an abbreviation of Betti's four canons of interpretation into two movements. Of course the theoretical assumptions of Fazlur Rahman's hermeneutic carried a faint echo of the views of the ninth-century Muʿtazila doctrine, especially the relative autonomy of values, which Hourani described as rationalistic objectivism.[41] Rational, objective, and autonomous values that consciousness could discover are characteristic of both Fazlur Rahman and Betti. According to Betti:

> A value is something absolute that has an ideal existence-in-itself as its essence; something that contains the basis for its own validity; an entity

36. Ibid.
37. Ibid., p. 59.
38. Ibid.
39. Ibid., p. 62.
40. Ibid., p. 85.
41. Hourani, *Islamic Rationalism*, p. 10.

> that remains removed from any change and any reduction through subjective arbitrariness – and which nevertheless remains an entity that can be reached by consciousness with the help of a mental structure that transcends the empirical self and incorporates it into a higher cosmos which is shared by those who have acquired the necessary spiritual maturity.[42]

They were both opposed to Gadamer's introduction of subjectivity into the hermeneutic circle. Therefore Fazlur Rahman found Gadamer's premise that our knowledge is fore-structured by our prejudices to be wholly unacceptable.[43] Gadamer's response to Betti, which is also applicable to Fazlur Rahman, was that his goal of philosophical hermeneutics was an attempt to discover what is common to all understanding, how such understanding is possible, and under what conditions. He argued that his project was to understand the ontological dimension of hermeneutics, as the primordial way of all Being. His critics, he said, were in search of a general methodology whose concerns are epistemological. Gadamer also believed that the hermeneutical object and subject unfolds in history, the main difference being that while Betti and Fazlur Rahman placed some distance between the object and subject of interpretation, Gadamer did not.

Fazlur Rahman's argument against Gadamer is that at times radical changes occurred within an intellectual or religious tradition. He cited the example of Christian thinkers such as Augustine, Aquinas, and Luther and among Muslim thinkers, figures such as al-Ghazālī and Ibn Taymiyya. All of these people brought about near-irreversible changes in their respective religious traditions. Such changes, he argued, occurred due to a self-aware and conscious critique on their part that also rejected aspects of the inherited tradition. Fazlur Rahman found Gadamer's claim that such self-aware changes in the tradition in themselves are pre-figured within the closed circuits of history to be untenable. He refused to accept Gadamer's near-mystical determinism of being. Conscious changes, he argued, occur in history if there is an objective ascertaining of the past and an equivalent response that is determined by contemporary values. Fazlur Rahman conceded, however, that Gadamer may have a point in his description of "effective history" as already being part of the conscious act of

42. Bleicher, *Contemporary Hermeneutics*, p. 28.
43. Fazlur Rahman, *Islam and Modernity*, p. 9.

understanding itself. What he could not accept was the overpowering and exclusive effect that Gadamer attributed to historical consciousness. Gadamer argued that the recognition of meaning and then the application of meaning, in other words the cognitive and normative functions of hermeneutics, are not two separate actions, but one process.[44] For Fazlur Rahman these are indeed separate moments.

Behind Fazlur Rahman's theory and disagreement with Gadamer lies the crux of his project. His was a radical project, in that he did not wish to control the flux of history or stabilize it. Rather, he wished to steer and direct the flux of history. "This means," he said, "that the process of questioning and changing a tradition – in the interests of preserving or restoring its normative quality in the case of its normative elements – can continue indefinitely and that there is no fixed or privileged point at which the predetermining effective history is immune from such questioning and then being consciously confirmed or consciously changed."[45] The change he advocated is not coded, tracked, or limited by tradition, but goes against the grain of tradition, if by the latter is meant conservation. His hermeneutic project is an axiology, a concern for constructing new values that are anchored in a left-wing liberal political philosophy, possibly resembling a Rawlsian model. So when Fazlur Rahman talked about a normative moral system, he did not have in mind the persistence of a historical tradition. Normativism to him meant contextual ethics. Here history engages transcendent revelation in order to create a new consciousness and new values for the emerging age. It was also not a static normativism, as much as it was a perpetually unfolding one. Gadamer and Fazlur Rahman agreed that an unchanging and infinite spirit labors beneath the historical transition. Fazlur Rahman, like Gadamer, also believed in the metaphysical distinction between objective meaning and ceaselessly changing expression. At the end, the truth for him was singular. Even though the truth may have multiple or overlapping expressions, it did not necessarily mean a multiplicity of truths. In that sense he was every bit a child of the modern Enlightenment.

Within late twentieth-century Muslim intellectual discourse Fazlur Rahman mapped the process by which human beings could objectify the eternal spirit or the mind of absolute consciousness. In his Qurʾānic

44. Gadamer, *Truth and Method*, p. 276.
45. Fazlur Rahman, *Islam and Modernity*, p. 11.

hermeneutic, one notion that looms large is that of *taqwā*, meaning "piety" or "reverential fear of God" or "consciousness." *Taqwā* is that inner torch that illuminates human character and mind, and provides it with a transcendental compass. He described it as a "mental state of responsibility from which an agent's actions proceed but which recognizes that the criterion of judgment upon them lies outside him."[46] It is also *taqwā* that is both activator of conscious history and the locus from which moral values derive. For this reason he distinguished between two kinds of values, namely historical values and moral values. Historical values include economic and social values that are peculiar to a particular society, a specific socio-economic context, and fall under the constraint of time and place. Such values only make sense within a given context. Moral values, in turn, are essentially transcendent. This means that while they do occur within a historical context, their "location at a point in history does not exhaust their practical impact or, one might even say, their meaning."[47] Employing an emanationist metaphor, he said that moral values "overflow" their specific contexts and history does not exhaust their validity. It is here that Fazlur Rahman and Betti, in my view, part ways. Betti believed in resurrecting meaning by ascertaining the intention in the mind of the original author. Fazlur Rahman for his part acknowledged the need to know the intention in the mind of the author, but insisted that the historical context of the author with all its complexities must be explored. This historicity of ideas was crucial to Fazlur Rahman and an aspect that tempered his Kantianism. The invisible context of ideas is not just mental, he said, but also environmental.[48]

The philosophy of history that permeates Fazlur Rahman's corpus is one that leans gently towards a liberal materialist analysis. Having said this, he has to be read carefully before one could say that he also accepted historicism. There is no doubt that he supported the early twentieth-century intellectual trends that favored history and historicism. This view of history entertained the idea that metaphysical truth, far from transcending history, was on the contrary the product of history. One of its effects were that it undermined an epistemology that was rooted in the stable universe of metaphysics. As an intellectual grappling with changing realities, he recognized that this metaphysical certainty was no longer

46. Ibid., p. 155.
47. Ibid., p. 5.
48. Ibid., p. 9.

available to him. That may also account, one suspects, for his mental and psychological anguish in the 1940's when he tried to grapple with questions of faith and history in the context of philosophy.[49] Rationality premised on metaphysics floundered against the wall of historicism. Ibn Sīnā's rationality, rooted in a stable metaphysics and cosmology and to which the younger Fazlur Rahman was beholden, lost its luster in the modern world. The thrust of historicism undermined the certainties inherited from Islam's medieval legacy. In place of the old metaphysics, the new metaphysical thesis asserted that only history brings to light the potentialities of a human being. The force of history itself as an agent of change displaces the notion of a permanent and fixed human nature. Faced with this challenge, it appears that Fazlur Rahman gradually held on to a singular metaphysical truth, that of revelation in active collaboration with history. Human nature as the ground for speculative and detached thought would no doubt be an objectifying construction. If, however, human nature existentially encounters history, it may lend itself to greater dynamism and creativity. Inspired by this spirit of the Qurʾān, we observe that in the latter part of his intellectual life Fazlur Rahman effectively abandoned his concerns with metaphysics. It is replaced by a singular preoccupation with the Qurʾān. He was "confident," he wrote in 1985, "of the eventual success of the pure Islam of the Qurʾān, which is fresh, promising, and progressive. It will take a few years and considerable effort, however, for the current obscurantism to be laid to rest in its grave. During the ensuing years of my life the bulk of my activity will be directed toward the realization of this end."[50] The Qurʾān now becomes not a pretext for philosophical hermeneutics as much as a historical hermeneutics with revealed truth as the centerpiece. Revelation represents the eternal and transcendent truth that unfolds and actualizes itself within history. After prophecy this task of actualizing truth is the function of the "learned," (ʿulamāʾ) who are, according to a famous tradition of the Prophet, the heirs to the legacy of prophets. It is their task to apply the revelation in every age and to renew the ethos of religion at relevant instances. So while there is no divinely sanctioned religio-moral instruction (*tashrīʿ*), such teaching will continue via the medium of creative and independent thinking (*ijtihād*).

49. Berman, "Fazlur Rahman," p. 155.
50. Ibid., p. 159.

Before Revival and Reform

Fazlur Rahman's Qur'ān-centered hermeneutics was in one sense a search for Islamic humanism in the modern age. His was a search for ethical values to address the needs of Muslim societies and their complex problems. In that quest he addressed critical issues such as the status of women in Muslim society, clearly one of the most important tests for modern Islam's ethical imagination. But there were also other matters that exercised him, such as Islam's view and acceptance of other religions; political ethics, the reinterpretation of Islamic law, and the development of contemporary ethics. His double-movement theory of hermeneutics was part of a larger ethical project that was vigilant against all kinds of complacency.

As with all thought processes there were also several inarticulate premises in his hermeneutic. Prominently lacking in Fazlur Rahman's thought was a systematic evaluation and critique of the present historical context, especially the political, economic, and aesthetic dimensions of this historical phase with which he urged Muslims to make a historical tryst. It becomes evident that he was not entirely comfortable with what can be called, for the lack of more precise terms, Western modernity. In several instances he showed disapproval of certain practices in the West. However, if one were to take his moral philosophy and ethical project seriously in order to apply values derived from the Qur'ān into the present context (the normative function), there is a need to undertake a critical analysis of the prevailing context. This he did not do in a systematic fashion and it remains a weakness of his hermeneutic.

It becomes very clear that a single dominant perspective of civilization is gradually overtaking our contemporary world driven by globalizing and homogenizing cultural, technological, scientific, and humanistic forces. This occurs despite the attempts of post-modern philosophy to resist such domination and celebrate the "other" in terms of that which is different, local, and non-rational. Everything from art to amnesia occurs along a single dominant vector that is Western. Most Third World countries in which Muslims find themselves today have lost the agency to determine their own futures under the dominant international economic, financial, and political institutions. Undemocratic and despotic regimes supported by multinational and international corporations and the political entities sponsoring their existence shape the context that will inevitably affect the project of rethinking Islam. In places where poverty, civil war, genocide, and underdevelopment are the features of society, talk about rethinking or reconstructing Islam may not only be viewed as a luxury, but may be met with deep cynicism when it does not address real-life issues. It goes without saying that rethinking Islam in Chittagong will be very different to that in Chicago.

All hermeneutics relate to the broader world and the facticity of life. This life is one of unrest, irregularity, unpredictability, indeterminacy, and insecurity. In order to be effective the hermeneutic project is always in a dialogic conversation with economic and political structures, as well as with art, aesthetics, culture, and the myriad of other dimensions of human existence. Fazlur Rahman, while being fully aware of the problems of the developed and developing countries, did not systematically address the issues of the facticity of life and the way these impact on religious thought. At times it appears that he subscribed to the liberal economic and political project of the 1960's and 1970's. On other occasions, he emphasized Islamic egalitarianism, redistribution of wealth, and democratic freedoms. Without any definitive statement from him it appears that he favored certain aspects of both socialism and capitalism, and possibly favored a form of leftist liberalism. One is aware that there is a limit to what one person can effectively accomplish in the massive task of reconstructing an intellectual tradition that spans several centuries and cultures. Reconstruction theory is normally oriented toward grounding a normative justification of the status quo. As he was one of the prominent Muslim reconstruction theorists of the twentieth century, Fazlur Rahman's limitations may also be viewed as the shortcomings of the project of reconstructing Islam. However, reconstruction is not only based on validating and justifying the status quo but is also designed to critique the existing conditions, in the manner that Fazlur Rahman did in his critical evaluation of contemporary revivalist groups and religio-political movements.

Rethinking Islam today takes place in the shadows of the genocide of Muslims in the Balkans and the pervasive sense of psychological defeat it brings to the collective Muslim psyche. In a world driven by media and cyber images this defeated sensibility has a trans-national quality. Foreign powers or dictatorships relentlessly attempt to defeat the spirit of resistance of the Muslim masses. Tragically, resistance to such oppressive forces manifests itself in violent reactions of rage and anger. In order to legitimize the use of violence and coercive measures, religious discourse is employed to validate the new forms of resistance. So powerful are the voices of militant Muslim discourse that even moderate voices are muffled and silenced. Such an environment is increasingly becoming a dominant feature of many Muslim societies. Under such conditions it is extremely difficult to rethink critical intellectual questions and propose a reconstruction. Any challenge to the remnants of the past that are embedded in the discourses of theology, law, philosophy, and other forms of thought is met with ferocious resistance and viewed as a threat to Islam itself. In modern and traditional institutions alike a sense of Islam as a historical and cultural phenomenon is radically subordinated to the notion of Islam as dogma, an artifact of the past. Yet, if history is any measure, then such conditions of crises and eventual exile, as in the case of Fazlur Rahman, create the opportunities and space for such critical reconstruction.

The body of thought that the project of rethinking or the reconstruction of Islam attempts to confront is premised on a triumphalist ideology: an age when Islam was a political entity and an empire. A cursory glance at this intellectual legacy will show how this ideology of Empire permeates theology, jurisprudence, ethics, and espouses a worldview that advances hierarchy. What adds to the frustration of millions of followers of Islam is the fact that this triumphalist creed and worldview is unable to deliver its adherents to its perceived goals of worldly success and leadership. In the post-Bosnian, post-Oslo, post-Kosovo Muslim world, to use a few dramatic illustrations, the conditions within many Muslim communities have deteriorated to the extent that not only space for dialogue with the "other" but also the space for intra-Muslim dialogue is rapidly diminishing. Any proposal regarding inter-faith dialogue, the establishment of academic positions for the teaching of Islam at secular universities, or even new approaches to Islamic thought are almost immediately, if not instinctively, viewed by sections of the Muslim community as elaborate conspiracies against Islam. One should also not be naïve and not recognize that some of the projects mentioned above have in the past been employed to serve Western imperial projects. The effects of the West as a colonial force and its impact on the general character of education in the Muslim world and on Islamic studies were "disastrous," in the words of Fazlur Rahman.[51] The first question addressed to any new project initiated by Muslims or by non-Muslims is: what is the catch? Why do "they" (non-Muslims) want to teach or study our Islam at universities? Why do "they" want to engage in dialogue? If Islam surrenders to dialogue, then will that act by itself not place Islam on a par with religions that lack validity? Is the burst of intellectual activity and interest in Islam in the West not a new kind of conquest, with knowledge being an instrument of power? The logic is as follows. The West has the economies of the developing world tied up with credit and debt to the World Bank and IMF, both seen as controlled by the United States. By opening up an intellectual and knowledge frontier onto Islam does it mean that new brands of Islam will be packaged to satisfy the needs of neo-imperialism? Muslims raise these questions and discussions on a daily basis in Islamabad, Khartoum, Brooklyn, Marseilles, Cairo, and Algiers. Proponents of radical Islam argue that the intellectual pursuit of Islam, especially in non-traditional institutions such as universities and colleges, is a new form of Orientalism. Those who advocate the reconstruction of Islam, such as Fazlur Rahman, are in particular singled out as being subversive. The paranoia is pervasive. The valuable books that both insiders and outsiders write mainly in Western languages hardly make it to the shelves of the intelligentsia of the Muslim world. If these ideas do reach those shores they appear in the form of banned or restricted literature and can hardly be acknowledged since their contents may be too explosive to be tried out in a living social laboratory. It is also true that only a handful of Islamicists working in the West read the works of their counterparts in the Muslim world, especially those written in indigenous languages. The frightening aspect of all this is the growing dominance and prevalence of negative attitudes in Muslim communities the world over, which make even bona fide and serious projects within Muslim scholarship appear suspect. It is now even more self-evident that the agencies of radical politics within Muslim communities are increasingly turning their attention to "insiders," whom they see as a bigger threat than those who are termed "outsiders." It therefore it comes as no surprise that dozens of Muslim intellectuals are

51. Fazlur Rahman, "Islamic Studies," p. 130.

either regularly hounded by frenzied mobs of religious activists and zealots or are censored by governments with sometimes an unholy alliance taking place between the zealots and dictatorships. Fazlur Rahman, in his astute and incisive manner, captured the prevailing psychological conditions of the post-colonial Muslim world when he said: "Their [Muslims'] ability to rethink their heritage with some rational distance and objectivity in order to reconstruct an Islamic future has been incalculably damaged. Instead of being able to create a rational distance vis à vis his heritage of the past, the average Muslim was pushed to cling to that past. What certain Muslim scholars could say, say in the seventeenth and eighteenth centuries, a Muslim scholar cannot say with impunity today."[52]

Having raised the question of international relations, politics, and economics, that does not mean that scholars of religion must become economists or political scientists. However, the study of religion will suffer if its insights do not take cognizance of how the discourses of politics, economics, and culture impact on the performance of religion and vice versa. In rethinking Islam Fazlur Rahman has argued that people outside the tradition can also play a meaningful role. The main responsibility devolves nevertheless upon those inside the intellectual tradition. This rethinking or reconstruction of Islam can optimally be achieved in a spirit of openness. Preferably, all parties should be aware of openness to the transcendence of ideas, religious values, and worldviews. This means recognizing the integrity of all the participants, while simultaneously being conscious of the ethics of politics and power. The last mentioned is of paramount importance, since without it we are doomed to more intense conflict.

Openness must also result in genuine pluralism within Muslim communities as well as outside the boundaries of religious communities. The statement attributed to the Prophet may now have greater relevance than before, when he said: "Differences among my community are a source of blessing." Diversity and differences must not be seen as a curse. At the same time "outsiders" ought to show genuine sensitivity and must prove unfounded, in word as well as in deed, the paranoia and fears that Muslim communities have of being undermined by outside forces. Rethinking Islam cannot occur in a fortress society or only in academic citadels: it needs living communities.

52. Ibid.

The canon(s) of Islamic thought is gradually being systematically interrogated in order to distinguish its various components, continuities, and discontinuities. In exploring this heritage of values, ideas, philosophies, patterns of spirituality, arts, cultures, and aesthetics comes a recognition of how its fabric and intricate tapestry have been constructed. This in turn will make it possible for dogmatism bred by the lack of enlightenment, or by the existence of fear, to be displaced by the torch of knowledge, understanding, and wisdom. The permanent will become evident from the contingent, as will the eternal from the temporal, the sacred from the mundane, without necessarily reducing such complexity to their essentials and essences. Reductionism and the dismemberment of an intellectual, historical, and cultural tradition is neither desirable nor is it a goal. The goal is to understand in order to think and know, and then to re-think, re-construct, then re-understand, and then to re-know. All this is done in order to live with integrity, justice, and a happiness that beckons.

1

EARLY SECTS AND FORMATION OF SUNNĪ ORTHODOXY

Introduction

It is a well-recognized fact by now that the rise of Sunnī orthodoxy in Islam as a body of doctrine and practice owes itself largely to earlier sectarian developments. Of course, as a "silent" majority tradition it antedates sects and represents a development from the earliest pre-reflective attitudes of the Muslim community at the point where the Prophet had left it. Despite the fact that Sunnism is a development from these earliest attitudes, and can thus claim to represent "original" Islam in an important sense, the purpose of this chapter is different. Here the attempt is to show that at the point where Sunnism gained self-reflection and formed its conscious being it had, in certain fundamental ways, undergone a radical change, indeed a metamorphosis, vis-à-vis its "original" state and the teaching of the Qurʾān. We shall try to underline those factors that were responsible for this metamorphosis in order to explain the nature of the metamorphosis itself. Later we shall portray the various historical attempts made in medieval Islam at the "reformation" of this orthodoxy in a bid to recapture the "original" spirit of Islam. While Sunnī orthodoxy will be our central concern we shall have to pay due attention to developments in Shīʿism both because of its intrinsic importance and meaning and because of its relationship with the larger Sunnī community.

The following analysis of the earliest sectarian proliferation in Islam is intended to reveal the nature of the crisis this young religion faced within two or three decades of the Prophet's death and how this crisis was gradually resolved. From the very first appearance of sectarian phenomena, both political and religious factors played a consistent and allied role on the sectarian side and on the side of the majority community and its political rulers, the Umayyads. The sectarians threatened not only the Umayyad state, which was then generally believed to have acted only in the interest of its own survival and suppressed its opponents, but also, more importantly and fundamentally, the integrity of the nascent community which generally supported the Umayyads and, later, the ᶜAbbāsids in its own interests of consolidation. That under the Prophet and the first two caliphs, Abū Bakr and ᶜUmar, the integrity of the state and the solidarity of the community was identical and, indeed, indivisible is obvious. Under the third caliph, the integrity of the state was, however, shaken, and so was that of the community, while under ᶜAlī the state was dismembered, and so was the community.

But when we come to the Umayyads, the terms of the state–community solidarity, although they retained a certain continuity, were nevertheless very weak: the original identity of those relations had changed. Although there was no total rupture between the two, there arose a duality nevertheless. The Umayyad state had primarily to look after its own survival interests, because the state was no longer the instrument of Islam, as it had been under the first four caliphs. It had its own goals and its own dynamics to realize those goals. It found, however, that its own interests were best served if it carried with it at least the larger part of the community, and thereby developed the ability to suppress those that threatened its existence. The community, on the other hand, faced its own dangers in terms of the proliferation of sectarian phenomena that threatened the very nucleus of its belief and practice. That is the starting-point for debates, arguments, and counter-arguments to win over the sectarians. But the arm of state power was indispensable. The state lent its arm to suppress heresies, but used it particularly against those heresies that were also a political threat to the state.

Under the dynamics of the new situation, a relationship of mutuality or reciprocity of interests was developed. It was no longer a simple identity of the community–state as in pristine Islam, where the being, the goal, and the function of both displayed a total homogeneity. Now state and community constituted a dyadic reality. When Muslims bemoan this change and say that the caliphate gave way to dynastic rule, what they really mean is precisely what we have stated here. "Dynastic rule" by itself is undesirable, but surely this is because one cannot guarantee that in a dynastic succession good and able rulers would always be forthcoming. However, if we suppose for a moment that Shīᶜī idealism about the "house of the Prophet" is actually true, then there would be nothing wrong with dynastic rule. Governance, dynastic or other, falls short of Islamic requirements when it develops power-dynamics of its own which are autonomous vis-à-vis the ideals and the dynamics of the community, i.e., when governance becomes secular or quasi-secular.

The adage "in Islam there is no separation between religion and state" is in some positive sense applicable to Umayyad rule and to all subsequent rulers in Islam. But it is not true in the fullness of the meaning it had prior to the rise of the Umayyads. Certainly, the basis of the Umayyad state was Islam: Islamic law, an Islamic judicial system, and Islamic disciplines of learning were developed. *Jihād* was presented in a way that reminds one of ᶜUmar I. Yet the Umayyads, with the exception of the intensely religious ᶜUmar b. ᶜAbd al-ᶜAzīz (d. 101/720), were "worldly" men whose ambitions and goals were not identical with the religious constitution of the community. This is what a pious and concerned Muslim means when he talks of a "traumatic fall" of Islam from the level of the earlier caliphs to that of the house of Marwān. It is this dyad of state–religion phenomenon of interdependence, rather than identity, that started effectively with the Umayyads and shaped the basic attitudes of the community through its early experiences with heresies and the nature of those heresies. These early attitudes – over the subsequent centuries – generated theological, legal, and spiritual rationales. These have become so entrenched and permanently settled that they have provided an unexceptionable and unique *framework* for whatever future elaboration, alteration, development, and reform may take place or had been attempted during the last thirteen centuries. As we shall see, there is great variety and richness to these developments in medieval Islam, indeed, in some ways a bewildering variety of opinions and views. Nevertheless, this framework – which we shall endeavor to delineate in the present chapter – and its matrix have remained effective throughout.

General Survey of the Early Schisms

Developments within Sunnī orthodoxy, as defined in the fourth/tenth century by Abū ᵓl-Ḥasan al-Ashᶜarī (d. 324/935), which was ascendant throughout medieval Islam, and to a lesser degree also influenced by his contemporary Abu ᵓl-Manṣūr al-Māturīdī (d. 333/944), can be viewed as the culmination of a process that was an immediate reaction against the Muᶜtazila, and to some extent against the Shīᶜī. The themes highlighted by this development generally appear to both Muslim and non-Muslim scholars to be the most important issues of sectarian controversy. The modern historian thus sees it as his task to trace and push backward, as far as possible, the rise and growth of doctrines and ideas connected with these issues. One takes, for example, the doctrine of the attributes of God and tries to find its origin in Islam or influences upon it from the outside. Another example is the doctrine of *qadar*, the doctrine that holds that human beings have the free will and power to produce actions for which they are, therefore, responsible, and so on. This is an exceptionally valid and valuable scholarly activity. For a person, however, who wants to gain an insight into the formation and development of religious attitudes and ideas in Islam, it is much more profitable, and indeed necessary, to start at the beginning, as far as possible, and to follow this unfolding history. This will put each issue in its proper place and help assign a historical and religious significance to it, thus yielding the possibility of an overall assessment, which is our task here. One will thus see, for example, that the doctrine of the attributes of God arose relatively late and somewhat indirectly in Islam and held a rather secondary position even in the early years of the second/eighth century. As for *qadar*, it comes into the limelight of history as a theological issue during the caliphate of ᶜAbd al-Malik b. Marwān (d. 86/705), who appears to have been keenly interested in promoting anti-qadarite views, as has been demonstrated by Josef van Ess in several works. Whether or not one agrees with his statement, this was indeed a "state enterprise" which was intended to save the Umayyad dynasty from active opposition.

The first active schism in Islam, as is well known, were the Khawārij who owe their name to the fact that they rebelled against ᶜAlī in 38/658. Some of their foremost leaders in the middle of the first century of Islam, such as Nāfiᶜ b. al-Azraq (d. 65/683–684), had supported the revolt against the third caliph, ᶜUthmān b. ᶜAffān. He also supported ᶜAlī's caliphate, until the latter submitted his claim to arbitration after which the Khawārij denounced him and then fought against him. Since they had rebelled on religio-ideological grounds, while the majority of the community did not join them, they had to explain and justify their stand. They were the ones who started religio-theological speculation and since then their political activism had been directed against what they perceived to be gross governmental injustice and misrule. Their very first statement naturally was that if a Muslim commits a grave wrong, without due repentance, he/she ceases to have faith and becomes an infidel. Later, during the fifties of the first century, a split occurred between Nāfiᶜ b. al-Azraq and the followers of Najda b. ᶜĀmir (d. 72/691–692).[1] The followers of al-Azraq, the extremist wing, held that anyone who did not join their rebellion-coup was an infidel, who must be opposed. They named their territory after the model of the Prophet's Madīna "the abode of immigration" (*dār al-hijra*), as opposed to the rest of the Muslim world which was "the abode of infidelity" (*dār al-kufr*) or "the abode of dissimulation" (*dār al-taqiyya*). They held that anyone who commits a grave sin also becomes an infidel and shall burn eternally in the fire. The followers of Najda, however, refused to subscribe to this view.

Most Khārijite interpretation of the Qurʾān is, on the whole, extremely strict. Nāfiᶜ, for example, held that in terms of the wording of the Qurʾān, the punishment of eighty lashes prescribed for the crime of a false accusation of sexual probity (Q. 24:4–5) only applied when the person slandered was a woman, and not a man. Further, the punishment of death by lapidation for adultery is unlawful he said, since there is no proof for it in the Qurʾān.[2] There is a good deal of evidence that many Khārijite leaders were highly learned men and capable of forming original opinions on points of law and doctrine. Nāfiᶜ b. al-Azraq was said to have been an unusually gifted *faqīh* (jurist) of his people, a term which does not just mean a "legist" in this early usage, but also meant a theologian. He had been a student of the Companion ᶜAbd Allāh b. al-ᶜAbbās and had composed a work titled *Questions*. Another very early Khārijite leader, ᶜImrān b. Ḥiṭṭān (who died at an advanced age in 84/703), is said to have been highly learned in *ḥadīth* and other branches of knowledge. He

1. Al-Ash'arī, *Maqālāt*, vol. 1, p. 159.
2. Ibid., vol. 1, p. 162.

belonged to the Ṣufriyya branch of the Khawārij, who were much like the Azraqites, except that they did not believe that the children and women of their opponents should be killed, as did the Azraqites. They also said that a Muslim who commits a grave sin such as theft or adultery cannot be called an "infidel" as the Azraqites claimed, but should only be called a "thief" or an "adulterer." The founder of the Ṣufriyya, Ziyād b. al-Aṣfar, belonged to the phenomenon of the very early Khawārij internal schisms, but the date of his death is not mentioned by any heresiologist. He is reported to have held that even those Khawārij (presumably his own followers) who were sure that they were "believers" could never be sure whether they were so in the eyes of God. This is an extraordinary statement for one of the Khawārij to make. They were usually very sure whether other people were real believers or not. We shall return to this when we talk about the reaction that developed within Khawārij circles and towards them under the discussion of *irjāʾ* (postponement).

The Khawārij leaders were inclined to the systematic discussion of religio-moral subjects as evidenced by the fact that we are told that Ṣāliḥ b. al-Musarriḥ (d. 76/695) used to discuss intra-Khawārij theological questions with another Khārijī named Dāwud on a regular basis.[3] When Ṣāliḥ was mortally wounded in a battle against the forces of the Umayyad governor Ḥajjāj b. Yūsuf, he appointed the famous Shabīb b. Yazīd (d. 77/696) as his successor, saying to his followers:

> I am appointing Shabīb as leader over you, although I know that among you are those who has more understanding of religion (*fiqh*) than him. However, he is an unusually courageous man and would inspire fear among your enemy. So, those of you who have a better understanding of religious issues should help him with their knowledge.[4]

Shabīb's only major innovation was that he allowed women to hold the highest political–military office, and, in fact, after his death his mother, Ghazāla, was elected caliph. We are told that a controversy had arisen over some of Ṣāliḥ's decisions. As a result of this, some of his followers abandoned him, most of whom returned later, while the majority remained faithful to him. Now Shabīb had taken up a "no-decision" *al-tawaqquf* approach on this controversy about a believer who commits a major sin.

3. Ibid., vol. 1, p. 186.
4. Muḥammad Muḥyī al-Dīn ʿAbd al-Ḥamīd, ed. of ibid., fn 1, 182, citing Dhahabī's, *Taʾrīkh al-Islām*.

Upon this, many of the Khawārij disowned or "abandoned" him and his followers. They were called the Murjiʾa of the Khawārij. Again, during Shabīb's brief leadership, a controversy arose as to why he had given, from the booty, a girdle and a turban to a certain person. "But what if this man is martyred and the things taken [by the enemy]?" asked the objectors, implying that in that case the person who really deserved them in a proper booty-distribution would be deprived of them. "Repent of your misdeed," the objectors demanded. Since Shabīb was unwilling to do so, he said: "I do not really think this calls for repentance." At this all the Khawārij "abandoned" him. Al-Ashʿarī comments: "So far as I know, no Khārijī 'owns' [i.e., approves of] him," adding: "They left the decision to God (*yurjiʾuna amrahu*) in his case; they do not call him an infidel, nor do they affirm that he was a believer."[5]

This shows that this group of the Khawārij belonged to the Ṣufriyya. We can see the development of a position that comes closer to that of the later Muʿtazila opinion and sometimes to the Sunnī attitude on the issue. But this position is generated by the inner dialectic of Khārijism itself. Finally, we would like to take notice of some more ideas of Najda b. ʿĀmir, whom we mentioned earlier in this section. Najda is an interesting figure among the Khawārij because some of his followers charged him with wrongdoing that strikingly remind one of charges against ʿUthmān b. ʿAffān. He was also killed by one of his own men, called Abū Fuḍayḥ in 72/691–692. He had apparently sent his son on an expedition against the Qaṭīf. There they captured booty as well as women, whom they married by some legal device, instead of distributing them as part of the booty. Najda said they had made a mistake but excused them on the ground that it was an error of *ijtihād* – an effort at finding a solution to a legal or moral problem. He then enunciated the principle that "he who fears that a *mujtahid* (a master jurist) who has made a mistake in *ijtihād* has incurred God's punishment before the mistake has been clearly proven, becomes an infidel."[6] This also shows that not all Khawārij admitted that one could always be sure whether a mistake had been committed or not – in matters that had not been decided by the Qurʾān. Najda had also removed the punishment for drinking alcohol (apparently because it had not been mentioned in the Qurʾān), and this was one of the charges against him.[7] As pointed out earlier, the

5. Ashʿarī, *Maqālāt*, vol. 1, p. 177.
6. Ibid., vol. 1, p. 163.
7. Ibid.

Khārijīs tended to adhere strictly to the Qurʾān's letter. Other charges against Najda included the allegation that he had distributed booty among the well-to-do people and deprived the poor thereof; that he had shown greater favors to land warriors than the naval warriors. Above all, it was alleged that when his men had captured ʿUthmān b. ʿAffān's daughter, and the caliph ʿAbd al-Malik had asked for her release, Najda purchased her for a large sum of money from the man who possessed her and returned her to the caliph.[8] Najda was asked to repent in terms of the Khārijī law, and he acquiesced. Later, his followers returned and said that their asking him to repent was a mistake because he was their leader (*imām*). They then repented of this and also asked him to repent of his earlier repentance, or else they would "disown him." Najda repented of his repentance! However, some people did not forgive him for what they probably correctly perceived to be his discriminatory attitude in favor of upper economic and social classes, and his soft attitude towards the caliphal authority. Abū Fuḍayḥ eventually killed him.

It is abundantly clear from the above account that the Khārijī demand was primarily for righteous conduct, particularly in the public sector and most particularly on the part of the administrative authority (*sulṭān*). A grave mistake, error, or sin calls for immediate repentance. If the authority does not repent then "disowning" or "abandonment" (*barāʾa*) is the only alternative, resulting in an active struggle for the restoration of the state of affairs. This, of course, assumes that errors can be clearly and decisively located. The frequency with which the words "repent!" and "we declare ourselves quit of you" occur in Khārijī political discourse – in addresses to their leaders or by their leaders to each other – is truly astonishing. There is no doubt that the Khārijīs were Bedouin tribesmen, a fact which explains their extreme fanaticism and intolerance. But there is also no doubt that their tribal character did not allow them to brook any palpable gap between the real and the ideal. It made them uncompromising idealists so far as issues of justice and injustice, righteousness and unrighteousness were concerned.

However, we have also seen that not infrequently this uncompromising attitude produced internal self-criticism and at times left many Khārijīs unsure whether an error had occurred. And if one had occurred, what was its true moral import? In such cases many of them

8. Ibid.

resorted to *irjāʾ*, i.e., they left the decision or judgment up to God. Indeed, even in the case of the Azāriqa, the most uncompromising of all the Khārijī sects, they demanded from their leader, Qaṭarī b. al-Fujāʾa (d. 78/697), who succeeded Nāfiʿ b. al-Azraq, that he repent as a consequence of a dispute. He refused to comply with the demand and was "disowned." He left for Ṭabaristān, where he later died fighting.[9] A very interesting and illuminating episode occurred among the Khawārij, the precise date of which is not known, but it probably took place in the sixties of the first century of the *hijra*. An Ibāḍī Khārijī leader, Ibrāhīm, issued an authoritative opinion (*fatwā*) that it was permissible to sell female slaves in the territory of the "infidels" – i.e., non-Khārijī Muslims. Many Khārijī sects made a distinction between Muslim and non-Muslim infidels in certain respects. Another man named Maymūn disapproved of it and "disowned" Ibrāhīm, while others expressed their "indecision" – *tawaqquf*. Outside Ibāḍī authorities supported Ibrāhīm and required both Maymūn and the "undecided" ones to repent and to "disown" a woman who was among the "undecided" but who had already died before the *fatwā* arrived. Further, Ibrāhīm himself was to repent for taking no action against those who had expressed their indecision. Abū Bayhas (d. 94/713), who in turn was responsible for several Khārijī subsects, declared that Ibrāhīm, Maymūn, and the "undecided" ones were infidels. He enunciated the important principle that "indecision is impossible with regard to people (*al-abdān*). Indecision is only possible with regard to a hypothetical question as to whether something is right or wrong. But as soon as the question becomes actual and ceases to be hypothetical, those present there must know decisively as to whose answer to it was right and whose was wrong."[10]

Irjāʾ can thus be formulated as the view that one is not always decisively clear that a certain error has been committed. And even more importantly, it is unclear as to what the precise nature and the moral weight of a particular error may be and that therefore final judgment must be left to God. Many Khārijīs frequently resorted to *irjāʾ* despite the emphatic formulation that they adopted the opposite principle, just cited above as the hallmark of Khārijism. The position of *irjāʾ* characteristically articulates

9. Ibid., vol. 1, p. 161.
10. Ibid., vol. 1, p. 175.

the attitudes of the larger body of the community which, by its inner logic, must eschew extremes, hold on to that which is practical and practicable, and always avoid theoretical decisions on polarities in the interests of practical compromises. As a practical attitude, therefore, *irjāʾ* necessarily characterized the majority of the community who refused to take sides either in the dispute between ᶜUthmān and his opponents or between ᶜAlī, on the one hand, and ᶜĀʾisha, Muᶜāwiya, Ṭalḥa, and Zubayr on the other. Although they believed that ᶜUthmān's murder was a mistake, there was no single person who in their eyes could be held responsible and blamed for it. The larger community was sure, however, that Khārijism was in error, namely the attitude that arrogates to itself the self-righteous claim to know precisely who is doing what amount of wrong and with what moral consequences. In other words, it was – besides being a "natural" and "confident" attitude of the "silent majority" – a reaction to the view held by most Khārijīs that those Muslims who are guilty of major errors (*kabāʾir*) become infidels, who must die in this world at the hands of the Khārijīs and must burn in hell eternally in the next world at the hands of God. *Irjāʾ*, then, is a reaction to this position of "threat" (*waᶜīd*) both in this life and the life after death.

But *irjāʾ*, when formulated as a doctrine, where it is no longer a question of a more practical attitude, can and indeed does also go to extremes, as we shall see below. Before taking up the discussion of the process whereby *irjāʾ* did become a doctrinal position in Islam, we have to examine another doctrine, that of *qadar*. This doctrine states that human beings possess free will, or that God has endowed humankind with a free will and that this will is efficacious so that a person is completely free to choose and to act. First of all we must note that unlike Khārijism, which was a practical phenomenon and only secondarily a doctrine, *qadar* is primarily the name of a doctrine, not of a practical attitude, although it may help a practical attitude. It should also be pointed out that whereas Khārijīs were Arabs – certainly Khārijī leaders were all Arabs – the qadarīyya, which was a school of thought, was largely (and primarily) a non-Arab affair, and included Persians and Egyptians, many of them from a Christian background. The Khārijīs were not *qadarīs*. Indeed, most of them believed that God created human acts. In fact, in the entire gamut of Khārijī subsects, al-Ashᶜarī names only two subdivisions of the sect of Ajārida, followers of ᶜAbd al-Karīm b. al-Ajrad[11] and the Maymūniyya, the followers of Maymūn b. ᶜImrān. Both of these men appear after the advent of qadarism in the latter half of the first century.

The opposite of irjāᵓ is *waᶜīdism*, meaning the unconditional threat of infidelity and the promise of hell for those guilty of serious error. Strictly speaking, the opposite of qadarism is not *irjāᵓ* but *jabr*, the doctrine of predestination. It must be repeated that whereas the first polarity primarily represents a practical attitude, the latter, *qadar–jabr* (free will–predestination) polarity is primarily a doctrinal affair, not a practical one. Thus, it is not necessary that a *qadarī* must be active or activist in actual life or even that he should preach activism. Nor is it true that activists, like Khārijīs, must necessarily hold *qadarī* (free will) views. In fact, they did not, although one would expect otherwise. It is true that *logically* at least *jabr* and *irjāᵓ* ought to go together as should *qadar* and *waᶜīdism*. In fact, the latter is what actually happened at the theoretical level at the hands of Muᶜtazilism. However, the Muᶜtazila were, by and large, not activists but scholars. This is why the founder of the Muᶜtazila school, Wāsil b. ᶜAṭāᵓ al-Ghazzāl (d. 131/749), and his comrade ᶜAmr b. ᶜUbayd (143/760–761) were sarcastically called "the eunuchs of the Khārijīs." This was because although like the Khārijīs they held those guilty of grave sins to be no longer Muslims, they never did anything practical about correcting the situation, as did the Khārijīs, even though the latter were mostly anti-*qadar*.

In recent Islamic history, the majority of Muslim modernist reformers of the nineteenth and twentieth centuries strongly emphasized free will over and against the medieval predestinarianism advocated by Ashᶜarism. Jamāl al-Dīn al-Afghānī (d. 1314/1897) when asked about this problem wrote in his journal *al-ᶜUrwat al-Wuthqa* in a strongly worded reply that the true Islamic belief is that God, not humanity, disposes of everything, including human destinies. His argument was partly utilitarian. He contended that belief in divine determinism made of Muslims a courageous people who were not afraid of death in battle because if God had preordained their death, nothing could save them. If not, no amount of danger could harm them. He further averred that, while Muslims believed strongly in divine

11. [ᶜAbd al-Karīm b. al-Ajrad, whose date of death I have not found anywhere, but who died in prison in Irāq in the days of the governorship of Khālid b. ᶜAbd Allāh al-Qaṣrī probably in the early years of the second century of the Hijra.]

predestination, they nevertheless also believed in *kasb* – the Ashʿarī doctrine that while God creates human acts, humankind nevertheless "acquires" or "appropriates" them, thus accommodating humanity's share in His action as well. One can very well imagine a Qaṭarī b. al-Fujāʾa or a Nāfiʿ b. al-Azraq subscribing to this type of belief. In fact, two followers of ʿAbd al-Karīm b. al-Ajrad, Maymūn and Shuʿayb, disputed on this matter. The former believed in *qadar*, while the latter believed in divine predeterminism, and both wrote to Ibn al-Ajrad in prison, asking his opinion. He replied: "We hold that whatever God wills happens and whatever He does not will does not happen, [but] we attribute no evil to Him."[12] This is a standard determinist reply. However, Maymūn managed to conclude that the master had supported his free-will thesis from the words "but we attribute no evil to Him." For if evil human acts also originate from God, then He cannot be free from attribution of evil. The conclusion, however, is incorrect since people such as the Ashʿarīs, who believe in God's authorship of evil as well as good, refuse to attribute evil to Him. We shall resume the development of *irjā'* from a practical attitude into a doctrine after we have briefly stated the *qadarī* doctrines. Our purpose is obviously not to give a comprehensive historical treatment of the *qadarī* views, but to consider these only to the extent that they are relevant to the rise of the Sunnī and (Imāmī) Shīʿī orthodoxies, the former rejecting them, the latter eventually adopting them. The salient *qadarī* doctrines are the following:

1. That God is one unique being, unlike any creature, possessing activity but no substantive attribute. Thus, He is living but has no substantive attribute of life; He knows but has no substantive attribute of knowledge. Because they denied the attribute of speech (*kalām*), they declared that the Qurʾān – as God's speech – was not an eternal attribute of God but something created (*makhlūq*).
2. That humankind is endowed with free will and the responsibility to create autonomous actions. God neither wills nor creates evil. Therefore, the evil that materializes occurs without and despite His will.
3. That a Muslim who commits a grave wrong or sin ceases to have faith (*īmān*), but does not become an infidel either as the Khārijīs insisted,

12. Ashʿarī, *Maqālāt*, vol. 1, p. 165.

but comes to occupy a "middle position" unless he or she repents. Deeds are, therefore, part of faith.

4. That God's activity is for the sake of the good (*maṣlaḥa*) of His creation. Therefore the laws that God has ordained for humankind have a purpose: the good of humanity.
5. That good and evil or right and wrong are discoverable by human reason unaided by revelation but that the ritual institutions of religion, such as daily prayers and fasting, cannot be known by pure reason but are known only through revelation.
6. That God's justice demands that just as He *must* reward good people for their good deeds, so must He punish people for their evil deeds, otherwise a distinction between the effects of good and evil deeds will disappear. Hence they denied God's forgiveness for sinners. Divine justice is a *quid pro quo* for every act, although of course, a grave sin wipes out all effects of good deeds, even of great good deeds.

Nuances there are many, but the above account sums up all the main theses of the qadarīyya in their developed form of the Muᶜtazila school which comes to prominence with Wāsil b. ᶜAṭāᵓ. The only thing omitted from this account is the Muᶜtazila denial that God will be seen by the faithful on the Day of Judgment as their opponents, the Sunnīs insisted.[13] But this is an isolated doctrine which makes little difference between the two sides, since the Sunnīs also said that God will not be seen with physical eyes, but through a special faculty created by God on that day.

The three "proto-qadarites" are said to be Maᶜbad al-Juhanī (d. 80/699), Ghaylān al-Dimashqī (d. 105/723), and al-Jaᶜd b. Dirham (d. 124/742–743). Of these three, only the first appears to be an Arab because of his relationship to the Juhayna tribe. It is conceivable, however, although I have not seen this mentioned anywhere, that he was a *mawlā* or a freed slave attached to that tribe, in which case he would be a non-Arab. In any case, he was originally a Baṣran, from where he subsequently traveled to Madīna where he spread his views on *qadar*, took part in the rebellion of Ibn al-Ashᶜath, was tried by the government of ᶜAbd al-Malik on charges of qadarism and was executed in 80/699. We do not know from where he

13. This is related to Q. 75:23: "There shall be faces on that Day resplendent with joy, looking at their Lord."

obtained his qadarite views. He is said to be "the first [Muslim] who held qadarite views." He is said to have learnt *ḥadīth* from Ibn ᶜAbbās and ᶜImrān b. Ḥusayn, both learned Companions of the Prophet. What is important to note is that since he had taken part in a rebellion, he was most probably executed because of this fact, and his being a qadarite was used as a pretext. Ghaylān is said to have been put to death on a charge of qadarism under the Umayyad ruler Hishām b. ᶜAbd al-Malik, probably in the middle of the second decade of the second century *hijrī*. In his *Anfänge Muslimischer Theologie* (1977), Josef van Ess has, I believe, persuasively shown that the real motives behind his death were also political.[14] Besides the fact that he was accused of having spread propaganda against the ruler while in the army on an expedition to Armenia, he openly held the view that rule could be vested in any Muslim. It was not necessary that the leader be a descendant of the Prophet through ᶜAlī and Fāṭima, as the Imāmī Twelver Shīᶜī hold, or in the Quraysh, which was actually the case and which the Sunnīs came to hold. He believed that leadership of the community could only be legitimized by the census of the community, an obviously dangerous position for the House of Marwān. As for al-Jaᶜd b. Dirham, who was also executed under Hishām in 124/742–743, he was a tutor of Marwān b. Muḥammad, a grandson of Marwān, the founder of the Marwānid–Umayyad dynasty (d. 65/685). Marwān b. Muḥammad, who was governor of al-Jazīra, later became the last of the Umayyad caliphs, and was known as a "follower of al-Jaᶜd" so much influence did al-Jaᶜd have upon him. We do not have any information of any possible political views he might have held. But the way he formulated and expressed his *qadarī* views on God was certainly sufficient to condemn him to death. Denying that God had attributes in a bid to remove all vestiges of anthropomorphism, he stated "God never spoke to Moses and He never took Abraham as a Friend," thus contradicting *verbatim* the statements of the Qurʾān (4:164; 4:125). If this is the case, then al-Jaᶜd was the first *qadarī* to be executed solely because of an extremely heretical formulation of a certain view of God, and apparently not on political grounds. This was despite the fact that he was so influential on such an important official personality as Marwān b. Muḥammad.

14. Van Ess, *Anfänge*, pp. 177–245.

The Role of ᶜAbd al-Malik b. Marwān

Before going further, I think we will do well to attempt to formulate some sort of a plausible picture of the sequence of development of qadarism and anti-qadarism in order to make sense of this very crucial turning-point in the religious history of Islam. Unless we can do this with adequate plausibility, this entire picture concerning the role of the "silent" community, the relevant groups of intellectuals, the role of the state or some important state personnel could become distorted. We have already seen that the Khawārij broke both with the rulers and the community on the issue as to what attitude should be taken vis-à-vis unrighteous human conduct. The community, although agreeing that right conduct is important and even crucially important, nevertheless rejected Khārijism, which claimed that an unrighteous act turns a Muslim into a *kāfir* (unbeliever) and that, therefore, the corrective-punitive use of the sword must be involved. The counter-attitude of the community is called *irjāʾ* as we have explained. In this picture, where is the starting-point of *qadar* or the doctrine of free and efficacious human will? It is known that in Iraq and Syria, particularly the latter, there existed an intellectually sophisticated tradition before Islam. But why did *this* particular doctrine arise in Islam at this particular time? We must look for an explanation within the Islamic context to explain that. The standard picture on the subject, reinvigorated recently by the scholarly endeavors of Professor van Ess, is that somehow qadarite ideas infiltrated Islam from the Hellenized Christian background in Syria and Iraq. This was deemed to be highly dangerous by the Umayyads, starting with ᶜAbd al-Malik b. Marwān who, therefore, deliberately adopted anti-qadarism as a state policy. He also pressed the services of certain highly important and influential religious leaders into the service of the state and created a climate of anti-qadarism and *irjāʾ* which was subsequently destined to be incarnated as the Islamic orthodoxy of the Ashᶜarites. In this incident one is reminded of the "Reformation" of Henry VIII in England.

Professor van Ess makes different statements on the subject. He repeatedly says that qadarism by itself was thought by the Umayyads to be innocuous, unless it was accompanied by anti-Umayyad political attitudes. This is the main thesis in his discussion of Ghaylān al-Dimashqī's fate in his *Anfänge Muslimischer Theologie*. To me this appears to be correct. He notes that there were several prominent qadarites both in Syria and Iraq who were generally held in high esteem and who were never touched by the Umayyad authorities. But since it is also one of van Ess's main theses that anti-qadarism was a state enterprise undertaken by ᶜAbd al-Malik, he has to hold that it was somehow dangerous to the state or at least that it was perceived as being dangerous by the Umayyad state. We are told that ᶜAbd al-Malik "wanted his subjects to believe that the power, the 'kingship' (*mulk*) given to him and his family was a possession [*mulk* sic.= *milk*] granted by God and inalienable according to His divine will."[15] He also states that qadarism or the free-will doctrine was not regarded as so dangerous when in Iraq but was deemed highly subversive when it appeared in Syria, for that was the center of Umayyad power. However, the qadarism of Ḥasan al-Baṣrī was questioned in Iraq by ᶜAbd al-Malik, in reply to which Ḥasan wrote his famous *Risāla* (Epistle), while that of the Syrian jurist and traditionist Makḥūl b. Abī Muslim ᶜAbd Allāh al-Shamī (d. c. 119/737) was apparently not. One might even plausibly argue that such a "dangerous" doctrine ought to be officially regarded as more dangerous in the outlying regions – because the subversion of state power is more liable to be caused there. Also, if predestinarianism was such an important state policy, why did Ḥasan al-Baṣrī get off so lightly after his blistering attack on this doctrine? Ḥajjāj b. Yūsuf al-Thaqafī, who had mercilessly treated men of great reputation and learning, including Companions of the Prophet, could have persecuted and even destroyed Ḥasan. On the contrary, the official note enclosing Ḥasan's reply praises the latter's unique learning.

What plausibly, and in a logical sense perhaps, necessarily happened was that when the community maintained its attitude of *irjāʾ* against Khārijism certain questions were naturally raised within certain circles in the larger community. The question was that, with the background of *irjāʾ*, whether one *can* indeed presume to pass judgment on human actions as the Khārijīs patently did, in view of the fact that nothing happens without God's all-powerful will. *Irjāʾ* was thus a fertile basis for the rise of the question as to a person's autonomous power to act – let alone such action being subject to human judgment. It is very natural for this question to arise in an atmosphere of constant debate and questioning. It is also very natural for committed Murjiʾites to resort, in turn, to predestinarianism. We are now

15. Ibid., p. 183.

speaking of *irjāʾ* as a kind of a doctrine, however crudely formulated, and not just as a practical attitude. This would, of course, provoke qadarism as a doctrinal response on the part of morally sensitive persons who were afraid of predestinarianism weakening the moral fiber of the faithful. Both sides could, and in the course of time did, avail themselves of the preexisting stock of ideas, but their genesis was to be explained in terms of the matrices of the moods of the community and the intellectual formulations of these moods. This is why Ḥasan al-Baṣrī says in his *Risāla*: "*We* have originated this *kalām* [i.e., on *qadar*] because some people have innovated a rejection of it."[16] It is clear from this that pro-*qadar* theological discourse (*kalām*) had been newly brought into being by Ḥasan (and probably others) in response to a dangerous *innovation* of predestinarianism. The latter had, therefore, in some sense preceded the rise of the *kalām* on free will. It is also interesting to note that the term *kalām* may not necessarily mean writing in a dialectical style. Unless Ḥasan had actually written some other work on the subject in a dialectical or question–answer style, for which there is no evidence, the term *kalām* may not necessarily mean dialectical theology, but a discourse in refutation of some thesis. For in this usage it is certainly referring to Ḥasan's refutation of the predestinarian thesis.

ᶜAbd al-Malik was educated at Madīna – he was the first Umayyad ruler to have been educated there. ᶜUmar b. ᶜAbd al-ᶜAzīz did the same a little later. Although Madīna, an important center of piety and learning, generally saw Umayyad rule as a traumatic fall from the standards of the early caliphate, it nevertheless tolerated them. Some Madinese also positively cooperated with them for the sake of political prudence and in the interests of the integrity of the community. The reply of the Madinese circles of piety and learning to rebellion and bloodshed was *irjāʾ* – not committing themselves one way or the other – as was the case of their attitude toward ᶜUthmān and his opponents and ᶜAlī and his opponents. Since Madīna was not just a center of piety, but also of learning and incipient religious thought, this *irjāʾ*, when it was theoretically grounded, led to predestinarianism – most probably of different shades. Thus, *irjāʾ* and predestinarianism were combined. And, although it is not necessary that they be combined, they do have a certain logical mutual accommodation. Otherwise, as we have seen, the Khawārij, although they

16. Fazlur Rahman, *Islam*, p. 56.

rejected *irjāʾ*, were mostly predestinarians. The Muᶜtazila, beginning with Wāsil b. ᶜAṭāʾ, were fellow free-willers, but unlike the Khārijites they were politically quiescent because they were a mere school of thought. Jahm b. Safwān was with the Muᶜtazila so far as the attributes of God are concerned, but unlike them he was an extreme predestinarian; yet he was politically active, took part in a long-drawn-out anti-Umayyad rebellion and was executed in 128/745.

The truth is that when *irjāʾ* develops into a theory and gives rise to predestinarianism, it ceases to have direct touch with actual practical attitudes. So is the case with free will when it becomes a theory. Now, ᶜAbd al-Malik and later others, such as ᶜUmar b. ᶜAbd al-ᶜAzīz, had learnt at Madīna that *irjāʾ* was primarily a personal belief and attitude. Later, when ᶜAbd al-Malik did become caliph, he might have also thought that at least *irjāʾ* would be helpful in discouraging rebellion and contributing to a consolidation of the state. But we must remember that *irjāʾ* was a response by the Muslim community or its religious leaders, and ᶜAbd al-Malik himself had learnt it from the community leaders. It would therefore have been impossible for ᶜAbd al-Malik simply to "hire," as Professor van Ess would have us believe, some leading religious personalities and ask them to write in defense of *irjāʾ* and predestinarianism, in the hope of changing the attitudes of the community. Van Ess has edited for the first time the *Kitāb al-Irjāʾ* of Ḥasan b. Muḥammad b. al Ḥanafiyya and his "Treatise in Refutation of the Qadarites," as well as a treatise of ᶜUmar b. ᶜAbd al-ᶜAzīz (d. 101/720) on qadarism, with erudite and excellent analyses.[17] He does nevertheless tend to take persons and their roles, particularly rulers and their policies, out of context from the general trends in the community as though they were acting in a vacuum.

Hence we hear that Muḥammad b. al-Ḥanafiyya (d. 81/700) and his son Ḥasan, author of the two aforementioned works (d. c. 100/718) on *irjāʾ* and determinism, may have been bought over by ᶜAbd al-Malik. Muḥammad b. al-Ḥanafiyya and his son were both educated at Madīna, like ᶜAbd al-Malik, and they were therefore part of the Madinese irjāʾist–determinist milieu like ᶜAbd al-Malik. Ibn al-Ḥanafiyya did not acknowledge ᶜAbd al-Malik as caliph until the total suppression by the latter of ᶜAbd Allāh b. al-Zubayr's rebellion in 73/693. In 66/686 the Shīᶜī al-Mukhtār actually staged a revolt in Irāq against Umayyad rule. Before the revolt, which was

17. Van Ess, *Anfänge.*

preceded by a process of gaining military support from various tribal chieftains and consolidating his power, he sent a message to Ibn al-Ḥanafiyya in Madīna. He told him that he was rising to avenge the blood of Ḥusayn, Muḥammad b. al-Ḥanafiyya's brother, killed earlier by Umayyad troops. To this message, Ibn al-Ḥanafiyya's reply was evasive. Upon his successful revolt in 66/686 and having established his government in Kūfa, al-Mukhtār again sent a messenger to Muḥammad b. al-Ḥanafiyya. This time he asked the latter to join him with a promise to deliver him from the surveillance of Ibn al-Zubayr who had set up a rebel government in Makka, Madīna, and elsewhere. Ibn al-Ḥanafiyya's reply was in the form of advice to al-Mukhtār, asking him to desist from bloodshed, and cultivate piety, adding politely that he was flattered to have so many supporters. When these events occurred, ᶜAbd al-Malik had barely come to power as yet, so there was no question of ᶜAbd al-Malik's financial largesse having any influence in winning supporters. Why did Ibn al-Ḥanafiyya reply to his supporters in this vein? Because, having cultivated the Madinese pacifist irjāᵓist outlook in the interest of the solidarity of the community, he wanted fighting to stop. He probably did not care at this stage (65–66/685–686) who won, whether it was ᶜAbd al-Malik or Ibn al-Zubayr, but it was important that whoever acquired power would be acknowledged. In 68/688, Ibn al-Ḥanafiyya performed the pilgrimage in the company of Ibn al-Zubayr, the Kharijite leader Najda, and an official representative of ᶜAbd al-Malik, making clear that he stood alongside no particular power. Ibn al-Ḥanafiyya was, therefore, already committed to Murjiᵓism, like the common run of the scholars of Madīna and indeed elsewhere, as was his son Ḥasan. That they subsequently received financial aid from the chancery would thus be a token of ᶜAbd al-Malik's gratitude to them, rather than their support of *irjāᵓ* and predeterminism being a token of *their* gratitude to the Marwānid.

Nor can Murjiᵓism be said to have begun with Ḥasan b. Muḥammad b. al-Ḥanafiyya's short treatise. I already pointed out some trace of Murjiᵓism when discussing the Khawārij leaders Ṣāliḥ b. al-Musarriḥ and his successor Shabīb b. Yazīd. When some people took sides in a dispute over al-Musarriḥ's actions, Shabīb remained non-committed and "neutral," resulting in his followers being dubbed "the Murjiᵓa of the Khawārij." This would have occurred before 76/695 since Ṣāliḥ was killed in battle that year. Further, the way the term "Murjiᵓa" was used in this context showed that it was not a new label, but a well-settled technical term. This also makes it probable, in fact very natural, that "neutralism" (*irjāʾ*) is a very early attitude that must have been consciously developed soon after the first civil war and resulted in the split of the Khārijīs with ʿAlī and their rebellions against him. The first application of the term was undoubtedly with reference to those wars and splits in the community. And the treatise of Ḥasan b. Muḥammad b. al-Ḥanafiyya primarily refers to these issues. But it naturally developed into a term meaning "neutralism" vis-à-vis alleged wrongdoings of any Muslim, in which meaning it was applied to characterize the stand of Shabīb. It is also noteworthy that although the treatise explicitly accuses only the followers of al-Mukhtār of denigrating and denouncing their opponents, it of course constitutes an equally serious indictment of the Umayyad rulers – including ʿAbd al-Malik himself – for cursing and denouncing ʿAlī in public from the pulpits. Actually, what ʿAbd al-Malik wanted, primarily through personal conviction but also most probably for reasons of state policy, was that tempers should calm down. For this *irjāʾ* was directly relevant, something that the community supported as the only viable practical alternative to mutual incrimination and civil wars. When, however, *irjāʾ* is raised to the level of a theory of the moral value of human acts, it is liable to generate the added theory of predeterminism. This actually happened in certain circles, which provoked the opposite theory of *qadar* or human free will, as is witnessed by Ḥasan al-Baṣrī's treatise. As *theories*, both free will and predeterminism are indeed remote from the concerns of the ordinary person and, therefore, from the moral milieu of the majority of the community. For no sensible person can be really persuaded to believe that they cannot do anything at all of their "own free will" nor that they can do anything they want to – knowing full well that nobody ever "chose" to be born, for example. It should be acknowledged, however, that given other social, economic, and moral factors, predeterminism and its opposite can contribute to the development of relevant attitudes to life, but the inherent limitations of their effectiveness must be duly recognized.

Law and Theology in Early Islam

In our book *Major Themes of the Qurʾān* we have elaborated on the fact that the Qurʾān both assumes and asserts human free will and also at a higher metaphysical level stresses the omnipotence of God. The Qurʾān not only sees no contradiction in this, but appears to believe that the human free-will activity as such, just like the activity of nature, depends upon and is conditioned by the divine will. In the Qurʾān, God's will is not additional to, a rival or a substitute for the human will. Such an attitude certainly underpinned the attitudes of the earliest Muslims, including those of the Khawārij. Under the impact no doubt of preexisting ideas in those lands some amount of reflection took place about this attitude. As soon as this intellectual activity reached the reflective stage and the predestinarians and free-willers formulated their doctrinal stands, human free will and divine omnipotence became directly antithetical to each other. This resulted in the power of God and the choice and efficiency of the human will becoming mutually exclusive concepts.

It is true that the purely theological schools became increasingly polarized in a theoretical sense. But it is highly interesting and significant that the lawyers, certainly the most prominent among them, also belonged to the Murjiʾa school as well. As lawyers one would certainly have expected them to be on the side of the theological school that upheld *qadar* or free will, and above all the ability of humans to judge human acts. They certainly do not appear to have perceived any obvious contradiction between their belief in *irjāʾ*, on the one hand, and their activity as jurists and lawyers, on the other. At this stage, of course, Sunnī predestinarianism had not yet reached the high watermark of al-Ashʿarī, let alone that of al-Bāqillānī (d. 403/1013) or Fakhr al-Dīn al-Rāzī (d. 606/1210).

There was of course a development in the concept of *irjāʾ* too. In the beginning it meant the adoption of a "neutral" attitude towards the participants in the earliest disputes and a refusal to decide who was in the right and who in the wrong: "The decision on this issue was left to God." This proposition was then extended, naturally enough, to a Muslim who professes Islamic faith but may be guilty of serious sins. Al-Shahrastānī, in *Kitāb al-Milal waʾl-Niḥal* (Book on Sects and Schisms) at the beginning of his account of the Murjiʾa gives four meanings to the term *irjāʾ*.[18] Strangely, the first meaning he gives is not the first that emerged historically and which we have given just now, but is the sense of "delay." He explains it as "delaying acts and regarding them as being after faith." This doctrine of a "gap" between faith and works, which seems to be a development from the

18. Al-Shahrastānī, *al-Milal*, vol. 1, p. 139.

original meaning, undoubtedly became the hallmark of the Murji'a "school," if it can be called such. This is because the Murjiᵓa actually came from otherwise very different, indeed conflicting, doctrinal schools – when the original attitude reached a formulation. It is in this sense that Abū Ḥanīfa, for example, was a Murjiᵓa, i.e. the idea that there is no necessary and organic relationship between faith and acts. Another allied meaning of *irjāᵓ* becomes apparent when a person does not *in principle* reject the cardinal duties of Islam, but also does not actually perform them either, but rather "postpones" them. That is when he or she says: "I will perform prayer or pilgrimage after I am free from such-and-such tasks." Such a person is a Muslim with faith. Al-Shahrastānī gives the second meaning of *irjāᵓ* as being derived from *rajāᵓ*, meaning "to give hope" to sinners that they would or might be forgiven by God on the Day of Judgment. Al-Shahrastānī then gives us the third meaning of the term which was actually historically its original meaning: to postpone the punishment of sinners until the judgment of God. His fourth meaning, which is not against the Khawārij and the Muᶜtazila, but against the Shīᶜī, i.e. to demote ᶜAlī to the fourth place after Abū Bakr, ᶜUmar, and ᶜUthmān, does not appear to be authentic. It has nothing to do with the question at issue, the status of a sinning Muslim, which was responsible for the entire religious and theological development of early Islam.

We must notice the change that had occurred in the Murjiᵓa position in this period, roughly the second century of Islam. The earliest position was, firstly, that a person *cannot* know and is thus unable to make a moral judgment as to whether there was a right and wrong position among the early disputants, ᶜUthmān, ᶜAlī, ᶜĀᵓisha, Ṭalḥā, Zubayr, and Muᶜāwiya. Secondly, if one could know, how could one make a judgment as to which person was right and who was wrong. Thirdly, those who were wrong were so wrong as to lose their faith altogether. For this reason God in His wisdom must finally judge these matters, which was, as we have recurrently said, essentially an anti-Khārijite position. From this position it soon followed logically, as it were, that a Muslim guilty of heinous sins still has faith and is a Muslim and is to be treated as such until God finally decides on the last day. It is from this stand that arises that genre of *ḥadīth* that seeks to create a clear distinction between faith and acts. It is reported, for example, that the Prophet once said repeatedly to his Companion Abū Dharr that a person who "professes that there is no God but God shall go to paradise even if he commits adultery and theft." This *ḥadīth* is not to be found in the writings of any pro- or anti-Murjiʾa champion in the first century. It therefore probably came into being in the first half of the second century. Probably along with this also arose the *aḥādīth* (reports) that support the doctrine of the intercession of the Prophet on behalf of the sinners of his community. Similarly there also arose *aḥādīth* that speak about the "punishment in the grave" (*ʿadhāb al-qabr*) for those who do not recognize the Prophet. For we are told that both the Khawārij and the Muʿtazilites rejected intercession and "punishment in the grave." We can clearly see where the community was going.

The primary meaning of *irjāʾ* in its first phase was to leave the final decision on sinners to God. From this followed a secondary conclusion that sinners nevertheless continue to be Muslims. In the second century, this last-mentioned meaning comes to predominate and a sharp distinction is made between faith and acts. The Murjiʾa, indeed, came to hold very different views about the definition of "faith." But common to all groups is the doctrine that works lie outside faith, and that faith neither increases nor decreases; or that it increases but does not decrease. Some, such as Jahm b. Safwān, believed that "faith" is the recognition of God and His Prophets by the heart and that such a person is a believer (*muʾmin*) even if he may verbally reject this. Others, such as Muḥammad b. Karrām (d. 255/869) and his followers, held that a person professing faith only by the tongue while rejecting it from the heart is a true believer. This means that that person is to be treated as a believer only in this world, and will burn in Hell. Most of the Murjiʾa, however, believed that faith comprises both the act of the heart (belief, love, and esteem) and its declaration by the tongue. The latter is also the view of Abū Ḥanīfa (d. 150/767). But it is reported that he distinguished between faith on the one hand, which for him meant that a Muslim must recognize the message of the Prophet only in general terms, and detailed knowledge which is not necessary, on the other. For example, a Muʿtazilite once asked him about the status of a person who knows and accepts that pilgrimage to the Kaʿba is obligatory, but does not know where the Kaʿba is located. In fact, the person erroneously says that it may be somewhere in India. Abū Ḥanīfa replied: "Such a person is a *muʾmin* (believer)." To another question about a person who knows and accepts that Muḥammad was God's Messenger but who does not know who Muḥammad was and thinks he was perhaps a negro. Abū Ḥanīifa replied: "Such a person is a *mu*ᵓ*min*." Incredible though such reports may seem to writers such as al-Khaṭīb al-Baghdādī (d. 463/1071) and al-Shahrastānī, I do not think they are implausible. This is also reflected in the difference between the elitist Ashᶜarites and, of course, the Muᶜtazilites on the one hand and the Ḥanafī–Māturīdīs on the other. The former held that a Muslim cannot claim to be a true Muslim without understanding the basis of Islam rationally. For the populist Ḥanafī–Māturīdīs "the Islam of the common Turk [in Central Asia] is perfectly good," even one who knows nothing about the rational bases of Islam. This, in fact, is the essence of *irjā*ᵓ in its new form in the second/eighth century. This view is correct if the least demands of Islam are met by the masses in terms of belief and action. In their consequences with respect to the quality of the Islam of the masses, the elitist and the populist views actually did not differ. The elitist view says that the Islam of the masses is worthless, but in its snobbery it does not expect them to do any better anyway. The populist view in turn is quite happy with the masses' Islam and does not see much need for improvement in their religiosity. In either case, the masses' Islam remains more or less at the minimal level. We shall see the consequences of this degraded state of popular Islam in the last chapter of this book, where we examine its adequacy for the possibility of establishing an Islamic democratic state, which is the clamor of the majority of Muslims today.[19]

Before examining the consequences of this *irjā*ᵓ for the moral foundations of Islamic law, we must also note that a rich crop of predestinarian *aḥādīth* arose in the second/eighth century. Neither Ḥasan al-Baṣrī in his pro-*qadarī* treatise nor yet Ḥasan b. Muḥammad b. al-Ḥanafiyya or ᶜUmar b. ᶜAbd al-ᶜAzīz in their anti-*qadar* treatises quote any *ḥadīth* from the Prophet on the subject. But jurists such as Mālik b. Anas (d. 179/796) in his *al-Muwaṭṭā* and the Ḥanafī, Abū Yūsuf (d.182/798) in his *Kitāb al-Āthār* include a good deal of strong predestinarian *ḥadīth*. According to one *ḥadīth* in the *al-Muwaṭṭā*, ᶜUmar b. al-Khaṭṭāb relates from the Prophet that, after creating Adam, God rubbed his (Adam's) back and brought out a group of his children. Thereupon God said: "I have created these for the Garden and they shall do the deeds of the people of the Garden." Then He rubbed Adam's back again, this time bringing out

19. [It is clear that Fazlur Rahman did not get to this chapter of this book as he intended.]

another lot of his progeny, and said: "These I have created for the Fire and actions of the people of Fire shall they do." The Prophet was asked: "On what basis, then, shall one perform any deeds?" The Prophet replied: "If God has created a servant [of His] for the Garden, He employs him to do the works of the people of the Garden, and if He has created a servant [of His] for the Fire, He employs him to do the works of the people of the Fire." In Abū Yūsuf's *al-Āthār*, a *ḥadīth* is narrated to the effect that some people asked the Prophet whether they were doing deeds that God had pre-written and (having been written) "the pens had run dry" (i.e., they could not be changed) or whether the future was still open.[20] The Prophet affirmed that it was the case that deeds had been pre-written; upon which the questioners asked why or on what basis should they act. The Prophet replied: "Go on doing works, because it is convenient for each person to do those [deeds] for which he or she has been created [or destined]."[21]

Let us now try to answer the question as to the relationship between law and theology, and the implications of each for the other. It is obvious that the *ḥadīth* quoted above and a lot more of this genre is heavily predestinarian. Law assumes that a person is the locus of legal–moral obligation and hence is charged with the responsibility of making a free choice and acting freely. When eminent jurists, such as Aḥmad b. Ḥanbal, express predestinarian views in their theology and deny any organic relationship between faith and action, we can look at this matter in two ways. We can either say their theological views were of a quite different provenance to that of their legal assumptions; therefore the two were not synchronized. In other words, they held contradictory doctrines about humankind. Or we can say that they saw no contradiction between their predestinarian theology and the moral foundations of their law. It seems that each of these ways of looking upon this matter has some truth. The fact is that the legal activity of these jurists was geared to purely practical life needs of action (ᶜ*amal*). Its theoretical foundations were simple enough. God had sent down the last revelation through the last Prophet on earth, disclosing the way human beings should conduct themselves in the various spheres of life and that it is their duty to obey. This obedience must, however, be facilitated for the Muslim by elaborating and systematizing the divine imperative into actual legal rules. As for theology, this is a matter of

20. Al-Anṣārī, *al-Āthār*, *ḥadīth* 581, 126.
21. Ibid.

belief *(īmān – ᶜaqīda)*. It is crucial, however, to hold correct beliefs. *Īmān* is not something that can be taken lightly, for the Qurᵓān is replete with this concept in all sorts of contexts. Now in the Qurᵓān, God is portrayed as all-merciful, just, etc., but He is also palpably represented as all-powerful without whose sovereign will nothing whatsoever happens. The *qadarī* free-willers, surely, pushed their thesis to anti-Qurᵓānic extremes when they denied any role to God whatsoever in the sphere of human moral action. Similarly, they pushed their thesis of divine justice to such extremes that they denuded God of the power to forgive sinners. Qadarism, therefore had to be rejected, irrespective of whether it had any relevance to the bases of law and action.

But the alternative view in the eyes of these lawyers, that predestinarianism as set out in this type of *ḥadīth* is not contradictory to the bases of law and human action, is also correct. For, at this stage of its development, the predestinarian view is formulated only in general terms. Indeed, the basis of free human action is built into this *ḥadith* literature. For this reason some reports state that a person who is destined for the Garden actually does the actions of the people of the Garden. Indeed, there is no hint at this stage that a person cannot act freely, let alone that they cannot act at all, a view Abu ᵓl-Ḥasan al-Ashᶜarī was to confirm about a century and a quarter later. God has preordained all that a human being will do in his/her lifetime. But unless a person actually does some specific action, he or she will never know that God had preordained it.

However, even if such a doctrine does not contradict or counter the basis of free human action, it certainly introduces a temper where the sense of *human* initiative is dulled. And, in conjunction with other factors that we shall speak of later in this chapter and the next, the human initiative may gradually become almost smothered. Further, the motivation to raise both the level and quality of one's action and preserve the sense of correcting one's conduct is weakened both by the doctrine of predestinarianism and *irjāᵓ* as well as the doctrine of prophetic intercession. That is to say, that with the introduction of this new temper – thanks to predestinarianism, intercessionism, and *irjāᵓ* – a moral trend does set in which runs counter to the Qurᵓān and its living, vibrant mission that aims at intensifying human moral energy.

Ashᶜarism, Māturīdism and Sunnism

As the debate between the Muᶜtazila (or the Qadarīyya) and their opponents, representatives of the emerging Sunnism, progressed, it naturally became more sophisticated and nuanced. The main theses proposed by the Muᶜtazila, which their opponents rejected, was enumerated above. This work is not a history of Islamic theology, nor indeed a religious history of Islam, therefore there is no intention to scan the intricate ramifications of all those theses and many others. The purpose is to locate and discuss these religious ideas, tenets, and trends that have concretely influenced the temper of the world Muslim community and have shaped its ethos and character. We shall, therefore, leave out the intra-God question of His essence and attributes. We may also leave out the question of whether God's attribute of "speech," of which the Qurʾān is the most consummate manifestation, is eternal or created. It was a controversy that certainly played its role in history when the ᶜAbbāsid caliph al-Maʾmūn raised the Muᶜtazilite doctrine to the status of state creed and persecuted Aḥmad b. Ḥanbal for not subscribing to the view that the Qurʾān was created. But it was a scholastic controversy having little to do with the concrete attitudes of the community. We shall instead take up the questions of God's justice, human free will, the nature of divine law, the definition of evil, and, indeed, the role of reason and how Ashᶜarism formulated their solutions.

Before going further, one point needs to be made. Any view sponsored by the state cannot ensure its success if it runs counter to the sensibilities of the community in general, and its "natural" leaders, namely religious and learned persons whom the community comes to trust. Al-Maʾmūn was far more sophisticated and powerful than an ᶜAbd al-Malik b. Marwān or ᶜUmar b. ᶜAbd al-ᶜAzīz who are generally credited by modern scholarship with having so strongly influenced the success of *irjāʾ* and predestinarianism. Yet al-Maʾmūn and his immediate successors were unable to make a dent in the opposition to the Muᶜtazilite creed. Finally, under al-Mutawakkil (d. 247/861) they had to abandon their support for the Muᶜtazila. Nor can one say that the ᶜAbbāsids were more democratically minded than were the Umayyads. If anything, the reverse may have a better claim to validity.

The primary motivation in all the solutions that al-Ashᶜarī proposed to the aforementioned problems was to uphold the uncompromising omnipotence and absolute will of God. The basic fault of the Mu^{c}tazila in the eyes of al-Ash^{c}arī is that they so defined the God–human relationship that God's power and will became compromised. On this point al-Ash^{c}arī unconditionally agreed with Ibn Ḥanbal even though he differed with him over the role of reason in religious thought. Once this happens, God's existence may well become superfluous at least for humankind, if not for nature. Islamic theology, like theologies of other religions, shows clear signs of action and reaction. Thus, on the subject of free will (*qadar)*, the Mu^{c}tazila were all agreed that in the sphere of volitional activity God did not actually play any role and that humanity was central in all. The Mu^{c}tazila were of course divided among themselves as to whether God still had the *power* to act in these spheres.

Al-Ash^{c}arī, in turn defined his extreme position by rejecting the idea that humanity can be validly said to act at all, let alone act freely. Humankind can be said to be an "actor" only metaphorically (*bi* ᵓ*l-majāz*). God creates all human acts and man only "acquires" them. When asked why he used the word "acquire" rather than "do" with reference to humankind, al-Ash^{c}arī replied that the Qurᵓān does so. The Qurᵓān, of course, patently uses the words "do" and "perform (*^{c}amal*)" with reference to human beings. The term "acquire (*kasb*)" is also used in the Qurᵓān fairly frequently. But the Qurᵓān seems to use this term when it wishes to emphasize not merely the performance of a deed but the *incurring of responsibility* for one's deeds, for good or for evil. Al-Ash^{c}arī, therefore, undoubtedly does violence to the meaning of the Qurᵓānic usage here. Much more incredible is al-Ash^{c}arī's attempt to prove from Q. 37:96 that God creates human acts: "He [God] has created you and what you make [as handiwork]." This is part of Abraham's speech to his idol-worshiping people. In the preceding verse Abraham says to them: "Do you worship that which you [yourselves] have carved?" (Q. 37:95). It is clear that this verse is also saying that it is God who has created you and those idols that you have made. But al-Ash^{c}arī replaces the words "what you make" with "what you do."[22] The Arabic *wa ma ta^{c}malun* is susceptible to both translations, but the context clearly is against al-Ash^{c}arī's interpretation. Perhaps nothing can bring out more strikingly al-Ash^{c}arī's anxiety to rob humankind of all power to act than the following passage which I quote *in extenso* despite its length, to illustrate al-Ash^{c}arī's technique of theological

22. Al-Ash^{c}arī, *al-Luma^{c}*, p. 116.

argumentation as well as his doctrine. The context of the passage is the Mu^{c}tazilite contention that if God, and not humanity, creates human actions, then God should become responsible for them, and not humanity. And in the case of evil actions, imputation of evil to God is unavoidable. Al-Ash^{c}arī has, in the preceding passages, replied that just as the thing in which motion is created is describable by the term "moving" but the agent who has created motion is not describable thus, similarly that is characterized by the term "evil" wherein God creates evil and not God Himself. Then we are told:

> If an opponent says: "Since God has commanded us to pray, our prayer consists of certain movements whereby we move when we pray. Now, a moving being [is described as] moving, because motion comes to inhere in it. [But surely] one who curses or lies becomes a cursing one or a liar, because he performs (*fa^{c}ala*) the [act] of cursing and [the act of] lying, not because these inhere in him." It will be said to him [in reply]: "If the reason (*^{c}illa*) for which we are being forced to admit that it is permissible for God to lie – He is supremely above all such accusation – is that [we allow that] He can command us to lie. It would then follow that in all the actions that He commands it would be permissible to describe Him by such acts. Thus, since He has ordered certain motions to inhere in ourselves and [thus] to offer prayers thereby, it would necessarily follow that it be considered allowable that He [too] cause certain motions to inhere in Himself and [thus] to offer prayers thereby." Should, however, the opponent say, that since it is permissible [on al-Ash^{c}arī's hypothesis] that God can command another being [a human] to lie, why is it not permissible for Him to create lying in that other in order that, that other becomes a liar. In the same manner that He had commanded another [human being] to pray, so that He creates in that other prayer, whereby that other person becomes a praying one? If the opponent puts to us this question in this manner, we shall accept its validity. [But the Mu^{c}tazila opponents] will be asked: "If it is permissible that God create prayer in another person in order that the other person becomes a praying one, why should it not be permissible for Him to create a will in another? [In so doing] that person becomes an intending one. Or [why not create] speech, whereby that person becomes a speaker?" If they say: "A speaker or an intending one, becomes a speaker or an intending one, purely because he/she *performs* [or *does*] speaking and willing [and not because speaking

> and willing occur to him/her or come to inhere in him/her like motion]." It will be said to them: "Then why do you deny that the one praying becomes a praying person because of performing the act of prayer in himself; or that a moving being moves, because he performs the act of motion in himself?" If, then, the opponent says: "Because sometimes one moves without doing motion to himself [i.e., he moves involuntarily]." It will be said to him: "And sometimes one wills and speaks without *doing* a will or a speech – like a lover who may so [intensely] love his beloved that he cannot desist from love. Or, like a person who talks during sleep or an epileptic fit, without any self-control." Should the opponent say: "The love of [such] a lover is no love in reality, nor is his/her will, a will in reality." Then the reply will be: "Nor is the speech of an epileptic or a sleeping person speech in reality*; nor is the speech of a waking person speech in reality,* nor is the will of a lover, will in reality. This is something, which anyone can understand."[23]

Waking persons do not have speech in reality for they only *acquire* speech created in them by God. Neither, of course, does God become a speaker by creating speech in a human. One wonders who is the speaker in reality, then! Al-Ashᶜarī and his followers denied potentialities or powers in things and humans. The Ashᶜarites had, therefore, to deny causation and adopt atomism both in time and space: before I raise my arm, I have no power to raise my arm; God creates this power in me at the time I actually raise my arm. As time went on, the Ash'arites gloried in finding ever new arguments to prove human impotency. According to a story, the systematic interpreter of the Ashᶜarī school, al-Bāqillānī (d. 403/1012), was once holding a discussion on *qadar* with the Buwayhid minister, the Muᶜtazilite al-Ṣāḥib b. ᶜAbbād (d. 382/995) in a garden. Ibn ᶜAbbād stood up and plucked a flower, and said to the Ashᶜarite scholar: "Do you want to tell me that *I* did not pluck this?" Al-Bāqillānī replied: "If *you*, indeed, *did* pluck it, then perhaps you can put it back also!" The idea is that power is indivisible; it cannot be for certain things and not for others. It is the same al-Bāqillānī who is reported to have advocated that all would-be orthodox Muslims must be required to believe in the atomistic structure of reality. Fakhr al-Dīn al-Rāzī (d. 606/1210), a great exponent of Ashᶜarism, held that a being who can be said "to act" in a real sense of that word must know all the consequences of the act. For example, if I move my finger, this sets in

23. Ibid., pp. 150–151.

motion an infinite chain of events, which I may not know and therefore I may not be properly said to move my finger. If for al-Bāqillānī acting in the real sense entailed omnipotence, for al-Rāzī it required omniscience.

This is how the vibrant message of the Qurʾān, inviting human beings to action, ended up three centuries later in the hands of the intellectual formulators of the creed of the mainstream of the Muslim community. We have already commented on how the predeterministic beliefs of the founders of Islamic law did in a sense mark a departure from the Qurʾān. It introduced a new temper in the community. Nevertheless, they were quite compatible with the bases of the law and were not necessarily injurious to moral action, since they represented predeterminism only in a general sense and were not action-specific. But with Ashᶜarism a totally new era of belief dawned upon Muslims. From then on, they could not act in reality; human action, indeed, became a mere metaphor devoid of any real meaning. Al-Ashᶜarī explicitly stated that even a waking person cannot speak in reality. This is certainly in stark contradiction to the very assumptions of law, that humans can choose and act freely, and therefore are responsible. It is true that this particular Ashᶜarī doctrine of human action is in the nature of a formula and, as such, has little direct bearing on real life. In real life, Muslims continued to go about their daily work. The truth is that Ashᶜarism held its sway right up until the twentieth century and holds sway even now in the citadels of Islamic conservatism. So when these formulas are trumpeted in the schoolrooms and from the pulpits, they cannot over a long period of time fail to affect the level of human activity, human initiative, and above all the frontiers of human imagination upon which these formulas must have a deadening effect. In the next chapter we shall see the marriage of this creed with the practical piety of Islam, i.e., Ṣūfism.

If this is the deterministic logic of Ashᶜarism, its concept of God's justice and the nature of divine law is still more spectacular. The Muᶜtazila had evolved a theory of rational ethics on the ground that good and bad are knowable by natural reason without the aid of revelation. This theory systematically worked out by al-Qāḍī ᶜAbd al-Jabbār (d. 411/1024–1025) has been masterfully presented by Professor George Hourani in his work *Islamic Rationalism*. The theory states that "primary" or general ethical truths about right and wrong are rationally discoverable by intuitive reason, but that for actual obligations of "secondary" ethical truths, humanity needs revelation. Humans, by reason alone, cannot determine those acts that must be done or avoided in order to come closer to pursuing a truly ethical life. The Muʿtazila did not hold that determination of actual do's and dont's is possible without the aid of the prohetic revelation. Firstly, they held that general ethical truths are purely rational and universal. Secondly, they believed that the practice of revealed obligations helps us to rise to the cultivation of those universal truths. This also shows why the Muʿtazila did not create a school of law: they did not hold that positive law was possible through pure reason alone.

But Ashʿarism responded by insisting that *no* right or wrong could be known, general or specific, through pure reason. The Ashʿarites held that without revelation, which began with Adam and ended with Muḥammad, neither murder nor lying nor any other act can be said to be good or bad. In a natural state the only law was self-interest. And, because human beings will deem all such things that promote their self-interest to be good, and those that thwart their self-interest as bad, therefore God has to declare, through revelation, what is good and what is evil. That pure reason yields no obligations or "reason is not a Legislator" (*inna l-ʿaql laysa bi-sharīʿ*) became the juristic axiom with all Muslim jurists. It is true that the Muʿtazila had given to the revelation only a secondary, though essential, place in their ethical theory. The really effective procedure would have been to erect a system of universal ethical values on the basis of an analysis of the moral objectives of the Qurʾān. But did the Sunnī jurists do that? This could have been achieved through developing a systematic ethical system derived from the Qurʾānic values, which are either there explicitly in the Qurʾān or could be extracted from its *rationes legis*. Instead the jurists were content to apply their legal principle of analogical reasoning (*qiyās*) quite unsystematically and in an *ad hoc* manner. The result is that today Muslims wishing to derive workable Islamic law from the Qurʾān have to make a fresh start by working out a genuine ethical value-system from the Qurʾān.

But the Ashʿarī anti-rationalism culminated in the assertion that God sends down laws through this revelation thanks to the sheer fiat of His will. The implication is that God does not thereby intend the well-being of His creation, as the Muʿtazila had contended. The real motivation of the

Ashʿarīs, no doubt, was to counter the excesses of the Muʿtazilite rationality. In terms of the latter's view God *cannot* do injustice, and hence He can neither punish the virtuous nor forgive the evildoer. For in that case the distinction between virtue and evil would evaporate. To the Ashʿarīs it seemed, and with good reason, that the Muʿtazila rationalism was imposing its own human categories upon God who must do this and must not do that. To this they replied with their own extreme formulation. They claimed that if God sent all virtuous persons to Hell and all evil persons to the Garden, all this would be perfect justice because He owed nothing to anyone. He is not under the will or command of anyone else. So contravening these commands on His part cannot be deemed to be wrong or a violation of the law. On the contrary, being the sole and absolute owner of His creatures, none of which had any claim to be created, He can do with them anything that He likes. And whatever He likes to do with them would be justice. Therefore, to search for ends and purposes in His laws is not only meaningless, but also grave disobedience to Him. This doctrine, of course, is purely theological.

In practice, Muslim jurists wrote a great deal on "the purposes of the Sacred Law" (*aghrāḍ al-sharīʿa*) and "the inner meanings of the religious laws" (*asrār al-dīn*). Works of Muslim jurists, which undoubtedly contain some of the most precious and brilliant intellectual products of Islamic thought, have, in fact, so far remained untouched by modern scholarship. Nevertheless, the general spiritual and intellectual atmosphere created by the orthodoxy and infinitely strengthened by Ashʿarism effectively militated, through long centuries, against the development of a new, comprehensive, and systematic attempt to interpret the Qurʾān into a really meaningful ethical and legal system. Ashʿarism, which succeeded only slowly in gaining general acceptance – thanks mainly to the influence of certain outstanding men such as al-Ghazālī (d. 505/1111) – held sway mainly in the Middle East. In the East, in Central Asia, and the Indian Subcontinent, the theology of Abū ʾl-Manṣūr al-Māturīdī, a Central Asian of Samarqand and a contemporary of al-Ashʿarī, gained currency. Unlike al-Ashʿarī, who belonged to the Shāfiʿī school of law, al-Māturīdī was a member of the Ḥanafī school which was predominant in these regions. Al-Māturīdī, on some crucial points, was close to the Muʿtazila and stands generally between the Muʿtazila and the Ashʿarites. Thus, on free will (*qadar*), he held that humanity was not devoid of power, as al-Ashᶜarī declared. Before the act, a human being has a certain power, which includes the physical power with which he or she is endowed. But at the time of the actual act this natural power is consummated by another power, so that the act necessarily and immediately follows. This second power is created by God in the agent at the time of the action, as al-Ashᶜarī held. He also held the Muᶜtazila view that right and wrong are natural realities and are discoverable by natural human reason, although he believed that revelation gives further moral strength to the agent to pursue good and avoid evil. He also affirmed that divine commands have purposes that are for the good of humankind. Although to an extent these views did remain alive among the Ḥanafī school of law, the spread of Ashᶜarism through the teaching of towering personalities such as al-Ghazālī and others to a large extent dampened the influence of Māturīdism. As we shall elaborate in the next chapter, it was the Ṣūfī spirituality of al-Ghazālī and of Ibn ᶜArabī that gave strong impetus to a *weltanschauung* where humanity was obliterated in the face of God and little room was left for human will and its efficacy. This state of affairs was naturally far more conducive to the theology of al-Ashᶜarī – for whom, as we have seen, a waking person's speech is just as little *his* act as is the delirium of a sleeping person or of an epileptic – than to the views of al-Māturīdī. Ḥanafī Sūfīs could differ but little from Shāfiᶜī and Mālikī ones.

Shīᶜism

Al-Ashᶜarī relates that the Imāmī Shīᶜī are unanimous on three issues.[24] Firstly, they all hold that Imāmate is established by a clear designation or text (*naṣṣ*) alone on the part of a predecessor in favor of his successor and not by election or consensus of the people as the Sunnīs do. Secondly, that no rebellion against an established government is allowed except through an Imām. Thirdly, that no *ijtihād* is permissible in the field of law (*aḥkām*), presumably as distinguished from theology. On the second point, it is well known that the Imāms of the Twelver Shīᶜī never rebelled after Ḥusayn, the Prophet's grandson, and since the sixth Imām Jaᶜfar al-Ṣādiq (d. 148/765), they have eschewed the acquisition of political power. The doctrine of abstention from rebellion, except through an Imām, seems to be a logical development from the stance of Jaᶜfar al-Ṣādiq and subsequent Imāms. It is

24. Ashᶜarī, *Maqālāt*, vol. 1, pp. 87–88.

not certain, but it is possible that Khumaynī started, soon after his successful rebellion in 1979, to call himself Imām. However, Khumaynī's whole concept of "rule by the clergy" (*wilāyat-i-faqīh*) seems to run counter to the Imāmī Shīᶜī tradition. As for the non-permissibility of *ijtihād* in the sphere of law, which al-Ashᶜarī states repeatedly is held unanimously by the Imamiyya, it is possible that it prevailed before the Shīᶜī started imbibing the Muᶜtazila legacy in the fourth/tenth century, which led to a change. This would be true particularly after the victory, in the twelfth/eighteenth century, of the Uṣūlīs, those who based law on principles (*uṣūl*), rather than on reports or traditions (*khabar*), of their opponents, the Akhbarīs or the "traditionalists.'

On free will, al-Ashᶜarī notes that while early Shīᶜī authorities (many of whom had a materialistic conception of God), such as Hishām b. al-Hakam (d. 179/795–796), held that a person possesses a certain power before the act itself, such as health, physical power, etc. The idea is comparable to the Māturīdī view. Human power is the consummating factor, whereas the act that follows necessarily is that which supplies the decisive impulse (*muhayyij*). The latter is described in a *ḥadīth* in al-Kulaynī as a "cause that arrives from God." Hishām b. al-Hakam also believed that God creates human acts. However, al-Ashᶜarī mentions several groups among the Shīᶜī who came to uphold, near or during his time, Muᶜtazila views on various issues and about whom he says: "They hold both views, those concerning the Imamate and those of the Muᶜtazila *(al-qāilūna bi ᵓl-iᶜtizāl wa ᵓl-imāma*)."[25] These groups rejected the materialistic conceptions of God held by earlier Shīᶜī theologians. Instead they adopted a spiritual view of God's nature, interpreted the anthropomorphic expressions of the Qurᵓān and the *ḥadith* à la Muᶜtazila, and believed humanity to be free agents whose acts were not created by God.

The Shīᶜī *ḥadīth* on God's role in human actions and on the issue of human powers is extremely interesting and highly nuanced. Shīᶜī *ḥadīth* was compiled several decades after the compilation of Sunnī *ḥadīth*, and was obviously influenced by much more sophisticated theological trends. The formula "There is no [absolute] determinism [of human acts] but neither is the human agent absolute (*la jabra wa la tafwīda*)" sums up the general stance of the Shīᶜī on this fundamental question. But within the understanding of this formula there are many nuances and progressions. To

25. Ibid., vol. 1, p. 111.

be sure, all these are traced to one of the Imāms, mostly to Ja^c^far al-Ṣādiq and occasionally to ^c^Alī himself. There are *aḥādīth* that emphasize God's role and there are *aḥādīth* that underline humanity's role. The general view that emerges is that both in God and humans there is a parallel process of determination. Thus, as we have seen, in humankind there are the factors of health, the relevant physical organ, the absence of impediments and, finally, there is the compelling motivation (*muhayyij*). On God's part, there is a process consisting of a general willingness (*mashī^ɔ^a*), a strong will (*irāda*), the measurement (of time and place called *qadar*), and, finally, the irrevocable determination (*qaḍā^ɔ^*). It appears that at the end of the process, when the act actually occurs, there is a coalescence of the divine determination and the human will. Hence, an action is a kind of collaboration between humanity and God. Further, the process can stop before the act, as a *ḥadīth* from Ja^c^far al-Ṣādiq says: "God willed that I should have power over something which He did not will that I actually do."[26] By the time of Ibn Bābwayh (d. 381/991–992), however, things had changed greatly and Shī^c^ism had come to accept the essentials of the Mu^c^tazila teaching. For example, the doctrinal formulation that whatever God does, He does for the well-being and in the best interest of His creation is a subject that forms a special chapter in Ibn Bābwayh's *Kitāb al-Tawḥīd.*[27] On *qadar*, Ibn Bābwayh decidedly interprets the term "will of God" as His determination of human acts, in the sense of God's command and prohibition of those acts. Ibn Bābwayh quotes a *ḥadīth*, which also exists in al-Kulaynī's *Kitāb al-Kāfī*, that Ḥamza b. Ḥumrān asked Ja^c^far al-Ṣādiq about human power, but the latter did not answer him. He went to him again and said to him: "May God bestow His goodness upon you, something has entered my mind about this [i.e., about the question of human power] which will not be removed except by something I hear from you!" He replied: "So long as it remains [only] in your mind, it will not harm you." "I said, 'May God bestow His goodness upon you! Believe that God, the Exalted, has not imposed obligations upon His servants except such as they are able to carry out and are within the limits of their power. Further, they cannot do anything of these [obligations] except through God's wish, His will, His measuring (*qadar*) and His absolute determination.' Ja^c^far al-Ṣādiq replied: 'This is the religion of God [i.e., religion that

26. Al-Kulaynī, *al-Kāfī*, vol. 1, p. 160.
27. Ibn Bābwayh, *al-Tawḥīd*, pp. 346–347.

He has revealed] espoused by me and my forefathers' – or words to that effect."[28]

This *ḥadīth* represents the standard teaching of the Shīᶜī *ḥadīth* outlined above, namely, that human acts are brought about by God's will as well as humanity's. But Ibn Bābwayh has commented on it: "God's wish and will," he says, "in so far as those matters are concerned which constitute obedience to God [positive religious duties], [only] mean that God has commanded these and that He is pleased [by their being carried out]. But in so far as those things are concerned that constitute disobedience [prohibitions], they mean that God has prohibited these and warned against them."[29] This clearly means that the role of God's will is here reduced from being a co-creative agency of the human act to strictly that of God's commanding an act or prohibiting it – which is a genuine Muᶜtazila position. The same author also interprets God's absolute and irrevocable determination (*qaḍāʾ*) concerning production of a human act in the same spirit. The Muᶜtazila gloss on Shīᶜī doctrine has come a long way indeed since these *aḥādīth* were first formulated.

With the introduction of philosophy into Shīᶜī theology in the seventh/thirteenth century by the Shīᶜī scientist and philosopher-theologian Nāṣir al-Dīn al-Ṭūsī (d. 673/1274) and his pupil Ibn al-Muṭahhar al-Ḥillī (d. 726/1325), the doctrine of *qadar* develops further. Al-Ṭūsī, in his famous compendium on theology, the *Kitāb al-Tajrīd*, a work which has several commentaries by both Shīᶜī and Sunnī theologians and was taught in both Sunnī and Shīᶜī institutions of learning, clearly states that a person is the "creator" of his or her own actions. This view had provoked the censure on the Muᶜtazila of being described as "the Magians of the Muslim community." That was because they believed like the Magians in two ultimate powers, God and humanity, if not God and Ahriman – and had materially contributed to their downfall. Since then, although Shīᶜī theology has remained distinct from philosophy proper, it has nevertheless been strongly influenced by philosophy in contrast to what happened in Sunnī Islam after the success of Ashᶜarism.

Conclusion

The splits that started early in the Muslim community were implicitly ideological, particularly the uprising against ᶜUthmān. Several later ones,

28. Al-Kulaynī, *al-Kāfī*, vol. 1, p. 162.
29. Ibn Bābwayh, *al-Tawḥīd*, pp. 346–347.

such as those of Muᶜāwiya against ᶜAlī and of Ṭalḥā and Zubayr against ᶜAlī were purely political power struggles. The rebellions in the name of justice and righteousness were conducted by the Khawārij. Later, beginning with Zayd, the great-grandson of ᶜAlī, whose followers were known as the Zaydīs, it continued. The Khawārij were extremely puritanical, idealistic, and egalitarian people in whose movement women also appear to have played important roles. But since they were Bedouins, they could not maintain any effective unity among themselves and there were constant accusations of infidelity (*kufr*) against each other. They were, therefore, in practice, no more than bands of warriors and not organized and unified rebels and were vanquished one after another by the armies of the Umayyad rulers – although after much trouble.

These Khārijī rebellions and civil wars produced a severe reaction in the Muslim populace in general. The community refused to justify rebellion and killing on charges of "grave errors and sins," an accusation not difficult to levy against their rulers. This popular reaction led to the acceptance of a pacifist or at least non-activist attitude in the community. This became known as *irjāᵓ*, the idea that rather than take a sword in one's hand and correct people's wrongs, one should leave the matter to God's decision and hope for His forgiveness. This pragmatic attitude, formulated as doctrine later, suited the Umayyad rulers who were almost by conviction of the same persuasion. It resulted in a lowering of the moral tension that the teaching of the Qurᵓān and the Prophet Muḥammad had aimed at creating, if not promoting an easy conscience.

This *irjāᵓ* soon generated the further belief that it is God's will, not that of humankind, that is effective in the final analysis and that a human being cannot go outside divine will. This quasi-predestinarianism, which was a theory and not just a practical attitude, provoked the oppositional doctrine of *qadar*. This meant that human beings produce their own actions and not God, and hence are responsible for them. The doctrine of *qadar*, though it was temporarily espoused by early ᶜAbbāsid rulers, made a very small dent in the irjāᵓist milieu that the community had come to espouse. It in fact produced a strong reaction in the form of Ashᶜarism, which gradually became the "official" theology of Islam. The new Ashᶜarī doctrine denied that humanity had the power to act at all in the real sense of the word. In this view humankind was, therefore, only a metaphysical actor. This attitude was bound to do severe damage to the human self-image as a repository of initiatives and originality and harmed the assumptions underlying law, which considered human beings as free and responsible agents.

2

DEVELOPMENTS FROM *IRJĀʾ*:

POLITICS, ṢŪFISM, AND GNOSTIC EXTREMISM

Introduction

The formulation of predestinarianism (*irjāʾ*) and its inculcation through *ḥadīth* and theology, traced out in the preceding chapter, manifests itself in two concrete aspects of the life of the community, politics and Ṣūfism (Islamic mysticism). If theological thought per se only indirectly influenced attitudes, then politics and Ṣūfism affected them directly, palpably, and profoundly. Indeed, throughout the medieval period, these two were the most salient factors determining Islamic life. Law continued to be operative, but as we have shown in the preceding chapter, even the metaphysics and ethics of law had become fairly heavily overlaid with a predestinarian and deterministic outlook, even at the hands of the great founders of the legal schools. Further inroads were made into the very fundamental character and rationale of the law by Ṣūfī metaphysics and ethics which both taught passivity. This Ṣūfī influence brought about a vicious dualism between the "inner life of the heart" and the "actions of the limbs."

It is of capital importance to understand the role of both these factors, the political and the spiritual in Islam in order adequately to appreciate the rise and nature of fundamentalist reform which we shall treat from the next chapter onwards. For indeed fundamentalist developments, as we shall see, are essentially reactions against both these factors and seek to eradicate or seriously modify Ṣūfī spirituality and drastically reform politics. Yet, as we shall also see, this fundamentalism is unable to free itself from its basic predestinarian framework and limitations but seeks reform within the terms of these postulates. Hence, its challenge to both the political and spiritual orders proves ineffective and temporary, unless it is able seriously to question and weaken the framework.

Of course, politics and Ṣūfism are basically negatively related to each other, the former dealing with the "external" life of the community, while the latter concentrates upon the "internal" life of the individual. But this mutual negation has, in actual history proved beneficial for both, since it has resulted in dividing life into autonomous zones. They may not collaborate but they need not fight each other either. In fact, they found a convenient if not a congenial *modus operandi* throughout the medieval period in the greater part of the Muslim world, even though they often clashed in popular rebellions in Turkey. Yet, despite their mutual exclusiveness, both have their origin in *irjāʾ*, albeit in different ways. So long as *irjāʾ*, continues to characterize Muslim life, fundamentalist reform has little hope of bringing any real and effective change to the *status quo*. On the contrary, it is destined to be reabsorbed into the *status quo*, except to the limited extent that it is able to breach the intellectual and ethical expressions created by the psychological barrier of *irjāʾ*. During the past two centuries of fundamentalist reform, very little of this has happened.

Islam and Political Life

Political quietism (*irjāʾ*) was, as can be expected, born at the same time as religious *irjāʾ*, for both were a reaction to Khārijism. However, as we shall presently see, political *irjāʾ* created for itself an independent, well-defined, and concrete basis by developing the twin concepts of the community (*umma*) and its *imām* (political leader) in a direction that was calculated to inculcate political quietism and passivity. The Sunnīs and the Shīʿī both shared this *irjāʾ* in somewhat different ways. Our aim in the following account is not to delve into the details of the two political traditions, but rather briefly to bring out their essential temper and basic similarities as well as differences. Each developed a rhythm of its own whereby it accommodated itself to the realities of political life, but on its own terms. Sunnism, squarely basing itself on *irjāʾ*, nevertheless managed to keep certain elements of idealism alive, while Shīʿism grounded itself in an idealism of passion, yet found ways of an uneasy though practically effective truce with reality. The two cannot be said to be antipodal to each other; yet their points of departure are antipodal and, therefore, the rhythms of their development and articulation of their political attitudes are, and indeed in some important ways, very different.

Naturally, the earliest and most seminal repository of the political views of both groups is to be found in their respective *ḥadīth*. In my *Islamic Methodology in History* (1965), I had quoted a good deal of Sunnī political *ḥadīth* to illustrate the evolving Sunnī political attitudes in conformity with the religious *irjāʾ*. The two most salient elements in this teaching are: (1) that Muslims must tenaciously stick to the majority of the community *(al-jamāᶜa)* and avoid schismatic and "peripheral" groups; and (2) that they must equally tenaciously stick to their political leader (*imām*). These two, the *imām* and the majority of the *umma*, are of course, interdependent and entail each other. The term *sunna* in the phrase *ahl al-sunna wa ʾl-jamāᶜa,* whereby the majority of the Muslim community describes itself, does not mean the Sunna of the Prophet, for no Muslim group ever denied that Sunna but means "the High Way," or "the Middle Way," as opposed to peripheral "trails." Abū Ḥanīfa's use of the term in his letter to ᶜUthmān al-Battī also has this meaning. In the Sunnī doctrine, in its subsequent development, the entire emphasis that the Qurʾān lays on the community shifts to the majority of the community's way as the Sunna. Now this Sunna is precisely *irjāʾ* both in the religious and the political sense. It was, no doubt, supposed to be a "mean" between two extremes. Politically, it claimed to represent the mean between Shīᶜī legitimism and Khārijī universalism, by insisting that rule belongs to the Quraysh, neither to the House of the Prophet nor to any Muslim who might happen to be the best "even though he be an Ethiopian slave," as the Khārijīs held. Religiously, they claimed to offer the mean between the absolute determinism of the jabarites and the absolute free will of the qadarites. But, as we showed in the preceding chapter, the religious mean turned out to be only nominal. In the hands of the Ashᶜarite theologians from Abu ʾl-Ḥasan al-Ashᶜarī to Fakhr al-Dīn al-Rāzī, the Sunnī doctrine became a form of pure determinism.

Perhaps the most interesting political *ḥadīth* in the authoritative Sunnī literature is the following one to be found in both the *Ṣaḥīḥ* (sound) works of Muslim b. al-Ḥajjāj (d. 261/875) and al-Bukhārī related on the authority of the Companion Ḥudhayfa b. al-Yamān:

> People used to ask the Messenger of God about good while I used to ask him about evil out of fear lest it [evil] should overtake me. I said: "O God's Messenger! We have been previously in a condition of paganism (*jāhiliyya*) and evil and then God brought us this good [through you]; will there be evil again after this good?" The Messenger replied: "Yes." Then I asked: "And will good come again after that evil?" He replied: "Yes, but there will be some corruption in that good." I asked him: "What will be its corruption?" He replied: "There will come a people who will follow a path [Sunna], other than mine and who will lead [people] to that which is different from my guidance. They will do some good things and some bad things." I asked him: "Will there be evil again after that [mixed] good?" He replied: "Yes. There will be propagandists standing at the gates of Hell – whoever responds to their call they will throw him therein." I asked the Prophet: "Describe them for us." He replied, "They will be from our own race [i.e., will be Arabs] and shall speak our tongue." I said to the Prophet: "So, what do you command me [to do], should that situation overtake me?" He replied, "That you stick to the majority of the Muslims and to their political leader." I said to him: "What if they have no majority [party], nor a political leader?" [He replied]: "Then, abandon all the groups even if you have to cling to the stem of a tree until death overtake you."[1]

In another version of this *ḥadīth*, Muslim adds: "The Prophet said: 'After me there will come political leaders who will not be guided by my guidance. There will be some men among them who will have a devil's heart in a human body.' Ḥudhayfa asked: 'What shall I do, O God's Messenger! If I find myself in such a situation?' He replied: 'Listen and obey the ruler; even if he should strike your back and wrest your property, you should but listen and obey.'"[2]

The first point to note in this *ḥadīth* is that it is undoubtedly a veiled commentary on the very early Islamic history, although it may not be easy to identify clearly the subject of each allusion or description. Probably "the evil that will come after the good brought by the Prophet" means the assassination of ᶜUthmān and the first civil war. The "mixed good" that will

1. Fazlur Rahman, *Methodology*, p. 56.
2. Ibid.

follow this first evil most probably refers to the rule of the Umayyads who substituted dynastic rule for the early caliphate which was condoned by the majority of the community but which was, nevertheless, seen by it and the majority of its religious leadership as a traumatic fall from the ideals of Islam. The second evil that follows upon this "mixed good" refers unambiguously to the early sectarian developments, particularly the Khawārij about whom we are told in another parallel *ḥadīth* that they would dart forth from (the panel of) Islam as an arrow darts forth from the bow.

This historical characterization then culminates in a statement of the political ideology whose most fundamental principle requires Muslims to stick to the majority of the Community and to be faithful to its political leader or ruler. The loyalty to the ruler is due even though he "strikes your back and confiscates your property." The experience of civil wars and their attendant chaos, particularly the incessant military campaigns of the Khawārij, resulted in a firm doctrinal commitment to political conformism for which the ground was effectively and simultaneously being prepared by religious *irjā*. Finally, this *ḥadīth* not only teaches political conformism but downright political quietism in the absence of a majority party and its leader. One should cling to the stem of a tree until one dies, rather than take part in political activity. This quietist teaching is spectacularly displayed in another *ḥadīth* recorded in the *Ṣaḥīḥ* of Muslim: The Messenger of God said: "There will be civil wars (*fitan*) during which to sit at home will be better than one who is standing up [i.e., in readiness to go forth into war], and one who is standing up will be better than one who is walking, and one who is walking will be better than one who is running [i.e., rushing into fight]."[3]

This principle of political quietism, forced by the excessive heat of political dissent, which advised Muslims to "stay at home" rather than go out, had as its other side an emphasis on conformity with the majority and obedience to its leader, as indicated above. A famous *ḥadīth* states that the Prophet said:

> Pray, God make that man prosper [or happy] who hears my words, preserves them well [in his mind] and then communicates them [to others]. For many a transmitter of [words of] wisdom does not himself understand [those words] and many a person transmits [words of] wisdom

3. Muslim, *al-Ṣaḥīḥ*, "Kitāb al-Fitan."

> to him who understands them better. There are three things about which the heart of a Muslim is never niggardly: sincerity of his actions for God, active good will for Muslims and sticking to the majority, for their mission comprehends all those who are outside their fold [i.e., sectarians].[4]

It was this line of political thought that prohibited rebellion against a sitting government, seeking support from Qurʾān 5:33, which recommends the direct punishment of those who "fight God and His Messenger and run around on the land corrupting it." Eventually, of course, successful usurpation or seizure of power came to be regarded by Sunnī political theoreticians as a valid principle of legitimization of power, and submission to tyrannical rule (*sulṭān jāʾir*) was recommended on the principle that "sixty years of tyrannical rule is better than one night without political authority."[5] It was in connection with the ruler's role as protector of law and order that he came to be described – particularly after the deep influence upon the Muslim mind of ancient Persian ideas of the king and kingly power – as "the shadow of God" and "the refuge of the World" (*jehān panāh*) and invested by men such as Niẓām al-Mulk with "divine glory" (*far-i īzdī*). Despite the grafting of the Persian elements upon the Qurʾānic ethos, the fabric of political theory appeared so seamless that even ultra-orthodox thinkers such as Ibn Taymiyya (d. 728/1328) could happily accept the characterization "shadow of God," although, of course, they would sternly reject any idea that attributed divinity to the ruler.

Certainly there is much in Sunnī Islam to argue in support of the ideal of political non-conformism as well. First of all, there is the principle that "there shall be no obedience to creation [i.e. the ruler] in disobedience to God," again in a form of a *ḥadīth*. This means that, irrespective of the personal character of the ruler himself, one must disobey him should he order something wrong to be said or done. Then there is the Sunnī contention against Shīʿī legitimism which requires that the ruler be an infallible Imām from the House of the Prophet. According to this contention, stated, for example, by al-Bāqillānī (d. 403/1012) the community may extract by force its rights from the ruler if he will not listen to correct advice, admonition, and warning. And, of course, the ruler

4. Fazlur Rahman, *Methodology*, p. 45.
5. Ibid., p. 144 n. 4.

can in theory be deposed. There is, in addition, the saying attributed to the Prophet that the "best deed in the sight of God is frankly to tell the truth in front of a tyrant." This *ḥadīth* has, indeed, historically inspired many a man of religion to show unusual courage to speak out the truth, sometimes even blurting out the truth before powerful and autocratic rulers, as can be seen from the biographies of so many prominent leaders. Although such literature is also filled with much fiction and wishful thinking, nevertheless the biographies of Aḥmad b. Ḥanbal, Ibn Taymiyya, Aḥmad Sirhindī, and countless others down the centuries is a record of which Sunnī Islam can justly be proud.

The point, however, is that basically Sunnism had settled for political *irjāʾ* or quietism and had developed an amazingly comprehensive arsenal of concepts and doctrines, first through the mechanism of *ḥadīth* and later through other political theories, to ensure that obedience to the ruler and political conformism was institutionalized. In this connection, we must not overlook the doctrine of *ijmāʿ* or the community's consensus, which, in view of the new developments in the political theory noted above, came to refer not so much to the community as to the "majority of the community." The doctrine of *ijmāʿ* has other important functions. For example, in the legal sphere it decides which belief or practice shall be normative; but in the political arena it plays no less important a role. It provides the basis for the ruler's unchallenged consolidation of power. And, despite the fact that Sunnī political theoreticians have forever been talking about the principle of "election" (*ikhtiyār*) of the ruler, the question of what constitutes an electoral college was left without any serious discussion. The institution of *shūrā*, the collective decision-making council through which the elders of a tribe arrived at decisions concerning momentous issues of peace and war in pre-Islamic Arabia, was stifled instead of being developed in later Islamic political theory. This was despite the Qurʾān's clear injunction: "Their [i.e. the community's] affairs shall be decided through their *collective or mutual discussion*" (Q. 42:38). Instead, *shūrā* came to mean that one man, the ruler, would "consult" such persons as he thought appropriate and then execute his will. No wonder, then, that it required real heroic courage to speak out the truth before an autocratic ruler! For the *shūrā* and the role of the community in the decision-making process explicitly enjoined by the Qurʾān vanished into thin air.

In the preceding chapter, we briefly portrayed the Shīʿī position on the question of free will as being a mean between total determinism and absolute freedom, although later, under the Muʿtazila influence, they tended to give complete autonomy to human agency. But, on the whole, the Shīʿī remained irjāʾists in a religious sense, maintaining that commission of a grave sin does not cause a person to become devoid of faith, as the Khawārij and the Muʿtazila held. Indeed, like the Sunnis, the Shīʿī also accept the well-known *ḥadīth* that a person professing that there is no God except Allāh and Muḥammad is his Messenger will enter the Garden even if guilty of heinous sins such as adultery and theft. This *ḥadīth*, which must have originated in the Murjiʾa circles, came to be accepted by both the Sunnī and the Shīʿī orthodoxies. Since the primary aim of this *ḥadīth* is to distinguish sharply between "faith" (*īmān*) and "works" (*ʿamal*) and to insure membership of the Muslim community solely on the basis of the profession of the faith, its real purpose is to contribute to the solidarity of the community and avoid internal dissension as far as possible. This is the hallmark of *irjāʾ*.

We also pointed out in the preceding chapter that the Imāmī Shīʿī eschewed rebellion against established rule except though an Imām and that their Imāms, beginning with Jaʿfar al-Ṣādiq, disavowed pursuit of political power. It is perfectly in line with political *irjāʾ* to hold that until the Imām appears from his occultation, political action against a state is prohibited. Indeed, the *ḥadīth* cited earlier where the Prophet is reported to emphasize the transmission of *ḥadīth* to men of understanding, and which ends with the necessity for a Muslim to act sincerely for God and stick to the majority of the Muslims etc., is also accepted by the author of the standard work of the Shīʿī *ḥadīth*, *al-Kāfī*. The only difference is that instead of the words "active good will for Muslims," the version of *al-Kāfī* has "active good will for the political leaders of Muslims," and this report, of course, comes down from Jaʿfar al-Ṣādiq. The Shīʿī, therefore, hold to political *irjāʾ* as the Sunnīs do.

Nevertheless, in the Shīʿī strain of political thought, as represented in their *ḥadīth*, one finds strong currents in reverse as well. This is starkly brought home by reinterpreting the self-same *ḥadīth* we have been discussing with a new turn. According to this version, an unnamed Makkan from the Quraysh stated that once Sufyān al-Thawrī (d. 161/777), a contemporary of Abū Ḥanīfa whom the Shīʿī mention in their *ḥadīth*, but whom they carefully disassociate from being a Sunnī, was asked to accompany him to visit Jaʿfar al-Ṣādiq. When they both arrived at al-Ṣādiq's place, they saw that he was already seated on a riding-animal ready to leave. When Sufyān asked him to relate to him the Prophet's report, referring to the *ḥadīth* under discussion earlier, Imām al-Ṣādiq said: "I am ready to leave now; let me return from my errand and I shall narrate the *ḥadīth* to you." Sufyān said: "I beseech you in the name of your kinship with the Prophet that you relate the *ḥadīth* to me now."[6] Al-Ṣādiq dismounted. Sufyān wanted to take down the *ḥadīth* and asked for pen and paper which the Imām asked to be brought forth. Then the Imām dictated the same *ḥadīth* that obliges Muslims to act out of sincerity for God, to have active good will for Muslim rulers, and to stick to the majority of the community. Sufyān, having written the text of the *ḥadīth*, had it checked by the Imām who departed thereafter. The person from Makka says that he and Sufyān then returned. On their way back, Sufyān stopped to reconsider the content of the *ḥadīth*. The Makkan said to Sufyān: "By God, Abū ʿAbd Allāh [Jaʿfar al-Ṣādiq] has hung around your neck something which you will never be able to shake off." "What is that?" asked Sufyān. The Makkan replied, referring to the words of the *ḥadīth*:

> "There are three things about which the heart of a Muslim can never be niggardly." Now, sincerity of action with respect to God I can understand. But as for "active goodwill for Muslim rulers," who are these rulers for whom we are obliged to have active goodwill? Are these Muʿāwiya, son of Abū Sufyān and Yazīd, son of Muʿāwiya and Marwān son of al-Hakam, and all those whose evidence in our view count as impermissible and who may not serve as prayer-leaders of Muslims? And as for his statement: "Stick to the majority party of the community," which party is meant here? That of a Murjiʾa who holds that a person may not pray, nor fast, nor bathe after sexual intercourse, indeed, he may marry his own mother, but still has faith [as pure as that] of Gabriel and Michael? Or that of a Qadarite who holds that what God wills may be frustrated and what Satan wills may be fulfilled? Or that of a Khārijite who declares himself quit of ʿAlī, son of Abū Ṭālib and, indeed, calls him an infidel? Or is it the party of a Jahmites [follower of Jahm ibn Safwān] who holds that faith consists only of recognition of God and nothing else?"

6. al-Kulaynī, *al-Kāfī*, vol. 1, pp. 403–404.

Upon this Sufyān al-Thawrī said to the Makkan: “Woe betide you! What do they [the Shīᶜī followers of Jaᶜfar al-Ṣādiq] say?” The Makkan answered: “They say ᶜAlī son of Abū Ṭālib is, by God, the ruler active good will for whom is incumbent upon us, and as for ‘sticking to their party,’ it means ᶜAlī’s household.” Upon this, Sufyān al-Thawrī took the document, tore it and said to the Makkan: “Do not tell anyone about this.”[7]

This story invites a good deal of commentary but we will note a few essential points from the point of view of our present discussion. First is the observation by the anonymous Makkan that Imām Jaᶜfar al-Ṣādiq had laid an unshakable obligation upon Sufyān al-Thawrī’s shoulders and then went on to provide his own detailed explanation, and not that of Jaᶜfar al-Ṣādiq. Secondly, there is a definite turn or twist to the meaning of the term *al-jamāᶜa* which means “the majority” or “the majority party” and cannot, therefore, mean “the house of ᶜAlī” or his followers. This also explains the nature of the Makkan’s apologetic and lengthy explanation. Finally there is al-Thawrī’s tearing up of the document after hearing the Makkan’s speech. Although this can per se carry contradictory explanations, it most probably means that his act of tearing up the document represents a disapproval of the Shīᶜī intepretation of the *ḥadīth* narrated by Jaᶜfar al-Ṣādiq and the interpretation given by the Makkan. The author of *al-Kāfī* relates yet another *ḥadīth* from Jaᶜfar al-Ṣādiq, which also exists in Sunnī sources (although not from al-Ṣādiq but from the Prophet) and according to which “whoever departs from the majority of the Muslims (*jamāᶜat al-muslimīn*), even by the span of a hand, has thrown off the responsibility of Islam from his neck.” The phrase *jamāᶜat al-muslimīn* obviously cannot mean a group or a sect, but must mean the majority of Muslims. According to another *ḥadīth* in the same work related again from Jaᶜfar al-Ṣādiq: “Whoever departs from the majority of Muslims and breaks his allegiance to the ruler, will be resurrected before God with his hand(s) cut off.”[8] There is thus a great deal of irjāᵓist *ḥadīth* in the most authoritative Shīᶜī traditions. Nevertheless there are factors in Shīᶜī Islam making for the opposite trend as well, which are much stronger than we encounter in the Sunnī stock of ideas. The Shīᶜī doctrine concretely and forcefully charges the ruler with ensuring the well-being of the subjects. This is again illustrated by the Shīᶜī *ḥadīth* in *Kitāb al-Kāfī*: “Muḥammad al-Bāqir [the fifth Imām] was

7. Ibid.
8. Ibid., vol. 1, p. 405.

asked what was the due of the ruler against his subjects. He replied that they owed him complete obedience. Then he was asked what was the due of the people against the ruler; he replied that he should equitably distribute wealth among them [from the public treasury] and do justice among them." "If this is done well [on both sides]," he added, "one should not worry about small breaches." According to another *ḥadīth* from Jaᶜfar al-Ṣādiq [the sixth Imām], Gabriel once came to the Prophet Muḥammad, after which the Prophet called together all Muslims, the Emigrants from Makka as well as the Helpers from Madīna to prayers and ordered them to wear weapons. The Prophet then ascended the pulpit, announced his impending death, while he was apparently healthy, and then declared: "I admonish him who will succeed me as ruler over my Community that he be merciful to the Community of Muslims. He should not harm and thus debase them, nor should he impoverish them and thus expose them to infidelity [*kufr* – apparently a reference to another *ḥadīth* according to which the Prophet declared poverty to verge on *kufr*]. He must not shut his gates upon them, lest their powerful consume their weak ones." According to Jaᶜfar al-Ṣādiq, this was the last speech the Prophet ever delivered from his pulpit.

Again, from Jaᶜfar al-Ṣādiq, the Prophet said: "I have greater claim over a faithful [one] than he has over himself, and after me ᶜAlī has the same claim over the faithful." Jaᶜfar was asked what this *ḥadīth* meant. He replied that the Prophet meant that if a person left behind him a debt or a liability, he (the Prophet) was responsible for it, but if a person left any property behind him, that would go to his inheritors (i.e. his family). This is because a person who possesses nothing has no right or claim over himself, nor can he exercise his authority to command or forbid anything to his family if he cannot provide their necessary expenditure. This obligation devolved upon the Prophet, upon ᶜAlī, and upon all subsequent rulers. This, then, is the reason why these have a greater claim upon the faithful than these latter have upon themselves. Jaᶜfar al-Ṣādiq added that it was only after this declaration from the Prophet that the large body of Jews became Muslims, since this constituted an insurance for them and for their families as well.

The Shīᶜī *ḥadīth* quoted here shows clearly that while the Shīᶜī accepted political *irjāʾ* in terms of conformity to the general community and obedience to the ruler, there are, nevertheless, very strong factors of idealism. We have seen in the *ḥadīth* involving Sufyān al-Thawrī how Jaᶜfar al-Ṣādiq narrated the *ḥadīth* about the obligation of both active good will for the community and obedience to the ruler, which can be found in any Sunnī *ḥadīth* almost verbatim. But then one can also see how it was interpreted to fit into the Shīʿī political ideology in clear disregard of the wording of the *ḥadīth*. In fact, this *ḥadīth* shows the enactment of this process of Shīʿaization clearly taking place before our eyes, as it were. Also, the Shīʿī *ḥadīth* emphasizes far more than does Sunnī *ḥadīth* the inalienable obligation, on the part of the ruler, to care for the well-being of his subjects. There is no counterpart in the Shīʿī *ḥadīth* to the Sunnī ones that enjoin *unconditional* obedience to the ruler, no matter if he be a tyrant, a transgressor against the law and usurps power. No doubt this idealism was facilitated by the lack of actual political power on the part of the Shīʿī. This kind of political attitude, when combined with strong ideas of human free will as developed by Ibn Bābwayh and later by al-Tūsī and al-Ḥillī, produces a strong idealist orientation. This idealism was, in practice, considerably tempered by the irjāʾist political attitudes outlined above, on the one hand, although, on the other, it was also augmented, while still in a state of quasi-dormancy in the medieval period, by Messianism and ever-intensified memories of Ḥusayn's death at Karbala. Once, however, this *irjāʾ* is weakened, not destroyed, as we shall see towards the end of this book, by some form of fundamentalism, this intense idealism, combined with insufficient intellectual equipment and enlightenment, is fixed into what may be called a form of "neo-Khārijism." This is precisely the Khumaynī phenomenon as will appear at the end of this work.

As for Sunnī Islam, we have highlighted its basic orientation as being politically Irjāʾist. The Sunnī *ḥadīth* is heavily predestinarian, loaded towards political docility and conformism and nurtured basically in the spirit of *laissez faire*. All of these numb the spirit of protest and the fiber of genuine moral activism. Yet one must not imagine that Sunnī conscience is dead if it is often numbed and dormant. We have already hinted above at certain powerful elements in Sunnī political theory which are calculated to make a ruler responsive to the needs of the community, if not altogether responsible to it. But he is also made responsible, if not directly to the community, certainly to God's law, the *Sharīʿa*, by which his conduct is to be judged and whose quardians are the ʿulamāʾ. It is the *Sharīʿa* that put checks on the unlimited exercise of power on the part of a ruler and prevented even headstrong rulers from becoming despotic. Above all, Sunnism, with all its realism, pragmatism, and even its expediency-oriented spirit, had to take notice of the fundamental teaching of the Qurʾān on justice and fair play which constitutes, besides monotheism, the essence of the revealed scripture. All jurists and constitutional theorists squarely charge the ruler with guaranteeing five basic rights to *all* his subjects: the right to life, to religion, to earn and own wealth, to human dignity, and to rational integrity or mind (*ᶜaql*). It should be noted that the fourth right, that of dignity, would apparently include some form of economic justice as well. The inclusion of this under a general notion of human rights is as recent as the United Nations Declaration on Human Rights. But the most interesting perhaps is the last – the right to rational integrity. It presupposes the belief that in the whole of creation humanity alone has reason which must be safeguarded. If rightly interpreted, this right would not only negate torture, physical or mental, which can interfere with rational processes, but even forms of indoctrination that render the human mind incapable of regaining its autonomy.

Thus, in Sunnī Islam too, despite the presence of *irjāʾ* elements, there are a host of other sources that make it possible to provide an interpretation that supports human initiative, dynamism, and idealism. These may remain dormant for long periods of time. But when injustice, expediency, compromise, or tyranny are perceived to go beyond a certain point these factors can be activated to create some form of active fundamentalism. Khārijite or quasi-Khārijite phenomena can be produced. Witness the Ahl al-Takfīr wa ʾl-Hijra group in Egypt who call the government of the day and its supporters *kāfir* and advocate emigration or the radical Ikhwān who, in November, 1979, occupied the Kaᶜba shrine at Makka.[9]

Ṣūfism

We hinted towards the end of the preceding chapter that even in those credal and theological systems, such as that of Māturīdī, that did not completely efface the moral, intellectual, and physical powers of humankind, belief in these human abilities was considerably eroded, both in theory and practice, by the growth and phenomenal spread of Ṣūfism. This occurred broadly speaking in two ways: one was by inculcating an attitude of passivity not only towards God, but towards the Ṣūfī shaykh

9. Sivan, *Radical Islam*, pp. 16, 85–88, 111–112, 120.

(teacher); secondly, at a more refined level, by turning the gaze inward. Both of these need some elaboration.

It is well known in scholarly circles that the beginnings of Ṣūfism are intimately connected with moral considerations of purification of the inner life, of sincere devotion to God and goodness, of keeping one's motivations free from extraneous admixture of "worldly" factors and hence of a constant inner examination of and vigil upon one's "heart." In ᶜIrāq, particularly in Baṣra, where this phenomenon thrived, there must obviously have been some pre-Islamic background that encouraged Ṣūfism. It was, however, the Qurᵓānic ideas of *īmān* (faith), *ikhlāṣ* (sincerity, inner purity) and *taqwā* (piety, guarding against moral danger) that had a singularly positive reaction in that milieu. Many sensitive Muslims felt that the mainstream practices of the faith had deviated in some vital sense from the path of original Islam and had become overly immersed in worldly interests and pursuits. Insofar as law and other institutions began to administer this "worldly" life and regulated overt human conduct, this new religious attitude of pure piety also came to regard social institutions as part of the outer, material world.

But this life of moral piety was active, not passive. The agent had actively to pursue and secure the goal of his/her spiritual perfection. This can be palpably brought home by an example from al-Junayd, the illustrious Ṣūfī of the second/third century A.H.–eighth/ninth century C.E., who particularly contributed so much to the development of the Ṣūfī doctrine of *fanāᵓ* (annihilation) and *baqāᵓ* (survival) in its earliest stages. In several of his works, al-Junayd repeatedly discusses this experience with experiential vividness. Now, the essence of this experience, according to al-Junayd, consists of three moments. At the first stage, the mystic sheds the lower human attributes and at the second, is invested with divine attributes. Having been so transformed in terms of attributes, the mystic comes to consider himself to have become identified with the being of God. He makes tall claims about his newly attained spiritual station and how he has left the world behind and become one with God. An interesting point here is that all this constitutes the moment of *fanāᵓ* only, while practically all later mystics claim that the stage of *fanāᵓ* consists of the mystic's getting rid of the lower attributes and that the attainment of divine attributes constitutes the stage of *baqāᵓ*. But for al-Junayd, the stage of *baqāᵓ* starts after the mystic has already attained divine attributes and comes to regard himself as having completely and once and for all transcended the hallmarks of lower creaturely life and secured union with God. When this happens, God shocks the mystic, arousing him from this state of felicitous repose and making him aware that this sense of unity with God is an illusion, that he is still essentially the creature that he was and must remain so, and that he must not and cannot aspire for more. Henceforward, the mystic, now returned to "sobriety" after his "intoxication," must live in a perpetually painful and grievous state of "suspension" or affliction where he cannot remain in union with God, nor yet can he return to his life prior to this experience.

What is to be noted in this account is that, apart from this temporary state of "intoxication," the mystic has an active and intense inner life. Indeed, after the experience of *fanāʾ*, it is a life of perpetual spiritual agony and travail which can be relieved by no diversion and no slumber. His loneliness is known to him alone. This doctrine of *fanāʾ* and *baqāʾ* is itself a development from the earliest phase of Ṣūfism whose essence was purely moral asceticism. But what follows later is something radically different in terms of the role of mystics and their conduct. Of course, later on one also encounters sober figures with spiritual self-awareness and vigilance such as al-Ghazālī and most Ṣūfīs of the Naqshbandī order. By and large, however, Ṣūfīs require that the novice adopt an attitude of complete obedience and withdrawal from the world. The positive *fanāʾ* of al-Junayd, wherein the mystic takes an active initiative and endures travail, is increasingly replaced by a placid and quasi-automatic development of the spiritual "stations" where the mystic is "stripped" of most human qualities (*fanāʾ*) and "invested" with divine attributes wherein he then "abides" (*baqāʾ*).

This momentous change coincides with the transformation of the Ṣūfī ideal itself. From a pursuit of moral purification and development, the character of Ṣūfism is now transformed into that of acquiring an infallible inner intuitive perception which, unlike the rational knowledge of the philosophers and the ʿulamāʾ, is certain and immune from doubts. This intellectual and intuitive Ṣūfism or "theosophy" is now substituted for intellectual and rational knowledge. But while rational knowledge, in its quality, is viewed as communicable and corrigible and, therefore, has an objective social dimension, the inner intuitive cognition of the mystic is communicable, incorrigible, and purely private. Again, rational knowledge applies to the outside world and religious rational knowledge is applicable to society for which it is meant, while mystic intuition is not transitive beyond the experiencing individual in this sense, but develops an inner, subjective dimension. Before we outline the consequences of this concentration upon the inner world, something must be said about the kind of psychology it inculcated and the worldview it produced.

The Ṣūfī initiate was required to form an attitude of passivity towards the master. Without this attitude it was impossible for the disciple to learn anything. This kind of teacher–student relationship also existed in the centers of orthodox learning, the *madrasas*, where the justification was expressed in the maxim that "water can flow only from a higher level to a lower level." Even here this approach could not be practiced or enforced completely because the process of orthodox instruction involved reasoning and to a limited extent encouraged argument and disputation with the teacher. However, procedures of the Ṣūfī path severely discouraged all this. Indeed, the practice of the Ṣūfī method required a definite psychological treatment of the disciple if not his/her total indoctrination. For this reason Ṣūfī shaykhs, who had often a keen and highly developed psychological insight, were usually very selective in terms of their disciples. Not infrequently, a master would advise a would-be disciple whom he had tested for some time to seek another master because "their temperaments were incompatible." From this arises the tremendous loyalty and affection of the Ṣūfī disciples to their masters. This becomes evident from the fact that the masters' biographies written by the disciples are full of miracles and prodigies which multiply with the passage of time. In the orthodox system, on the other hand, there is hardly any trace of this kind of extravagance; although a certain amount of aggrandizement of the great ᶜulamāᵓ does occur on the part of their spiritual progeny. Particularly with the passage of time biographies are inflated, but it is still within certain rationally plausible limits. An example of this latter type is the statement in Ibn Taymiyya's biography that the Mongol army had to withdraw from battle against the Mamlūk army due to stormy weather, which is interpreted as a consequence of Ibn Taymiyya's presence at the battlefield, as well as the Mongols' defeat at the hands of the Egyptian army at the subsequent confrontation.

This psychological passivity apart, the metaphysics that grew out of Ṣūfī theosophy in the later medieval centuries and whose master architect was the great Spanish shaykh Ibn ʿArabī (d. 638/1240) was thoroughly monistic. This monism at the metaphysical level is undoubtedly pantheistic. To say that everything is a manifestation of God in its own measure is a form of polytheism. This metaphysical level should be distinguished from the psychological plane where Ibn ʿArabī does distinguish between each person and his or her God (*rabb*).

Ibn ʿArabī's ideas, made popular through poetry, particularly by Rūmī and ʿIrāqī in the first instance and then their successors, for centuries in Persian, Turkish, Arabic, and Urdu, became common household stock with practically every educated Muslim. It can be said without a doubt that these monistic–pantheistic ideas literally supplanted the orthodox belief almost universally at a public level in the Islamic world, despite severe critiques of Ibn ʿArabī at the hands of many orthodox ʿulamāʾ and Ṣūfīs. In this new religious ideology, God is the only reality, all else being a shadow existence and, insofar as this latter has any being, it is the being of God. All religious truth and morality is relative. In order to approximate reality, one must not negate any creed but accept all creeds. Satan himself is blessed because, in supplying the necessary principle of friction with God and thus making the world movement possible, he is performing his function faithfully. He must be congratulated for this. This new spiritual teaching produced an outlook that, in numerous fundamental respects, was the very antithesis of the Qurʾānic ethos. While the essence of the Qurʾānic teaching is ethical endeavor and an ever keen sense of right and wrong, Ibn ʿArabī's message, which even regards Satan as virtuous, taught relativism in truth and morality. Indeed, if Ibn ʿArabī knew of any absolute at the human level and in the human–God relationship, it is this relativism. Further, God being the only reality, everything is determined. God Himself has a will but no choice and freedom.

If one looks back at the distance one has traveled from the early days of Khārijism to the spiritual milieu of Ibn ʿArabī and his followers, one cannot help feeling giddy. The reaction of *irjāʾ* to Khārijism had been in itself an understandable development although it rendered the ethical dynamism of the Qurʾān essentially inoperable and helped lower the moral tension of the human self. This *irjāʾ* was then followed by a belief in divine determinism of human acts, as though the latter were a logical consequence of the former. *Irjāʾ* had demanded the minimum from the faithful in terms of belief, knowledge, and, indeed, action. This determinism was, in turn, followed by the Ashʿarite teaching which asserted not just that human actions were predetermined by God but that, indeed, humankind had *no action* at all in the real sense of that word. According to Ashʿarism a human being could be called a doer or an actor only metaphorically. In fact, there was no agent of human actions on al-Ashʿarī's showing: for in his view God did not perform actions, but created them, yet neither did humans perform them, except metaphorically by "acquiring" them and were hence responsible for these actions. At the fourth stage of these successive developments came Ibn ʿArabī's pantheism and moral–religious relativism. Whereas al-Ashʿarī and his followers taught that only God can act and that the application of this term to other beings was metaphorical, so now Ibn ʿArabī and his disciples taught that only God exists in reality and the application of this term to others is metaphorical. While Ashʿarism rendered the concept of human action pretty much vacuous, Ibn ʿArabism rendered the very concept of human existence totally inane. If this entire development is put beside the Qurʾān and the performance of the Prophet Muḥammad, the stark irony of it stares us in the face.

One important literary development arising out of the Ṣūfī phenomenon was that through its alienation from orthodox or legal Islam at the popular level, it provided a pretext for the semi-religious semi-secular poets to express publicly their feelings of dissatisfaction and scoff at what they perceived to be the narrowness and stolidity of the orthodox system of belief and practice. As popular Ṣūfism drifted further and further from orthodox Islam and, particularly after the rise and popularity of pantheistic Ṣūfism, these expressions of liberation from restraints of orthodoxy became more and more popular. This phenomenon is unique to Islam among the revealed Western religions. It is also to be noted that such expressions were made and tolerated only in poetry. This poetry, particularly in Persian, is unique in its charm, beauty, and grace and, indeed, its intoxicating effects. In its pantheistic and ubiquitous love, it is often impossible to say whether the poet is talking about divine love or earthly love. Ibn ʿArabī himself had composed, while in Makka, a poem titled "The Interpretor of Desires (*Tarjumān al-Ashwāq*)." When his critics accused him of singing therein, not of divine love, as he had professed, but of his love for a learned lady friend by the name of Niẓām, he himself wrote a commentary to show that he was, indeed, talking about divine love. The following examples will give us some idea of this "liberated" poetic milieu. The illustrious Persian poet Hafīz (d. 792/1389) says:

I am not the kind of drunkard who ever gives up cup and wine,
The Muḥtasib knows that I'm seldom guilty of this.

The *muḥtasib* was the official in charge of public morality who administered punishments to merchants guilty of fraudulent practices or people who drank alcohol. Says ᶜUmar Khayyām (d.527/1132):

If you don't drink, [at least] don't accuse the drunk ones.
Whenever I get the opportunity, I'll repent to the Lord.
You boast of the fact that You don't drink
Yet You do a hundred things before which drinking pales into insignificance.

Here is Bedil's (d.1721) riposte to the orthodox:

The Kaᶜba pilgrims worship only a gate (and its walls);
The jurists worship only a stack of books. Cast away Your veil (O God!) and let it be known
That we lovers worship Someone quite different!

One could go on indefinitely with citations from this genre of poetry, but I will stop with the following crowning example from the Persian *diwān* of the Indian poet Ghālib (d. 1869):

This wretched and reckless drunkard could just as well prostrate before God (as before his idol);
But his idol refused to share (*shirk*) his forehead in prostration (with God)!

This attitude of sarcasm and rejection of the orthodoxy in poetry was accompanied by Ṣūfism's stark challenge to the authority of the Prophet himself as law-giver. This challenge emerges clearly by the ninth century C.E. through the development of the concept of the "Seal of the Saints" in conscious contrast to the expression "Seal of the Prophets" (*khātam al-nabīyyīn*) applied by the Qurʾān to Muḥammad (Q. 33:40). Some Ṣūfīs had contended that a saint is superior to a prophet because the former is "with God" while the latter is "with men," because he has to legislate for them. Hence the "Seal of the Saints" is superior to the "Seal of the Prophets," since spirituality denotes a higher station than legislation. This view is starkly articulated by Ibn ᶜArabī who says that Muḥammad had an "exterior" life, that of the Sharīᶜa, and an "inner" life, that of spirituality, and strongly suggests that he (Ibn ᶜArabī) constitutes the inner or spiritual perfection of Muḥammad. According to a *ḥadīth* the Prophet said: "Prophethood is like a building; it was all complete except that the place of one brick was empty, so I became that brick." Commenting upon this *ḥadīth* Ibn ᶜArabī says: "When the Prophet said this, he was seeing that building only with one eye – the external eye of Prophethood [and not with the inner eye]. Otherwise, there was actually an empty space for two bricks, a golden brick [the inner spirituality] and a silver brick [the external law] and the Prophet himself filled both of them." Inasmuch as it was left to Ibn ᶜArabī to perceive this truth, however, he brought Muḥammad's inner, spiritual life to perfection.

The rebellion of the Ṣūfīs and poets against the Sharīᶜa orthodoxy was no doubt basically generated by the fact that the orthodox systems of law and theology had become formal, rigid, and shorn of their source in the springs of inner life. But there is also little doubt that, since Islam's central effort is aimed at the establishment of an ethically based social world order, the Sharīᶜa must remain its essence. This opposition of the self-righteous Ṣūfī spirituality to the Sharīᶜa was ameliorated to a certain extent by the teaching of al-Ghazālī and after him a long line of the orthodox Ṣūfīs, particularly those of the Naqshbandī and Khalwatiyya orders. But their goal, except in rare cases such as those of the Indians Aḥmad Sirhindī (d. 1034/1624) and Shāh Walī Allāh of Delhi (d. 1176/1762), remained individual rather than social reconstruction. Al-Ghazālī, though endowed with extraordinary intelligence and perception, definitely regarded law, state, and social action as lying outside the orbit of true spirituality. For him, only that knowledge directly conducive to the success in the hereafter (*ᶜilm al-ākhira*) deserves the name in the true sense of the word. This knowledge is totally esoteric and explores the depths of the Ṣūfī encounter with God. He regarded the law and the state as useful and beneficial because, by regulating and controlling society, they facilitate the development of esoteric knowledge. But, for him, they have no direct spiritual value whatsoever. The devaluation of the Sharīᶜa law can be gauged, among numerous other remarks, by the following dubious anecdote related by al-Ghazālī. Abū Yūsuf, the pupil of Abū Ḥanīfa, as is well known, wrote a book titled *Kitāb al-Ḥiyal* (The Book of Legal Fictions), containing the legal arguments whereby one could circumvent the law. It is also alleged that, in order to avoid payment of the *zakāt* tax which falls due when one full year has passed in ownership of wealth or property, a man would transfer it to his wife after six months and, similarly, she would transfer it back to her husband after another six months. In this way they would avoid paying the compulsory tax since no one person owned the property for a full financial year. Now, al-Ghazālī states that this matter was reported to Abū Ḥanīfa in the form of a complaint against Abū Yūsuf's conduct. Abū Ḥanīfa replied that Abū Yūsuf was perfectly justified in what he did, because he was a lawyer and law, as such, allows such manipulation! As indicated above, the ascription of this statement to Abū Ḥanīfa is very dubious since it is not to be found in early historical sources. The point, however, is that al-Ghazālī seems to hold that the *intention* of the law can be violated with impunity because, for him the Sharīᶜa law, as such, does not belong to the field of religion (*dīn*) but pertains to activities related to "this world" (*dunyā*), in other words a secular sphere.

We pointed out how the monistic–pantheistic mentality produced a new type of fatalism that could not fail to numb the moral faculties. The intellectual–spiritual milieu for this had already been prepared by Ashᶜarite theology. Earlier I indicated that Māturīdism did not share the Ashᶜarite theologians' view that humanity was incapable of acting. Indeed, al-Māturīdī insisted that a human being is an "actor" in reality and not metaphorically. Nevertheless the development of the Ṣūfī mentality and its wide diffusion in Islamic society made the spiritual environment unconducive to the fruition of Māturīdism as an effective creed. To its credit the Ḥanafī–Māturīdī tradition generally tended to adopt the Naqshbandī Ṣūfī order which was highly orthodox and inculcated a positive attitude to this world, and was often involved with politics to reform governments. Yet we observe that not even Naqshbandism could for long gainsay the influence of Ibn ᶜArabī's theosophy of "Unity of Being" (*waḥdat ʾl-wujūd*). Even the highly influential and original Aḥmad

Sirhindī, who rejected this doctrine, could not free himself from its substantive effects. While severely criticizing what he saw as Ibn ᶜArabī's elimination of all essential distinction between good and evil, Sirhindī equally criticized the ᶜulamāᵓ for "attributing real existence *to this world besides God*" (*ghayr-i wujūd ra wujūd thābit kardan*).[10] The truth is that once Ṣūfism bridged the metaphysical – as distinguished from the ethical – dualism between God and the world and developed it under the impact of neo-Platonic teaching, there was no going back on it. Sirhindī, despite himself, had effectively to accept it. Within Ṣūfism his reform is undoubtedly radical. He proclaimed that on all points where Ṣūfīs differ from the ᶜulamāᵓ, the truth invariably lies with the ᶜulamāᵓ. This contrasts strikingly with, for example, Ibn Taymiyya's declaration that on those points where there is a difference between the *ijtihād* of the ᶜulamāᵓ and the intuition of the Ṣūfīs, the truth cannot be said to lie automatically on either side. Both sides must compete for the validity of the point of view on the basis of Sharīᶜa proofs. With all this, however, so far as Ṣūfī theosophy or metaphysics is concerned, there was no way to give up monism, which was the only form in which it could comprehend monotheism. In our study of the philosophy of Mullā Ṣadrā (Ṣadr al-Dīn al-Shīrāzī) we have shown the demanding nature of monism.[11] Mullā Ṣadrā was an existentialist with a vengeance and regarded all existence as consisting of unique and irreducible individuals (*afrād*). Yet the pull of monism is so strong that he frequently stated that reality is one and only one, God, and all other beings are inane and vacuous. They are not even entities related to and dependent upon God, but are mere relations to God. In this relation only one term is real, that of God, the other term being nothing at all.

Under the titanic grasp of this monism, even Māturīdism could not develop its proper ethos. Indeed, no creed could. The greatest irony is the case of Ibn ᶜArabī himself. For in his creed and his legal persuasion he belonged to the literalist (Ẓāhirī) school. But once he entered Ṣūfī theosophy and uncoiled his labyrinth of esoteric interpretations, there was no way to return to his literalist creed which was no more than a formal facade.

In the later Ṣūfī theosophy, there developed in Islam a belief in the existence of a "World of Images or Symbols" (*ᶜālam al-mithāl*) which, with

10. Fazlur Rahman, *Selected Letters*.
11. Fazlur Rahman, *Mulla Ṣadrā*.

the passage of time, grew so strong that it became one of the major preoccupations of Muslim intellectuals and refined minds. It represents sheer introversion of the Muslim mind away from the world and society. The spiritual–intellectual life of the world of Islam in the thirteenth to the eighteenth centuries cannot be adequately understood, let alone fully appreciated, without some idea of the meaning and importance of the "World of Images" in later Islam. No other spiritual–intellectual and cultural tradition has a parallel to it. The original reason for this curious doctrine was to render intelligible the phenomena of afterlife, physical resurrection, judgment, punishment, happiness, etc. Al-Ghazālī had suggested that such phenomena as the "chastisement of the grave" (*ʿadhāb al-qabr*) could be understood in two ways. These phenomena could either be understood as purely metaphorical expressions, which cannot do justice to religion; or they could be understood as realities occurring in a world of their own, i.e. not the material world, a belief which religious truth requires. After al-Ghazālī, the first formal announcement about the existence of a "World of Suspended Images" *(ʿālam al-Ashbāh al-Muʿallaqa)* was made by al-Suhrawardī (d. 587/1191) who claimed that he had experienced this "world" several times and it contained some very ugly, repulsive, and frightening figures and some highly pleasurable and attractive ones. These were, then, hell and heaven respectively.

According to this doctrine, just as in the human mind there lies an intermediary phenomenon of imagination between percepts on the one hand and the intellectual concepts on the other, so also in the constitution of the universe there exists, between the world of material bodies and the intelligible spiritual realm, an intermediate "World of Images" which mediates between the two and acts as their transit, as it were. This world was often identified with the faculty of imagination of the outermost celestial sphere which moved itself and also moved the entire contents of the universe, thanks to the succession of images in its own mind. Spiritually developed and sophisticated minds can, and indeed must, contact this world of images, to enrich themselves with the contents of that world. This is because, before events take place in this material world, they can be experienced in that intermediary world. Just as in our minds, the image of a dollar bill, for example, displays all the qualities of a material dollar bill, except that it has no matter and therefore does not occupy space, so too the objects in the world of images are just like objects in this world except that they are not material, and therefore that world, although it contains "pure quantity" (*miqdār khāliṣ*), has no space. Ibn ᶜArabī has left us a detailed description of a world, including its cities and other contents, which he had experienced, so large that all the heavens and the earth of this world of ours can go into a small corner of it. This world was created by God from an infinitesimal piece of clay left over from the material from which He had fashioned the physical frame of Adam.

We have dealt with the world of images at some length because it is hardly known to modern scholarship, except in the works of Henri Corbin, who interprets it in terms of Jungian archetypes. And yet, as indicated above, it is an extremely important feature of the intellectual–spiritual culture of Islam in late medieval centuries. "Miracles" of saints were often located there. On its basis was achieved high sophistication in the Islamic doctrine of physical resurrection: the body in the afterlife will not be the carnal body humans have in this life. Once disintegrated this body can never be restored. The body after death will be an externalized expression or image-symbol of the internal states and dispositions of the soul. It will not be characterized by growth and decay as this carnal body is, but will be static like a shadow. While in this life the soul is "in" the body, in the afterlife the body will be "in" the soul. This image-body, like the soul, will experience pleasure and pain, so that revealed statements about physical pleasure and punishment are not metaphorically but literally true.

The Extremists (Ghulāt and the Ismāᶜīlīs)

The early impact of Islam on the peoples around the Arabian peninsula, particularly in Iraq, produced a tremendous ferment of the ideas and ideologies already there. To view this ferment as "reform" would certainly be far fetched, but it appears that it did leave its mark on certain Islamic developments notably on the Imamology of Shīᶜism and Islamic esotericism in general. The chief phenomenon among these preexisting doctrines from our present perspective is that gnosticism, which under the umbrella of Shīᶜism embraced a certain Islamic nomenclature as a guise, constituted its utter perversion. A striking feature of gnosticism is its crass materialism and in all its versions it rejects the law. It is strange, however, to see that Marshall Hodgson regards the anthropomorphism of the Ghulāt as having been "inspired by the Qur᾽ān."[12] Indeed, in his *The Venture of Islam*, he considered the Ghulāt doctrines and even their antinomianism to be in some sense an authentic Islamic development.[13] We give below a translation of al-Ashᶜarī's account of two of the well-known Ghulāt, al-Mughayra b. Saᶜīd al-Bajalī (d. c.119/737) and Abū Manṣūr al-ᶜIjlī (d.c. 120/738)[14] as a representative sample of the Ghulāt's beliefs before commenting on these points.

> The fourth group [or sect] from among them [i.e. from the Ghulāt] are the Mughīrites, followers of al-Mughayra Ibn Saᶜīd. They state that he [al-Mughayra] used to say that he is a prophet (*nabī*) and that he knows the great name of God. They [also say] that their object of worship is a man of light with a crown on his head. He has organs and a shape like those of a man: he has a stomach and a heart from where wisdom rushes forth. And that the letters of the alphabet in the word, *abī jād*, were in conformity with the number of his [the divine's] organs. Thus the letter alif corresponds to his feet because of its crooked shape. He [Mughayra] also said that if you saw the place [on the body of the divine] that corresponds to [the letter] ha, you would witness something tremendous. He was [obviously] referring to the pudendum [of the divinity]. And he even mentioned that he had seen it, may God curse him! He also asserted that he revives the dead, thanks to the Great Name (*ismuhu ᾽l-aᶜẓam*) [of God]. And that he showed his followers several things including wonders and talismans.
>
> He told them how God began His Creation, and asserted that God – whose name be exalted – was alone and nothing was with Him. When He wished to create the things, He uttered His Great Name. It flew away and settled on His head like a crown. In this connection, al-Mughayra referred to the statement in the Qur᾽ān: "Clarify the name of your Lord." (Q.87:1). Al-Mughayra continued: Then He wrote with His finger upon His palm all the acts of humans, evil ones and good ones. His anger was so aroused by the evil acts that He perspired. His perspiration formed two oceans: one saline and dark and the other light and sweet [water]. Then He looked into the ocean and spotted His own shadow. He then moved to get hold of it, but it flew away. He then ripped off the eye of His shadow. From it [the eye] He created a sun which obliterated His shadow, saying: "It is not proper that there be another God besides Me." He then created

12. Marshall G. S. Hodgson, *EI* 2, s.v. "Ghulāt," p. 1094.
13. Hodgson, *Venture of Islam*, vol. 1, p. 266.
14. Also see al-ᶜUqaylī, *al-Ḍuᶜafā᾽*, vol. 4, p. 177.

all creation from these two oceans: the infidels from the saline dark ocean and the faithful from the light sweet one.

He also created the shadows of people. He first created Muḥammad, peace and blessings of God be upon Him, and this is the meaning of His Qurʾānic verse: "Say (O Muḥammad!) if the Merciful One had a son, then I would be the first to worship [Him]." (Q. 43:81). We then sent Muḥammad to the entire humanity, and he was a shadow. He [God] then proposed to the heavens that they prevent ᶜAlī, son of Abū Ṭālib, may God be pleased with him [from becoming successor to Muḥammad] but they refused. Then He proposed the same to the earth and the mountains, but they also refused. He then proposed the same to all humanity; ᶜUmar b. al-Khaṭṭāb stood up and went to Abū Bakr asking him to bear the burden of preventing [ᶜAlī from succession] and to betray him. Abū Bakr then did so, which episode is referred to in God's statement in the Qurʾān: "We presented the trust to the heavens and the earth and the mountains" (Q. 33:72). According to al-Mughayra, ᶜUmar said [to Abū Bakr]: "I will aid you against ᶜAlī on condition that you hand over the Caliphate to me." That is in reference to God's statement: "Like Satan, when he tells a person: Become an infidel." (Q. 59:16). And Satan, according to him [Mughayra] is ᶜUmar. He also claimed that the earth will spew out the dead who will return to this world. When Khālid b. ᶜAbd Allāh [the Umayyad governor of Iraq] heard of al-Mughayra's views, he executed him.[15]

A little further on, al-Ashᶜarī gives an account of the Manṣūrites, followers of Abū Manṣūr al-ᶜIjlī:

They assert that the Imām after Abū Jaᶜfar Muḥammad [al-Bāqir] b. ᶜAlī b. al-Ḥusayn b. ᶜAlī, is Abū Manṣūr, who said: The family of the prophet Muḥammad are the heaven, the Shīᶜī are the earth and that he [Abū Manṣūr] is a part of the sky that had fallen [reference to Q. 52:44] on the earth from Banū Hāshim. This Abū Manṣūr was from the Banū ᶜIjl. He also claimed that he ascended to the heaven where his deity touched his head with His hand and then said to him, "Oh my son! Go and deliver my message [to humankind]." Then he came down to earth. The phrase by which his followers would take an oath was: "Lo, by the Word!" [Referring presumably to God's word addressed to Abū Manṣūr]. Abū Manṣūr said that Jesus was the first being created by God, then ᶜAlī, and

15. Al-Ashᶜarī, *Maqālāt*, vol. 1, pp. 68–73.

> that the appointment of God's Messengers never ever ceased. He denied the reality of Paradise and Hell, asserting that both Paradise and Hell are men. He declared all women, including those forbidden by Law, to be lawful for his followers. He also said that the corpse, the spilt blood [of animals], the flesh of the swine, alcohol and games of chance [all forbidden in the Qurᵓān] and other prohibited things are all lawful. None of these things, he said, had been forbidden for us. And nothing had been forbidden that might strengthen our souls. Indeed, these are but names of men whose authority/governance (*wilāya*) God had prohibited. To justify all this, he interpreted by taking recourse to the word of God the exalted: "There is no harm, for those who have faith and do good deeds in whatever they may taste." (Q. 5:93). He also annulled the shares of inheritance saying these are names of men whose governance is compulsory. He declared it lawful to strangle hypocrites (*munāfiqūn*) and to seize their wealth. Yūsuf b. ᶜUmar al-Thaqafī, the Umayyad governor of ᶜIrāq finally captured and executed him.[16]

Al-Ashᶜari notes that the distinguishing feature of the Ghulāt was that they wrested the privilege of Imamate from Banū Hāshim, the clan of the Prophet Muḥammad, and claimed it for themselves. And although the followers of Abū ᵓl-Khaṭṭāb also worshiped Jaᶜfar al-Ṣādiq, nevertheless they believed in the godhead of Abu ᵓl- Khaṭṭāb as well. As for the rest of the fifteen sects of the Ghulāt, most believe in the divinity of the Imāms and many also of Muḥammad. One can at once see from the above quotations that this is pure gnosticism employing certain Qurᵓānic phrases and verses. But the employment of such phrases and verses is, surely, a far cry from Marshall Hodgson's and, following him, Steve Wasserstrom's Islamic evaluation of this phenomenon.[17] Wasserstrom in an otherwise rich and useful article on al-Mughayra b. Saᶜīd tells us that "the most significant such attempt was that of Marshall G.S. Hodgson who recognized that the *ghulāt* alone in Islam at that time were dealing with problems that Ṣūfīs later took up, no doubt with partial success; certain questions about personal religious experience – about revelation, morality and spirit."[18] It was Hodgson who observed that in the Ghulāt speculations "we get a sense of large issues debated."[19] I think it is also unwarranted to speak of any

16. Ibid., pp. 74–75.
17. Wasserstrom, "Moving Finger"; Hodgson, "Early Shīᶜa."
18. Wasserstrom, "Moving Finger,"; p. 3.
19. Hodgson, "Early Shīᶜa," p. 8.

genuine "religious experience" in the case of most of the Ghulāt. It is essentially a case of unsuccessful attempts on the part of the Ghulāt to transfer gnostic symbols onto Islam. Wasserstrom, in his gnostic euphoria, goes so far as to fasten gnostic concepts on to the Qur᾽ān itself.

It is, however, clear that this gnosticism contributed seminally to the development not only of Nuṣayrī and Ismāᶜīlī beliefs, but, indeed, to the Twelver Shīᶜī belief in the impeccable, infallible, omniscient Imām, besides the contributions of the pre-Islamic Iranian doctrine of the divine king. In my book *Islam* I wrote: "Exactly by what stages these motives and ideas were fused to develop the idea of the Mahdī into a divine personage, and who precisely were the persons that wrought the amalgam or vitally contributed to it, we cannot say at the present stage of research since the early doctrinal evolution of Shīᶜism is still very obscure."[20] This gap has now been filled by the new literature on the role of gnosticism in Islam, particularly through the Ghulāt, the latest contribution being that of Wasserstrom. But if we must reject the Ghulāt as reformers of Islam, does Ismāᶜīlism warrant such a valuation? We may start by saying that whereas the Ghulāt were an extremely peripheral and transient phenomenon, Ismāᶜīlism has not only survived until today but at one time – during the tenth and eleventh centuries – it was a phenomenon of vast proportions in the world of Islam. So much so that an observer situated at that time could have regarded it a distinct possibility that Ismāᶜīlism might capture Islam entirely and make short work of "official" Islam. Our analysis will attempt to show that if Ismāᶜīlism failed in this, it did so because of its inherent weaknessess as a spiritual–philosophical system. For so far as politico-military power is concerned, it had an abundance of it in the tenth and eleventh centuries. Yet, on closer examination, Ismāᶜīlism has to be taken seriously and can by no means be dismissed as a peripheral and extrinsic force. Marshall Hodgson's advice would here serve us well: he observed that the scholarly observer must render the mental and practical behavior of a group understandable in terms available in the observer's own mental resources.

If the Ghulāt can by no reasonable measure be judged to be Muslims, the Ismāᶜīlīs cannot be denied the credit of having taken Islam seriously indeed. Whereas the Ghulāt set at naught the entirety of the Sharīᶜa, the Ismāᶜīlīs took the Sharīᶜa seriously, despite the fact that they looked

20. Fazlur Rahman, *Islam*, p. 172.

forward to the abrogation of the Sharīʿa by some universalist version. The question before us is twofold: why did Ismāʿīlism take the path of esotericism that it actually did take? And why did it, in the last analysis, fail? The answer to the first question, why it broke with both Twelver Shīʿism and Sunnism and insisted on a separate esoteric and subterranean propaganda path, is that both these traditions, which we have previously discussed in detail in their relation to *irjāʾ*, on the one hand, and the living call of the Qurʾān on the other, developed a "flat" religious and moral character that was intellectually uninspiring. Unless a way could be found to produce spiritual, moral, and intellectual movement within the body of these traditions, there was little prospect of their attracting creative minds. At a later stage philosophy and Ṣūfism appeared and the latter gained many supporters; particularly after the eleventh and twelfth centuries it encroached upon Sunnī Islam. Shīʿism never allowed Ṣūfism to grow on its soil, and also contributed to the swift decline of Ismāʿīlism. As for philosophy, Sunnī Islam rejected it more often than accepting it. This was largely because of its eccentric character, being derived from Greek thought. In most cases there was at least an attempt to integrate it into Sunnī Islam. Later, it found a haven in Shīʿism but by that time it had already assumed a particular ideological character. It played a role in Shīʿī law as well as in the *kalām* theology and it became the mainstay of both traditions. Shīʿism, *as a tradition*, remained a hodge-podge of law, *kalām* and a gnostically generated Imamology which could not be put to use for any genuinely religious purpose. True, the Shīʿī insisted that an infallible source of religious knowledge was needed which would put it beyond the realm of human certainty and doubt, but the effects of it are nowhere visible, whether objectively or by claims in Shīʿī law or *kalām*.

The two main traditions of Islam, then, both irjāʾist, being unable to contain the restless spirits that demanded room for creativity particularly moral and spiritual, and a possibility for political reform of the social structure, were incapable of accommodating radicalism. Sunnī Islam, in particular, became impervious to anything that might ruffle either its conscience or its mind. All it thought necessary for its continued success was to keep the community consolidated at all cost, no matter how much it retreated from the Qurʾān, even without being really aware of this, and to cling to a real or artificial past: both of these factors being summed up in its self-bestowed title *ahl al-sunna wa ᵓl-jamāᶜa* (people of the original tradition and the solidarity of the community). On closer examination, the separate existence of the Twelver Shīᶜī community is even far less warranted than that of the Sunnīs for, as we said earlier, the Shīᶜī Imām neither has nor can have any effect on the products of Shīᶜī lawyers and theologians. He is a purely gratuitous and vacuous postulate. If the purpose is to inject a factor of idealism, then the Qurᵓān is there in its concrete ethos. The Shīᶜī through the centuries showed little regard for the Qurᵓān, despite producing a large number of commentaries. They have especially wrought havoc with their ecstatic and allegorical interpretations. The truth is that while the Sunnīs have imperceptibly but surely receded from the Qurᵓān and the real legacy of the Prophet, the Shīᶜī have cast the Qurᵓān into systematic oblivion, and both disrupted and distorted the real legacy of Muḥammad. But once the Imām is removed, what is left except the dry bones of the law and the intellectual husk that is *kalām* theology, which are common to both intellectual traditions. In the final analysis the only justification for the Shīᶜī as a separate entity is purely negative: their anti-Sunnism.

While it cannot be denied that many may have joined esoteric cults in the early centuries of Islam through purely political motivations to subvert the new community and bring down Arab Muslim hegemony – and this seems to me to be true of the Ghulāt as a whole, there was undoubtedly also a very genuine trend, which we hope to have demonstrated above, of trying to find ways to a clearer sense of the message of the Qurᵓān than the legal efforts of the jurists and the dry formalism of the theologians could afford. The Qurᵓān definitely oozes out of the deep springs of life of which the *kalām* is little more than a controversy. As for law, it is obviously necessary for any organized life. But the schools of Islamic law, including the Shīᶜī, hardly do justice to the living impulse of the Qurᵓān. Their atomistic approach to the Qurᵓān does not make for a cohesive system. More important, although there is to use Weber's terms a good deal of "formal rationality" in Islamic law, there is hardly enough. One may say there is an almost total lack of "substantive rationality" which means the basing of law on higher, non-legal, specially moral principles. Islamic law usually juxtaposes the moral propositions with the legal, which is certainly better than the absence of moral principles, but hardly does justice to the moral principles of the Qurᵓān. The principles of the Qurᵓān deserve systematization and then from these law should be systematically derived.

To come back to the performance of Ismāᶜīlism, what did it achieve in the light of our foregoing observations? It gained extensive political power in the form of the Fāṭimid dynasty, starting from North Africa in the early tenth century; by the middle of that century it dominated Egypt as well. The Fāṭimids built opulent commercial networks and a powerful navy in the Mediterranean. But it is obvious that they were quite unprepared for putting their ideals into practice, even if they had formulated them, which they did not. Their most illustrious legist, Qāḍī Nuᶜmān (d. 363/974), formulated a legal system on the basis of the Twelver Shīᶜī system of law. The reason given by the great Qaḍī was that the Ismāᶜīlī revolution will have to be the work of several eschatological personages (Mahdīs) and, therefore, the Ismāᶜīlī rule should take its point of departure from the basis of an already existing legal system.[21] The truth, however, was that the vast majority of their subjects were non-Ismāᶜīlīs, and the rulers could not overcome this impediment. But all revolutionary fervor had gone from the Ismāᶜīlī ideologues, once they began to rule. They settled down happily with the status quo just as any other Muslim state was doing.

When we look at Ismāᶜīlī doctrine, however, the scene is much less flattering. It is a hodge-podge of ideas, doctrines, and symbols taken from gnosticism, some form of Pythagoreanism, and, later, neo-Platonism. A hang-up on the mysteries of the number seven which was applied to all sorts of phenomena – religious, philosophic, and scientific – and a preoccupation, like the Ghulāt, with esoteric properties of the letters of the alphabet were hardly calculated to yield a satisfactorily rational worldview. Even though in their neo-Platonic heritage – in the Epistles of the Brethren of Purity (Ikhwān al-Ṣafā), for example – there are to be found tangible ingredients of rationalism. But neo-Platonism is hardly suitable for constructing a rational account of physical nature. But the most fundamental failure of Ismāᶜīlism, as indeed, of all esoteric (Bāṭinī) ideologies is their method of interpreting the Qurᵓān, if one can call this "mumbo jumbo" a method at all. This interpretation represents the most arbitrary treatment of the Qurᵓān. We have already stated that both the

21. [Here Fazlur Rahman added: "If we take a contemporary parallel viz., that of the Communist revolution. Its protagonists also say that they are not yet Communists, but are only at the stage of socialism. But even as socialists they have wrought a wholesale transformation on the life of their people, for example, in the USSR."]

kalām and legal interpretations of the Qurʾān were superficial. Much of *kalām* even when forced was not as capricious as the alleged esoteric "method" was. A deeper understanding of the Qurʾān was certainly necessary. And it was because no such understanding was attempted that Islamic law remained a lifeless body (except for the efforts of men such as al-Ghazālī of whom we shall treat in the next section), and *kalām* became a purely extrinsic and formalistic discipline. But if Ismāᶜīlism wanted to remedy the situation, it ought to have taken its point of departure from the Qurʾān and then integrated whatever elements it found compatible elsewhere to illuminate its message. But the Ismāᶜīlīs made the Qurʾān literally a plaything of their fancy, which they tried to exalt by characterizing it as *taʾwīl* or "the discovery of the ultimate meaning." As I pointed out in my review of Henri Corbin's edition of Nāṣir-i Khusrou's *Jāmiᶜ at al-Ḥikmatayn*, there was absolutely no attempt made by any Ismāᶜīlī thinker to formulate any laws of symbolization and, in fact, none could be established. We know of certain interpretations of the Holy Book by Muslim philosophers. Light, for example, represents knowledge, in Ibn Sīnā's interpretation of the Verse of the Light in the Qurʾān. But interpretation itself sufficiently makes clear in these cases why certain symbols are taken to stand for certain entities. These relationships are in themselves rational. But generally speaking no such relationship obtains in the Ismāᶜīlī *taʾwīl*. It will be sheer torture to cite examples here, but the above work of Nasir-i Khusrou is a specimen in point – in fact it is one of the more reasonable specimens. Under such conditions what possibilities did the Ismāᶜīlī interpretation (*taʾwīl*) have of gaining acceptance at the hands of Muslims? This explains Qāḍī Nuᶜmān's assertion that since more than one Mahdī was needed to fulfill the Ismāᶜīlī dream, there was no need to spell out an Ismāᶜīlī law or ideology.

Conclusion

After going through the developments sketched out in these two chapters, both at the popular and the elite levels, one can imagine the spiritual and moral state of the Islamic society. The moral apathy induced by the doctrine and attitude of *irjāʾ* characterized not only the theology, but through doctrines of predeterminism also affected the concrete attitudes. This we have found more true of Sunnism than of Shīᶜism. In the political field again, Sunnism suffered more from attitudes of conformism and docility to the political forces, although in its theoretical makeup there have been important counterbalancing factors, such as the idea of the consensus of the community, election of the head of state, and his implicit responsibility to the community. The Twelver Shīʿī, who had no state until the late fifteenth century C.E., also upheld the consensus and unity of the community, the wellbeing of the community, and the necessity to obey the political ruler, as is shown by the Shīʿī *aḥādīth* quoted in the first part of this chapter. The Shīʿī *aḥādīth* however, put much greater emphasis on the duties of the ruler towards the well-being of his subjects. These materials exhort the ruler to be kind to the point of taking personal care of subjects, an emphasis not found in the Sunnī *ḥadīth* and constitutional literature. The Shīʿī doctrine, however, by its espousal of a transcendent Imām who gets his validation from God rather than through election by the community, puts him beyond questioning by humans.

Lastly, Ṣūfism, through its various ramifications, crowns the irjāʾist mentality by inculcating an attitude of sheer passivity. The doctrine of monism which overwhelmed Ṣūfism in its later developments denied any reality except God's being, and, although it generated a certain attitude of liberalism, nevertheless tended to numb the moral faculties. Its important spiritual child, belief in a world of images, turned the vision of the more sophisticated and refined minds totally inward in the enjoyment of an esoteric world as an escape from the unpredictable and harsh social, economic, and political realities.

3

EARLY MEDIEVAL REFORM:

THE ṢŪFĪ REFORM AND THE ROLE OF AL-GHAZĀLĪ

Ṣūfī Developments

We have seen why Ismāᶜīlī "reform" failed although it made a serious, sustained and large-scale effort to produce an alternative to the "official" version of Islam. Despite its aims to create a just socio-political order, it was bound to fail because it could not produce a credible interpretation of the Qurᵓān, but rather produced a spiritualized version which had no intelligible connection with the Holy Book. In fact, like the Ghulāt, the starting point of Bāṭinism or Ismāᶜīlism was hardly ever the Qurᵓān, despite what Marshall Hodgson claims. But Ṣūfism, the phenomenon we are going to consider, has gained far greater centrality in Islam precisely because its starting point was orthodox Qurᵓānic piety. And, even though its esoteric adventures, particularly in the later centuries, often were unwarranted and fanciful, it nevertheless never cut itself off from its pietistic roots in the Qurᵓān. Hodgson tells us: "Even more than among the Bāṭiniyya, the Ṣūfīs' starting point was ever the Qurᵓān, whose inward meanings they explored, attempting to get behind the surface of the words. Their technique was less allegorical or symbolical than that of the Bāṭinīs and focused instead on the personal experience that the words seemed to crystallize; even so, there were points of contact between the two ways of more deeply reading the Qurᵓān."[1] As we have noted earlier, the starting point of the Bāṭinīs can hardly be said to be the Qurᵓān – except of course in the field of law, as far as the Ismāᶜīlīs are concerned, where there is hardly any obsession

1. Hodgson, *Venture of Islam*, vol. 1, p. 394.

with the number seven or the letters of the alphabet, or any vestige of esotericism.

It is important to note that esotericism is not equivalent to religious experience as is very often stated and implied by so many modern Western writers, such as Hodgson. The esoteric doctrine of the Bāṭinīs per se implied no religious experience. They were doctrines that their followers did not want to divulge publicly. They even developed secret codes to communicate these doctrines to their fellow adepts. A mystic experience is sometimes called esoteric, because it is inherently ineffable. It would be better to call it personal or private experience, like feeling pain or pleasure. But the term esoteric is out of place, since here esoteric means something that is deliberately kept hidden. There is no reason to believe that the Bāṭinīs had religious experiences. It was fear of persecution that prevented them from making these doctrines public. Nor is there the slightest warrant to regard these "esoteric" doctrines about the "hidden meanings" of the Qurʾān as "deep or profound." A truth publicly stated may be far more profound than an "esoteric" one. Lately, it has become a fad in certain intellectual circles in the West to equate the esoteric with that which is more true or the more profound.

When we come to Ṣūfism, however, we can speak of a genuine religious experience because this apparently constitutes the essence of Ṣūfism. Here again there are parallel pitfalls similar to what we have said about Bāṭinī esotericism. This is because the word "experience" is highly ambiguous. I think in our present context, experience may be defined as a more or less sudden spiritual happening, accompanied by at least a certain degree of amazement or a sense of wonder or being "taken aback," which reveals a new meaning to reality as a whole. To the extent that this happening is sudden and brings home the awareness of something new, it may be ineffable, but it need not be so. Certain philosophers and thinkers such as Plotinus (d. c. 270) and al-Suhrawardī (d. 587/1191) also experienced sudden illuminations. These were intellectual in content and thus quite communicable. The fact of these happenings is, of course, ineffable and thus constitutes them as experiences. Then there are moral experiences where people have converted to more spiritually productive and meaningful lifestyles. Most Ṣūfī experiences are of this kind, or aesthetic experiences which may be religiously or mystically charged, but not always necessarily so.

All great Ṣūfīs undoubtedly had some experience – religious, spiritual, moral, or aesthetic. The first three kinds are probably all present in a single experience. The aesthetic may or may not be present, or may not always be present prominently, although it is sometimes very powerful. But most Ṣūfīs did not have an experience in the sense in which we have defined it: a sudden illuminative or transforming event. In most cases, the subject had a gradual spiritual–moral development, normally under the direction of a shaykh, but on occasions spontaneously. Whenever a person develops an "inner" life, whether through an "experience" or gradual development, they can be called a Ṣūfī or a mystic, unless we can characterize gradual development also as a kind of an experience. Thomas E. Homerin, in his research on Ibn al-Fāriḍ (d. 632/1235) makes the point that Ibn al-Fāriḍ, who in his day was regarded as a great mystic-poet, became over the centuries a saint with a lot of "miracles" attributed to him.[2] Now, miracles and sainthood are primarily features of popular religion, not of the religion of the intellectual elite, although some of this elite too were influenced by popular religion. Homerin raises the very interesting and important question in this connection as to whether Ibn al-Fāriḍ, and others like him, can be called genuine Ṣūfīs even though they wrote great Ṣūfī poetry. When, in the post-classical period of Islam, a brilliant poetic tradition (mostly Persian) developed, it was heavily laden with Ṣūfī terminology, imagery, idiom etc. Yet most of this literature is totally secular. The famous nineteenth-century Indian poet of Persian and Urdu, Mirzā Asad Allāh Khān Ghālib (d. 1869) says addressing himself:

> These subtle points of Ṣūfism and their brilliant explanations – O Ghālib!
> You could be considered a saint, but for your voracious consumption of wine!

So is the case with many quatrains of ᶜUmar Khayyām, if their attribution to him is genuine. However, in the case of Ibn al-Fāriḍ, it is difficult to conceive merely conventional Ṣūfī versification, for in several of his poems he rises to an unmistakable ecstatic pitch.

However, one very important question must be answered with regard to Ṣūfism, before we go to the heart of the Ṣūfī reform in Islam. In the bewildering variety of Ṣūfī doctrines and ideals, three kinds of catchwords stand out so prominently that they must be regarded as the pivots of Ṣūfism:

2. Homerin, *Poet to Saint*.

love of God, gnosis (*ma^crifa*) of God, and the moral ideal, obedience to God (*ṭā^ca*). The first two are certainly not the same. Although it is often said that love results in gnosis, love is essentially an independent ideal. The protagonists of gnosis seldom if at all talk of divine love in any important sense. Basically these two are different ideals. While we shall discuss the moral ideal at some length below when we talk about orthodox Ṣūfism, culminating in al-Ghazālī, we must start by making some observations about the gnostic ideal of cognition and the ecstatic ideal of love. Both these ideals undoubtedly hold something valuable for the faithful, but the manner in which many Ṣūfīs employ them often makes them questionable. As for love, there is no doubt that the Qur^ɔān recognizes a strong love motive in worship where the aesthetic element is powerfully present. Anyone who has recited the Sūra al-Rahman (Sūra 55) which sings the glories of God as spread out in nature, a theme so frequently repeated in the Qur^ɔān, can hardly fail to be moved to ecstasy. The Qur^ɔān insists that these glories of God are sung by the entire creation; on the Day of Judgment, "You shall see the Angels encircling [in utter devotion] the Throne of God, hymning the praises of their Lord" (39:75; cf. also 9:13). The love and aesthetic element is, therefore, patently there and is an inalienable element in worship. However, whenever the Qur^ɔān hymns to God in celebration of the beauty, grandeur, and the great design of nature, it finds a serious purpose in it, rather than a sport and it asks man to serve and further these purposes and be grateful to God in worship. In the above-mentioned Sūra 55 where the wonders of God's creation are recounted, the burden of the question is: "Which, then, of the favors of your Lord will you disavow?" Again, for example, in Sūra 3:191: "Indeed, in the creation of the heavens and the earth and the succession of night and day, there are signs for those who have intelligence. Those who remember God while standing, sitting and lying down and reflect upon the creation of the heavens and the earth and exclaim: 'Our Lord! You have not created all this in frivolity– Glory be to you, save us from the torture of fire.'"

Thus while there is a powerful ecstatic component in the Qur^ɔānic teaching, ecstasy cannot be an end in itself, even in worship. It must lead to serious reflection. It has little to do with the artificially induced ecstatic fits of later adepts, particularly at the popular level. Nor were the Prophet and his Companions known to have ever "chanted the name of God" and danced ecstatically to the rhythm of *dhikr*. As for the cognitive ideal of gnosis (*maʿrifa*), again the Qurʾān surely supports it. For the Qurʾān, however, all knowledge – intellectual, scientific, or intuitive – comes from God. David's expertise in making coats of mail comes from God. Joseph's expertise in interpreting dreams comes from God. Scribes who can write down documents of agreements, wills, etc. are also "taught by God" (21:80; 12:37; 2:282). "Knowledge" (*ʿilm*) and its derivatives appears hundreds of times in the Qurʾān which, besides belief in monotheism, sets the highest value on knowledge and excludes no category of knowing whatsoever. Among the highest attributes of God is knowledge (*ʿilm*). Indeed, knowledge is literally infinite because: "Over every person of knowledge is One who knows" (Q. 12:76). However, the primary orientation of cognition in Islam is decidedly towards action. For Islam is concerned with building a certain socio-moral order in this world. Cognition thus serves a practical value, finding its justification and referent in knowledge. Without knowledge as a referent the truth-value of cognitive statements cannot be established.

Now, with the exception of moral Ṣūfism, of which we shall speak in some detail, neither the ecstatic nor the cognitive forms of Ṣūfism paid even the most scant regard for this fundamental orientation of Islamic spirituality. All Ṣūfīs claimed a kind of supra-intellectual knowledge and lashed reason with scorn. It would perhaps be going too far to say that with such supra-rational intutitive claims Ṣūfīs wanted to jettison all intellectual truth and responsibility. In fact, many of them held that there can be no contradiction between intuition and reason. And, the more philosophically minded among them even believed that there is an organic relationship between the two. Nevertheless, the overall effect of their statements has been a disparagement of reason. The Ashʿarite orthodoxy had already disparaged reason vis-à-vis revelation, and when the Ṣūfīs also disparaged reason in favor of an alleged knowledge immune from error, called unveiling (*kashf*), a powerful anti-rational impulse was bound to be generated. This in fact did happen. In Ṣūfī utterances particularly, as well as in the ultra-right wing circles of the orthodoxy, there was so much anti-rationalism that Ṣūfīs came to be looked upon as potent, professional anti-rationalists.

Yet the content of this cognitive Ṣūfism is intellectual. The most eminent representative of this type of Ṣūfism which seemed to overwhelm practically all other forms in the later medieval centuries is Ibn ᶜArabī (d. 638/1240), who was born in Spain and died in Syria. Although he worked mostly by imagination and association of ideas rather than by logical processes, nevertheless his mysticism has an intellectual content through and through. However, he claimed both intuitive channels and intuitive certainty for his deliverances. His *magnum opus* is titled "Makkan Openings" (*Fatuḥāt Makkīyya*), while his other important, and more organized, work titled "Ringstones of Wisdom" (*Fuṣūṣ al-Ḥikam*) claims in the preface to have been given to him by the prophet Muḥammad *in toto* for transmission to the Muslim community, without him, Ibn ᶜArabī, having added anything to it of his own! Here we come to the nub of cognitive Ṣūfī claims: it is a disclosure or revelation of mysteries. We all know where we are. Ever since the advent of gnosticism into Islam in various forms, mystery-mongering has been an increasing preoccupation. The object of knowledge is hidden and the way to reach it is equally mysterious. This is not the "unknown" (*ghayb*) of the Qurᵓān. First of all, the *al-ghayb* of the Qurᵓān, i.e. the totality of the unknown, is known only to God. However, this unknown can be partially made known to some people (prophets): "Do these people [the pagans] have a knowledge of the *ghayb* [totality of unknown] so that they can write it down in a book?" (Q. 52:41; 68:47). "Does this person have a knowledge of the *ghayb* so he can see?' (Q. 53:35). We have also seen above that God teaches all sorts of knowledge and skills to humans; although this is not called the unknown (*ghayb*) by the Qurᵓān, it is certain that it falls in the same category. This is illustrated, for example, in the story of the teacher and companion of Moses (Q. 18:65). *Ghayb* is also relative. It may be known to some people, but remain unknown (*ghayb*) to others, or something may be *ghayb* to someone now, but it may become known later on. This is brought out by the story of the *jinn* who went on laboring for Solomon in the Temple even after his death, thinking he was still alive. But when moths ate up Solomon's staff on which his corpse was reclining and he fell, they discovered "that if they could have known the *ghayb*, they need not have remained in this reviling servitude" (Q. 34:14).

The second most important lesson the Qurᵓān teaches about the *ghayb* is that although it is unknown, there is nothing mysterious or occult about it. The entire ethos of the Qurᵓānic doctrine of cognition is that it is diametrically opposed to gnosticism and all mysterious cults. The most that can be said is that the prophets have a special avenue of knowledge called *waḥy* whereby unknown matters are disclosed to them. *Waḥy* was also given to the mother of Moses (Q. 20:38); and given to bees (Q. 16:68). It is a kind of intuitive knowledge but it does not require any particular exercise or rites of initiation. Above all, the unknown of the Qurʾān, when it is disclosed, is perfectly "natural" knowledge as is clear from all the examples given above. But much of the Ṣūfī theory of knowledge turns mysticism into mystification, to use Evelyn Underhill's expression.[3] Many Ṣūfīs were after "hidden" and "mysterious" matters and meanings. It is not at all clear why hidden things are superior to manifest things and more valuable than these. We have seen from the Qurʾān that its *ghayb* is simply unknown, and when it becomes known, it is of the same order as other known things.

This, then, is the crux of this cognitive Ṣūfism vis-à-vis Islam's most fundamental ethos. The *ghayb* of the Qurʾān, when it comes into the arena of the known, produces changes therein, revolutionary changes, or else it prefers to remain hidden. Delving into the *ghayb* is absolutely essential. For indeed a perpetual immersion in this sensory world tends to sap one's moral energies, disorients the mind, and produces the corrosive acids of secularism. But when the window from the *ghayb* opens, it oxygenates the petrified bloodstreams of this sensory realm and breathes new life into it: "What about him [Muḥammad] who was dead and We gave life to him and bestowed upon him a light whereby he walks about people [i.e. he does not retire to a hermitage]" (Q. 6:22). To seek the *ghayb*, it is necessary to be a recluse in the "Cave of Ḥīra," but once the window opens it must free one to come into the arena of the moral world to teach, struggle, and fight. It is on this touchstone that cognitive Ṣūfism largely fails. Talk about miracles (and hidden mysteries) become "the toys of this path" as Aḥmad Sirhindī (d. 1034/1624), himself a great Ṣūfī puts it. Ibn Qayyim al-Jawziyya (d. 751/1350) told us that when a Ṣūfī becomes absorbed in his divine love and forgets about mankind and even obedience to God, because he enjoys and relishes that love for its own sake, there remains no essential difference between him and a person who becomes similarly absorbed in human love and enjoys and relishes it. Surely this is also true of cognitive Ṣūfism. Ibn Taymiyya's judgment is much harsher. He asserts that when a Ṣūfī divests

3. Underhill, *Mysticism*.

his mind of all its positive content in order to "devote himself exclusively to God," as he claims, then the devil comes to inhabit his empty mind and freely does his work there.

From the perspective of the problem with which we have been preoccupied since chapter 1 of the present study and which has really become *the problem* for this study, namely that of *irjāʾ*, the Ṣūfīs cannot be called Murjiʾa in a technical sense. But their overall impact on the moral life of the community has been, from this vantage point, even more disastrous than *irjāʾ*. Ṣūfism has left us an extraordinarily rich legacy both of profound ideas and outstanding personalities of moral caliber and spiritual achievement. Ṣūfīs, by definition, were people who gave up desire of this world and devoted themselves to moral and spiritual purification. Most of them also helped all sorts of people often without consideration of race, creed, or sex. They were, in thought and practice, ultra-humanitarians. But by the same token they encouraged moral relativism which was exploited and misused by their popular followers, who were no more than spiritual jugglers for the masses. After the massive injection of Ibn ʿArabī's ideas into the spiritual life of the community at the mass level, an anomianism and even anti-nomianism emerged, which went beyond the control of the ʿulamāʾ. There is no doubt that Ibn ʿArabī's intention in promulgating his doctrine of *wahdat ʾal-wujūd* or "unity of being" was to introduce a radical humanism into Islam, in which God and humanity appear as identical and as utterly interdependent. No matter how much intellectual ingenuity and skill has been deployed by recent scholars to absolve this theosoph of the charge of pantheism, it is undeniable that both its intention and actual impact, particularly at the popular level, was to abolish all distinction between the Creator and creature. "God is the servant and the servant is God" remains the essence of this message, despite all the dialectical exercises and paradoxical expressions. While *irjāʾ* would relax the moral tension of the self by promises of God's forgiveness in the next world, *wahdat ʾal-wujūd* all but proclaimed total moral nihilism in this world. In the aesthetic field, love of divine beauty degenerated to a point where loving adolescent youths was openly advocated by many Ṣūfīs. In this atmosphere of moral depravity, a *ḥadīth* came into circulation according to which the Prophet had said that God Himself dwells in adolescent youths (*amārid*), a *ḥadīth* apparently so widely accepted in these circles that Sirhindī had to take it seriously and interpret it away.

Ṣūfism, there is no doubt, had originated within Islam in response to certain verses of the Qurʾān emphasizing the transient nature of this world vis-à-vis God. It was to inculcate sincerity of faith in Him and the notion of reward and punishment in the hereafter. It was a response by spiritually sensitive spirits to the milieu of worldliness and materialism that the Muslim community was seen to have fallen into with the establishment of the Muslim empire and its governing institutions. Most important among these institutions was the law that sought to regulate only the external behavior of a person. These sensitive spirits reacted against Islam's message being expressed primarily, if not exclusively, in such an external mold. Al-Ghazālī was later to characterize law as a "discipline that is purely this-worldly, having nothing to do with the science of the Hereafter (*ᶜilm al-ākhira*)."[4] In the beginning there was no hostility between the spiritualists and the legists. On the contrary, we find that for the most part the spiritualists were also legists and traditionists (*muḥaddithūn*). It was most probably this same group of people who augmented *ḥadīth* by adding certain characteristically Ṣūfī elements to the corpus of *ḥadīth*, particularly *ḥadīth qudsī*, prophetic reports containing material where God directly speaks to Muḥammad but which do not form part of the Qurʾān. Ibn Ḥanbal's enmity towards and later persecution of the great early Ṣūfī al-Muḥāsibī (d. 223/837) seems to have been influenced by such hostility.

The most basic feature of this early Ṣūfism is a peculiar type of moral élan called *zuhd* – saving oneself from immersion in the temptations of this world – and a strong motive of contrition that accompanied it. These Ṣūfīs were not celibate monks. A few of them were, but then quite a few of the orthodox ᶜulamāʾ were celibate too, a fact that has nothing to do with the influence of Christian or Buddhist monasticism. On the contrary, as a rule most Sūfīs were married. However, the kind of moral wakefulness and alertness that some of the early Ṣūfīs displayed must be regarded as peculiar in the light of the Qurʾān. The Qurʾān normally speaks of *taqwā*, or being conscious of God's presence in all one's acts and dealings. Now, the word *taqwā* does not just mean "being careful" but being conscious that whatever a person does or thinks is witnessed by God, and therefore inspires a sense of awe and reverence for God. God is not just another item

4. Al-Ghazālī, *Iḥyā*, pp. 28–29.

among the items of the universe. This is the reason why He deserves complete worship and total obedience. The Qurʾān speaks of the hearts of the faithful trembling in awe when God is mentioned (Q. 8:2; 22:35). It speaks of their "skins trembling from the [reading] of the Qurʾān … and then their skins and their hearts soften up [naturally, without being forced by the pressure of will] to the remembrance of God or to prayers" (Q. 39:23). Again, "only those believe in our verses who, when these are recited to them, they fall prostrate [before God] and glorify God with their praise and are not puffed up with pride. Their sides [i.e. bodies] rise from their beds [for night vigils] when they call their Lord, out of fear and hope and they spend [on the needy] out of what We have given by way of sustenance" (Q. 32:15–16).

It should be pointed out that most of the above-quoted verses that talk about the psychological trembling state of the hearts also mention good deeds in the same breath. For the Qurʾān, deeds that do not issue from such a state of mind of *taqwā* are barren and sterile in terms of their consequences. What all this amounts to is the deepest possible sense of responsibility, which is very different indeed from the secular idea of responsibility (literally a mock responsibility) developed in modern Western thought. Yet it is also very far from being the kind of moral responsibility (which is equally a mock responsibility) indulged in by the early Ṣūfīs of Islam. Ḥasan of Baṣrā (d. 110/728) in his letter of advice to the pious Umayyad caliph ʿUmar b. ʿAbd al-ʿAzīz (d.101/720) quotes what later became a Ṣūfī *ḥadīth* according to which God has created nothing more hateful to him than this world, and from the day He created it He has not looked upon it. On the contrary, the Qurʾān constantly calls nature (this world) the great "sign" (*āya*) of God and ceaselessly upholds natural phenomena as its wonders. In particular, the Qurʾān tirelessly reminds humanity of the blessings of food, drink, comforts etc., which He has provided. "This world" in fact becomes evil and poison only if it turns into a veil concealing God from humanity instead of revealing God to humanity.

Thus it is then that even this "moral" Ṣūfism from the beginning, in some of its major aspects, manages to twist the Qurʾānic doctrine. In fact, even to call it "moral" is to misuse that term. For morality governs intra-human relationships and Qurʾānic morality does this with a strong sense of the presence of God. But the Ṣūfī doctrine of contrition and ascetic self-denial turns this positive morality of the Qurʾān into a struggle against oneself. Human beings are asked to wrestle with themselves. The dimension of intra-human relationship, which is the essence of the Qurʾānic morality, is practically eliminated. If this had not happened, Ṣūfism would have been the most positive spiritual asset of Islam. But when, in the moral struggle, one term is eliminated and one's own self as evil or Satan is substituted, surely a moral vacuum is created, providing justification for the harsh criticism of Ibn Taymiyya noted above. But this is not all. Soon Ṣūfism reached a stage where humanity began to wrestle with God. In this process, an inspired paradox (*shaṭḥ*) or change of personality takes place, as we have seen above in Ibn ᶜArabī. God becomes humanity, and humanity God. Ibn ᶜArabī is, of course, an intellectual Ṣūfī, the greatest of all intellectual Ṣūfīs. But long before that, we have Abū Yazīd al-Bistāmī (d. 262/875), the "intoxicated Ṣūfī" who stated: "then He changed me out of my identity into His selfhood … Then I command with Him with the tongue of His Grace, saying: 'how fares it with me with Thee?' He said: 'I am thine through Thee: there is no God but Thee.'" Often, of course, instead of the change of identity, humanity completely disappears (through moral effacement) and only God remains (or humanity becomes God). Al-Bistamī says: "Once He raised me up and stationed me before Him, and said to me, 'O Abū Yazīd! Truly, My creation desired to see Thee?' I said: "Adorn me in Thy unity, and clothe me in Thy selfhood, and raise me up to Thy oneness, so that when Thy creation see me they will say: "We have seen Thee: and then wilt be that, and I shall not be there at all.'" Finally, this whole drama grows out of a moral experience of extraordinary contrition. Once again, al-Bistāmī tells us, "For twelve years, I was the smith of myself and for five years the mirror of my heart. For a whole year, I spied between myself and my heart" (possibly a reference to Qurʾan 8:4: "God intervenes between man and his heart"). "I then discovered a hand of infidelity (*zunnār*) [a reference to the Hindu band worn on one's shoulder as a token of slavery to a deity-idol], which was fettering me from the outside [i.e, the world]. It took me twelve years to cut it. Then I discovered an internal fetter which took me five years to cut. Finally, I had an illumination. I contemplated the creation and I saw that [for me] it had turned into a corpse and I said four *takbīrs* over it, I pronounced Allahu Akbar four times, that is to say buried it."

This, then, is the odyssey of the massive transformation of Qurʾānic morality into Ṣūfī spiritual smithery – a moral wrestling with oneself, and finally wrestling with God where humankind drops out of sight. Not all Ṣūfīs were the same, of course, even in the early stages (ninth century). A more sober strand of Ṣūfism that started with al-Muḥāsibī found its most effective representative in al-Junayd (d. 298/910). Massignon, in his *Passion of al-Ḥallāj*, drastically berated al-Junayd and declared *tout court* that al-Junayd was merely a theoretician of Ṣūfism who never had a mystic experience.[5] The reason is that he found al-Junayd at a polar distance from the "intoxicated" Manṣūr al-Ḥallāj. But when he came to write his *Essai sur les origines du lexique technique de la mystique musulmane* (first published in 1922), Massignon noted that a good many doctrines of al-Junayd had been taken over by al-Ḥallāj, which called for an apology for his earlier error.[6] Nonetheless, Massignon still characterized al-Junayd as a "savant prudent et timide," apparently because the latter made a sharp distinction between God and humanity. It is difficult to know how much of the original works of al-Junayd was available to Massignon because both in the *Passion* and the *Essai* almost all his quotations and references are taken from later sources, and a collection of the treatises of al-Junayd with an English translation was only published by A.H. Abdel-Kader in 1962, the year of Massignon's death.[7] In this work not only does al-Junayd speak of his own mystic experiences, but his descriptions throughout imply that he is giving an account of his own experiences.

The esssence of the doctrine of al-Junayd, whose mystical ethos has been justly compared to that of St. John of the Cross (d. 1591) as found in his *Dark Night of the Soul*, is precisely the insistence that humankind *cannot* be God. He characterized al-Bistamī's experience as immature although he wrote a commentary on some of the latter's works and interpreted them in a more orthodox tradition.[8] He affirms, indeed, that the mystic does have an experience of union with God, where his being is "taken over" by God's being. However, he maintained, as Sirhindī would say much later, that the mystic inevitably returns from that state of unity and regains his "otherness" which is accompanied by pain and travail. All the treatises of al-Junayd that treat the mystic's inner transformation tell

5. Massignon, *Passion of al-Hallāj*, vol. 1, pp. 76–77.
6. Massignon, *Essai*, p. 206.
7. Al-Junayd, *Rasāʾil*.
8. Al-Ṭūṣī, *al-Lumaʿ*, pp. 280–281.

exactly the same story in almost exactly the same language, albeit sometimes in longer and shorter versions. His doctrine becomes clear by a summary of his longest treaty on the subject, *Kitāb al-Fanāʾ* (The Book of Annihilation) in the following points.

Before the creation of humankind, God in pre-eternity had made a covenant (*mīthāq*) with them, as the Qurʾān (7:171) has it. It is clear that human beings did not have any existence of their own at that stage, nor did their souls exist in pre-eternity. All existence, therefore, was but God's own existence and the human existence also, as ideas in God's mind, was but God's existence. Since humankind had no existence, they had no attribute there either. In that state, it is correct to say that it was God who had sought humanity – since the initiative was His – and not humanity who sought God. God's will was operative in humankind, who had no will of their own. Humanity in that state enjoyed the most perfect existence, a divine existence which ruled absolutely on humanity. In fact, humanity per se cannot even know it. This is the state that can be described as the perfect annihilation-in-survival (*fanāʾ fī ʾl-baqāʾ*) and perfect survival-in-annihilation (*baqāʾ fī ʾl-fanāʾ*). After creation, humankind became self-conscious. But after this, positive existence, the procedure of pre-eternity is reversed. Humankind then sought God, but in a self-conscious manner. According to a well-known *ḥadīth*, God said: "My servant progressively draws nigh unto Me by works of supererogation and I love him; and when I love him, I am his ear, so that he hears by me, and his eye, so that he sees by me."[9] Thus, a human being can and does lose him or herself in God, but self-consciously. For this reason, the human experience of God entails a conscious loss and an extraordinary effort and fatigue, because people know that they are lost in God and "absent" from the world, and their enjoyment of this state of bliss is also in the state of conscious "absences." This is the reason that mystics, when they are absent from the world and lost, still talk.[10]

But here lies the point of danger of this whole experience. Ṣūfīs are liable to become enamored by this experience, which is certainly extraordinarily pleasurable. They not only feel exhilaration in their experience, but also begin to proclaim how God had favored them and how they have become lost in Him. They begin to exert pressure upon God and

9. Al-Junayd, *Rasāʾil*, p. 154.
10. Ibid., 153.

take Him for granted. They are so pleased with their remembrance (*dhikr)* of God that they start to boast of their spiritual gains and pleasures, and the fact that the total sway of God is upon them. In fact, if they were totally lost in God and united with Him, they could not feel and utter these things. It is only because they have kept themselves separate from God and are not completely lost in Him that they can do so. This must necessarily be the case, since their creation entailed a self-consciousness. (This possibly was al-Junayd's elliptical critique of al-Bistāmī and al-Ḥallāj). At this point, God completely restores their self-consciousness, which constitutes a painful tragedy, since it entails extreme pain and travail. Some Ṣūfīs at this point of their return to the world console themselves by looking at beautiful scenes and figures and lovely gardens and indulge their taste in aesthetic enjoyment because they cannot face the stark and painful sense of loss. But many of them, the real Ṣūfīs, endure the pain and travail for they know they are destined not to attain real unity with God. They embark upon a hard life of trial, and stare the stark truth in the face but keep the flame of their desire for God alive. They are the true spiritual heroes, ever ready to make any sacrifice for their beloved and await with grinding uncertainty His final decision for them.

Al-Junayd's doctrine can be summed up in the well-known beautiful Arabic verse:

> I will to unite with him, but he wills seperation.
> I abandon my will for the sake of his will.

This brief summary of al-Junayd's extremely difficult formulation of both his mystic experience and doctrine was the start of a long development of orthodox Ṣūfism that preferred the state of "sobriety" to "intoxication." It finally culminated in the grand synthesis at the hands of al-Ghazālī in the eleventh century between Ṣūfism and orthodox Islam. For an analysis of this synthesis and an assessment of its importance for the future of Islam we must now turn to al-Ghazālī.

Al-Ghazālī's Reformist Synthesis

Abū Ḥāmid al-Ghazālī (450/1058–505/1111) is the most influential and impressive religious personality in post-classical Islam. At the age of thirty-three he had achieved enough work of brilliance and originality in the traditional Islamic sciences of law and theology to be appointed rector of the Niẓāmiyya College at Baghdad by Niẓām al-Mulk, the illustrious Saljūq minister (*wazīr*). He was a towering personality and his career a resounding success. But right at the zenith of his glory he resigned his rectorship, having held it for four years. He was troubled both by doubts in his faith which rested on traditional theological (*kalām*) arguments and his practical life. His doubts almost crippled him physically for two months as he tells us in his "spiritual autobiography," *al-Munqidh min al-Ḍalāl* (Deliverance from Error). He then took to seclusion, and wandered for ten years in Syria, Egypt, and the holy cities of Islam. His thought and spiritual concentration culminated in his magnum opus, *Iḥyāʾ ʿUlūm al-Dīn* (Revivification of the Sciences of Religion).

After ten years he reemerged in his native region in 1086, and accepted the rectorship of the Niẓāmiyya at Nishapur at the insistence of Niẓām al-Mulk's son, Fakhr al-Mulk, upon whose assassination by the Ismāʿīlīs in 1106 he again quit this post. He then returned to his native Tus, taught there, and wrote his last great work on jurisprudence, *al-Mustaṣfā* (The Quintessence). What is equally puzzling and irresistibly fascinating is precisely this spiritual odyssey, this restless and vicissitudinous intellectual spiritual career of al-Ghazālī. Before we can say something decisive about his performance, a brief analysis of his inner life is absolutely necessary in order genuinely to understand his spiritual life and his work. For al-Ghazālī is one of those rare thinkers whose actual inner life is bound up with his work. This is why someone such as Ibn Taymiyya, for example, who even doubted whether al-Ghazālī's Islam was acceptable, nevertheless insisted on his sincerity, besides his unusual intelligence and "ocean-like" knowledge. Let us first clarify the nature of the "doubts" that al-Ghazālī developed. This doubt was two-pronged: it was both personal (moral) and intellectual. If it had been only cognitive–intellectual, it was hardly necessary for him to resign his post suddenly the way he did. He could have proceeded to resolve such doubt without throwing away his career all at once. But it was his personal and moral crisis, the realization that his pursuit of pomp, power, and glory was not only worthless, but dangerously harmful if he was a genuine seeker of truth. Such "doubt" might have attacked him even if he had not been a man of high academic accomplishments, even if he had been, say, a successful businessman.

But, of course, if he wanted to pursue the truth, then he must not only reject his pompous lifestyle but equally his academic preoccupation with theology (*kalām*) and law (*fiqh*), because neither of them yielded ultimate truth. Both were unreal in a sense. *Kalām* was an intellectual artifice whereby theologians defended the fundamentals of the faith against objections, innovations, and intellectual doubts. *Kalām* did not and could not establish faith; it presupposed the truth of faith and defended it, with disputation (*jadal*) as its weapon and method. As for law, it was of course necessary to order society. Yet the purpose of law is to ward off harm and evil affecting society. Law cannot and does not claim to be an avenue to truth. We shall have more to say presently on al-Ghazālī's re-valorization of these traditional Islamic sciences, but for the moment we must pursue the broader question of his doubt.

Al-Ghazālīi explicitly states in *al-Munqidh* (Deliverance):

> From the various sciences that I had mastered and the methods I had practiced in investigating, the two types of knowledge, the traditional and rational, I had already obtained an unshakeable faith in God, Prophethood and the Last Day. Faith in these three principles had become deeply ingrained in my soul, not by any definite abstract proof but rather through a host of reasons, indications and experiences whose detail cannot be comprehended by any enumeration."[11]

It is clear that this doubt is not at all of the same nature as the Cartesian "doubt" which was self-induced and formal and which was also remedied by a purely abstract and formal proof. In *his* doubt, al-Ghazālī found his personal fate at stake. Secondly, it is perfectly intelligible why al-Ghazālī might at once have believed and believed so deeply in God, prophethood, and the Last Day – that this belief was not just intellectually entertained like *kalām* propositions. These beliefs had become the very stuff of his mind, as he himself says, and yet he pursued the realization of these truths for himself. It is naive to think that the two are incompatible, which is the pivotal point of Farid Jabre's argument about al-Ghazālī. On the contrary, it is commonplace in life that the simultaneous coexistence of certainty and skepticism is sufficient to drive one to greater realization. For the Qur᾿ān, it is something quite natural: cf. Qur᾿ān 2:260 on Abraham's faith. Ibn

11. Al-Ghazālī, *al-Munqidh*, p. 59; also see al-Ṣarīfīnī, "al-Muntakhab," fol. 20 a–b.

Taymiyya characterized this faith of al-Ghazālī as "undifferentiated faith" (*īmān mujmal*).

Al-Ghazālī tells us that he found only four paths to go about the task before him: those of the theologians (*mutakallimūn*), the Ismāᶜīlīs (*Bāṭinīs*), the philosophers (rationalists), and the Ṣūfīs. Then he states: "I said to myself, truth cannot lie beyond these four types, for these are the only ones who are seeking the way of truth. Should truth be blocked to them, there is no hope of ever finding it."[12] Thus, what al-Ghazālī was seeking was a correct and effective method of realizing and appropriating the truth in a new and deeper way. He found this in Ṣūfism. First of all, Ṣūfism resolved his double crisis mentioned above. At the personal level, it saved him from attachment to the worldly enticements of power, fame, and monetary acquisitiveness. At the intellectual and spiritual level, it helped him realize and re-appropriate the ultimate religious truths with a new depth and meaningfulness. It is now clear that when he rejected theology and philosophy, he rejected them as methods (dialectic and logical rationality respectively), not necessarily all their content. In fact, he re-appropriated basic *kalām* propositions through mystical experience. And indeed, he retained much of a philosophical–speculative outlook, through Ṣūfism. It must be noted that particularly through Ibn Sīnā's philosophy, a melange between Ṣūfism and speculative rational thought had already occurred. Bāṭinism had in a sense shared both, although it cannot be characterized either as Ṣūfism or as rational philosophy. Its esoteric doctrines offered a rich crop of symbolism which both philosophy and Ṣūfism could readily appropriate.

Above all, Ṣūfism reinvigorated al-Ghazālī's Ashᶜarism. Ashᶜarism had taught that human beings could not be said to act in a real sense, but only in a metaphysical sense, since God was the real "actor.' Ṣūfism proclaimed that only God exists. Both Ashᶜarism and Ṣūfism taught passivity vis-à-vis God, since both subscribed to the inanity of natural and human voluntary causations. Al-Ghazālī, in fact, devoted one whole section of his polemical work against certain major theses of the Muslim philosophers in *Tahāfut al-Falāsifa* (The Incoherence of the Philosophers) to refute the whole concept of causation. It is this vigorous juncture of Ṣūfism and Ashᶜarī *kalām* that makes him proclaim, in his *Jawāhir al-Qurʾān* (Gems of the Qurʾān), an important work belonging to his middle Ṣūfī period, that "indeed, there is

12. Al-Ghazālī, *al-Munqidh*, p. 31.

nothing in existence except God and His acts, for whatever is there besides Him in His act."[13] In fact, Ashᶜarism, just like Ṣūfism, had rendered God a concentrate of power and will, just as the Muᶜtazila had made Him a concentrate of justice and rationality. However, Ṣūfism also brought to the fore the element of universal divine mercy, which the Muᶜtazila practically denied and the Ashᶜarīs ignored. Al-Ghazālī's Ṣūfism thus enabled him to supplement his Ashᶜarism in an important way.

What is puzzling in al-Ghazālī's spiritual odyssey is his different evaluation of certain sciences, of which we are here particularly concerned with *kalām* and *fiqh*, particularly the latter. For it is his assessment of law (*fiqh*) that would enable us to judge his real relationship with the orthodox or the kerygmatic tradition, as Hodgson calls it. Upon the nature of this relationship the extent and quality of al-Ghazālī's contribution to Islam and Islamic reconstruction will turn. Before we go further, however, a note of caution is in order. Al-Ghazālī, because his mind was gripped by a certain mood at a given time, and also due to his prolific speed of writing, sometimes expressed himself in an exaggerated manner about certain matters. Thus, in his *Iḥyā*ᵓ (Revivification) he denounced law as a "purely this-worldly science," having nothing to do with religion which consists only of "the science of the hereafter." But in the same work he assigned to it an essential religious status, albeit that of an instrumental one. Again, in the *Jawāhir al-Qur*ᵓ*ān* he said about sciences such as medicine, astronomy, and physics that although these are genuine sciences, no benefit either in this life or the next is attached to them.[14] Now, we know that although he evaluated medicine, for example, as being lower than the religious sciences, he nevertheless regarded it as religiously essential, and declared it to be *farḍ kifāya*, a religious duty which devolves upon the community as a whole. In his Criterion of Action (*Mīzān al-*ᶜ*Amal*), which must belong to the early days of his conversion to Ṣūfism, he made the startling statement that praying without understanding the meaning of the content of prayer is just as "religious" as dancing, since both consist of purely physical movements. Occurrences such as these are not uncommon in his writings, but in such cases it is not difficult to find out his real intent.

But the case of *kalām* and *fiqh* poses a complicated problem when viewed in the context of the entire history of his thought. His first period,

13. Al-Ghazālī, *Jawāhir*, p. 11.
14. Ibid., p. 25.

that of external success, was, as we have seen, marked by devotion, teaching, and writing on these two central disciplines of orthodox Islam. In the middle period lasting for ten years, he was devoted to Ṣūfism, internal development, and writing about the inner spiritual life. He wrote a good many works in this period, including his most celebrated work, the great *Iḥyāʾ*. In this work, as we have pointed out above, he regarded only the "science of the hereafter" as being the truly religious science and possessing absolute value, while he assigned an instrumental value to *fiqh*, sometimes even condemning it as "a science concerned only with this world."[15] He particularly lashed out at the bearers of this science, the *fuqahāʾ*, as corrupt men of this world. He wrote a separate work, *Iljām al-ʿAwām min ʿIlm al-Kalām*, (Restraining the Masses from [the Harm] of Theology) where he characterized the *mutakillimūn* as immature children to whom spiritual truths must never be divulged. Positively, he wrote the work Moderation in Creed (*al-Iqtiṣād fī ʾl-Iʿtiqād*), where he strongly advised avoidance of the extravagances of the *kalām* but where he inserted basic *kalām* formulas as true creed but as interpreted through a very moderate Ṣūfism. But it is in his *Jawāhir al-Qurʾān* (Gems of the Qurʾān) that he makes repeated and highly interesting attempts to give a religious evaluation of *kalām* and *fiqh*. In all these statements Ṣūfism, Ṣūfized philosophy that has some resonance with the Ismāʿīlī *Rasāʾil Ikhwān al-Ṣafā* (Epistles of the Brethren of Purity), as well as the influences of *kalām*, *fiqh* (or *kalām-fiqh*), and the discourse of mosque preachers seem to dominate. He says that the importance of *fiqh* stems from the need of society for law. *Kalām* is needed to combat those who innovate and sow doubts in the minds of others. Thus, he declared that the jurist and the theologian are close to each other. Again, "as for the relationship of these two to the goal [knowledge of God and His attributes] and to the path to the goal [i.e. the Ṣūfī way] is this. The jurists (*fuqahāʾ*) are to be regarded as the builders of hospices and other facilities on the way to Makka for the sake of the pilgrimage, while the position of the theologians (*mutakallimūn*) is like that of the guides to the pilgrimage and guardians along the way."[16] Immediately al-Ghazālī adds: "If these people add to their arts [i.e. *kalām* and *fiqh*], the following of the [Ṣūfi] path to God by cutting through the steep passes of the soul and disengagement from worldly attractions and

15. Al-Ghazālī, *Iḥyā*, vol. 1, pp. 28–29.
16. Al-Ghazālī, *Jawāhir*, p. 23.

making God their sole concern, their excellence over all others would be like the excellence of the sun over the moon. But if they cannot do this, their rank is very low, indeed."[17]

In this work, al-Ghazālī expresses some regret over his own previous preoccupation with writing on *fiqh*, despite the fact that he rated it high in the scale of religious sciences.

> This is a science for which there is universal need because it is related to betterment, first, of this life and then of the life to come. For this reason, one who possesses this science is additionally priviliged by fame, honor and priority over others – preachers, those who tell [Qur$^{\circ}$ānic] stories and the theologians (*mutakallimūn*). And for this reason, this knowledge has had the fortune of being the beneficiary of a great deal of discussion and lengthy investigations in proportion to the need for it so that works on it have multiplied, particularly on those issues where opinions differ. This, despite the fact that these differences are not very large and even error in legal matters is not far from the truth, for nearly all legal thinkers (*mujtahidūn*) can be said to be right or it can [at least] be said that every *mujtahid* deserves one reward [from God] while one who hits the right opinion gets a double reward. However, since a great deal of pomp and glory is dependent upon it, legal thinkers are heavily motivated to go to excesses in building up its details. I myself wasted a considerable part of my life in writing about disputed matters in the field and spent a good part of it in authoring works of the [Shāfi^{c}ī] school and in organizing these into long, middle and small ones, indulging in far too excessive elaboration and detail. However, what I deposited into my 'Abridgement of the Abridgement', being my fourth and shortest work [on the subject] is quite sufficient [as a law guide].[18]

The substance of al-Ghazālī's *Jawāhir* (Gems) consists of his selections from the Qur$^{\circ}$ān which he divides into theoretical (giving knowledge of God) and practical (by which he means ethical, not legal). A most telling illustration of the way in which al-Ghazālī came to underrate law and legal science is to be found in his introduction to the *Jawāhir*. In answer to a possible objection as to why al-Ghazālī, in this work, dares to propose to classify the verses of the Qur$^{\circ}$ān in different ranks of importance (verses

17. Ibid.
18. Ibid., p. 22.

about God, the Ṣūfī path, the practical verses etc.) while the Qur'ān claims to be one, indivisible Word of God, he says:

> You should know that if the light of your inner sight cannot guide you to see the difference between the import of the verse of the "Throne" [Q. 2:255] and the verse concerning loans [Q. 2:282] or between the chapter [sūra] of God's "Uniqueness" [Q. 112] and the chapter cursing Abu Lahab [Q. 111]; and, if your deviant soul immersed in the blind acceptance of authority (*taqlīd*) is frightened of making such differentiations, then you should accept the authority of the Messenger (Peace and blessings of God be upon him) himself to whom the Qur'ān was revealed. For several reports from him indicate the nobility and high status of certain passages of the Qur'ān [relative to others].[19]

Here, al-Ghazālī emphasizes the radical difference in the import of Q. 2:255, which speaks of God's glory, omniscience, and majesty, on the one hand, and verse Q. 2:282, which lays down rules for incurring loans, their recording, witnessing etc., on the other.

After his return to teaching, first publicly at Nishapūr and then privately at his home in Tus, al-Ghazālī wrote at least two works: one on jurisprudence, *al-Mustaṣfā* (The Quintessence) and the other his spiritual autobiography, *al-Munqidh min al-Ḍalāl* (Deliverance from Error). In the latter, he exalts the Ṣūfī way as being the only way to God. He views it as a kind of introduction to prophethood, being beyond pure rationality although neither alien nor contradictory to it. This is in basic conformity with the attitude of his middle period, the period of Ṣūfism. However, in the introduction (*khuṭba*) to *al-Mustaṣfā*, we read as follows:

> Sciences are of three kinds, first, purely rational which the *sharīᶜa* neither incites against, nor does it invite to them, for example, mathematics, geometry, astronomy etc. The position of these is an amalgam of false guesses – and some guesses are *sinful* (Q. 49:12)[20] – and correct knowledge which, however, has no benefit – and we seek refuge in God from knowledge that does not benefit. For no benefit lies in enjoyment of the present and pompous worldly prosperity, since these are merely transitory, the real benefits being in the reward of the next Abode. Secondly, there are the purely traditionally transmitted sciences for

19. Ibid., p. 37.
20. The Qur'ān, however, is not talking of sciences but of wrongfully guessing at other people's motivations.

example, *ḥadīth* and commentaries of the Qur'ān ... There is little of importance in these, for all big and small can acquire them equally, since transmission requires sheer power of memory and demands no rational activity.

The noblest of sciences are those that combine both reason and tradition; and personal thought as well as revealed authority. Now, law and jurisprudence belongs to this category because it takes a balanced path, by taking the choicest of revelation (*sharᶜ*) and reason. Neither is it a manipulation by pure reason, which is not welcomed by the *sharᶜ*. Nor is it based on blind acceptance of pure authority which reason cannot certify to be correct nor support. It is because of the nobility of the science of law (*fiqh*) and its cause [which is a combination of authority and reason] that God has made abundant the motivations of people to acquire it and those who are learned in it are the highest of scholars in rank and the greatest of them in prestige; and they have the largest number of colleagues as followers.

In my early youth, specialization in this science brought religious and secular benefits, as well as rewards in the afterlife and the first life, requiring of me to devote to it a good part of my life and expend on it alone a considerable portion of my effective activity. I, therefore, authored several works, concerned with law and jurisprudence. After that, I turned myself to the science of the path of the hereafter [and acquisition of] the knowledge of the secrets of religion [i.e. Ṣūfism]. Thus, I authored on this topic comprehensive works like the Revivification of the Sciences of Religion [*Ihyā' ᶜUlūm al-Dīn*], and small works, like Gems of the Qur'ān [*Jawāhir al-Qur'ān*] and middle [length] ones like The Alchemy of Happiness (*Kīmiyā' al-Saᶜāda*). Then, divine decree drove me to return to teaching and thereby benefit others. So a group of experts in the science of law proposed that I write a work on jurisprudence.[21]

The language of this passage is apparently in striking contrast to the preceding one quoted from *Jawāhir*. There, al-Ghazālī regretfully says that in his earlier life he "wasted" much of his time in writing works on points of difference among the jurists and particularly spent needless time in writing lengthy and detailed works on law, whereas brief compendiums would have sufficed. In *al-Mustaṣfā* he seems to recall not only nonchalantly, but with a measure of approval and pleasure, that he had been occupied with law in

21. Al-Ghazālī, *al-Mustaṣfā*, pp. 3–4.

his early youth. In *Jawāhir*, he says that unless a jurist and a theologian also cultivate the inner discipline of Ṣūfism his rank is very low indeed. In his later work a jurist *deserves* the high popular status, but in earlier work law comes not only after Ṣūfism, but repeatedly comes after theology. In fact, in *al-Mustaṣfā* law belonged to the category of "the noblest sciences." In the *Jawāhir*, and particularly in the *Ihyāʾ*, the jurists are described as corrupt people because they enjoy such good worldly fortune, pomp, and glory and law appears only as a "this-worldly science." In *al-Mustaṣfā* law (*fiqh*) partakes not only of this-worldly goodness but also that of the next life, and the pomp and glory of the jurists are justified by their real service to the faith. Also, the language al-Ghazālī uses in the passage of *al-Mustaṣfā* describing his Ṣūfī career and then his going back to law appears to be loaded with significance. About his conversion to Ṣūfism he says, "I turned myself to" (*aqbaltu*) while about his resumption of public teaching and returning to the law, he says, "divine decree led me" (*sāqanī qadarullāh*).[22] Finally, in the same passage, he recounts the works he had written in neutral, non-committed terms, while in the *Jawāhir* and other spiritual works he mentions his spiritual writing with satisfaction and praise.

How is this enigma to be resolved? For we cannot put it down to mere careless writing, similar to the examples cited earlier. And the enigma becomes more intriguing if we consider that al-Ghazālī wrote his *al-Munqidh*, which gives decisive preference to Ṣūfism, at about the same time as *al-Mustaṣfā*. First of all, in this last work of his, we note here that although al-Ghazālī mentions his spiritual works casually, he does not indicate his disapproval of them as he had earlier denounced his legal works in the *Jawāhir* as a "waste of time." Indeed, the tone indicates that he felt as if going back to the law and teaching were normal and natural occupational shifts and moves he was required to make. There is, then, no other conclusion to be drawn from this except that with his return to public teaching and occupying himself with law, he did not retract from Ṣūfism. The fact is that when al-Ghazālī became a Ṣūfī he did degrade *fiqh* but never dismissed it completely, and his harsh words in the *Ihyāʾ* are meant to be directed more against the "*ʿfuqahāʾ* of these days" rather than against *fiqh* itself. When he resumed writing on *fiqh* at the insistence of certain *fuqahāʾ*, as he tells us in *al-Mustaṣfā*, Ṣūfism was very much with him. He was in all likelihood mentally prepared to do so, in addition to whatever

22. Ibid., p. 4.

pressure his patron, Fakhr al-Mulk, other *fuqahā*ᵓ, and the political circumstances put upon him.

The question remains as to why al-Ghazālī describes *fiqh* as "belonging to the category of the highest or noblest sciences," having previously relegated it to a very low rank. The same question applies to *kalām*, which he had disparaged during his mystical phase, but a theme that is sprinkled all over the pages of *al-Mustaṣfā*. One answer given by Professor Anne K. Lambton, strongly suggested by Professor Henri Laoust, and accepted by Professor Bernard Lewis is that al-Ghazālī was pressured by Fakhr al-Mulk to resume public teaching. I think that my analysis, given above, of the status of *al-Mustaṣfā* as well as the status of law in *al-Mustaṣfā*, supports this interpretation in general. But accepting such a conclusion without further questioning also creates its own problems. Al-Ghazālī had immersed himself in Ṣūfī spirituality for a full decade. During this phase he untiringly emphasized honesty, sincerity of motivation, turning one's back upon worldly considerations, and fixing one's gaze exclusively on the hereafter. Seen from this perspective he radically devalued *fiqh* and *kalām*. How could he now simply resume his interests in these disciplines and yield to political pressure from a sulṭān? How does one explain this somersault, especially when he made resounding and critical remarks about the scholars (ᶜulamāᵓ) who had truck with the rulers. And, if one cannot help having links, then it is less evil for a scholar (ᶜ*ālim*) to be visited by a ruler than to pay visits to the ruler!

We have already mentioned that al-Ghazālī's writings naturally reflected his own inner personality and experiences. His writings are certainly for the educated, and particularly the religiously educated, public. But they are equally a mirror of his inner spiritual personality. We also saw from our quotation from the *Jawāhir* that he had degraded *fiqh* and *kalām* only when he perceived their possessors to be devoid of spiritual life. However, those who combined *fiqh* or *kalām* with Ṣūfism and infused the former with the spiritual meaning of the latter were distinguished from their fellow ᶜulamāᵓ with "the excellence of the sun over the moon." Al-Ghazālī himself had now thoroughly imbibed and cultivated spirituality and had given inner depth and meaning to the Sharīᶜa. Why should he not return to the "outer" disciplines of the Sharīᶜa and serve the cause of the solidarity of the community and the kerygmatic tradition? This analysis is confirmed by the account of ᶜAbd al-Ghāfir (d. 529/1134), a contemporary of al-Ghazālī who knew him personally and appears to have been quite objective, both in his criticism and appreciation of this notable scholar. His views are also by far the most reliable guide besides al-Ghazālī's own statements about himself. Space does not allow here, otherwise this entire statement is worthwhile quoting. On the subject of Fakhr al-Mulk's forcing him to teach, ᶜAbd al-Ghāfir says:

> Then [i.e., after his ten-year spiritual odyssey] he returned to his home confining himself to his house and occupying himself with thought as well as observing Ṣūfī practices. He was the object of visit by many and was a treasure of people's hearts, whosoever visited him. This lasted for quite a while. His works appeared and became widely known. During these days he was not the target of any opposition, nor did any objection [or refutation] appear by anyone against what he said. Then the turn came for the great Fakhr al-Mulk . . . and Khurasan came to be adorned by his power and rule. He came to recognize al-Ghazālī's station and stature and [was impressed by] his condition, his clean belief and pure life. Fakhr al-Mulk sought to be blessed by him and so went into his presence and listened to his discourse.
>
> He asked al-Ghazālī not to let his precious knowledge and thoughts remain barren so that no one benefited from them . . . and he insisted to the utmost and intensified his proposal [that al-Ghazālī resume public teaching] until al-Ghazālī agreed to go [out of his house] and was taken to Nishapur [the capital of Khurasan]. All this time, the lion had been absent from his den and the matter had been hidden under the unknown and secret decree of God. He was asked to take up teaching in the blessed madrassa Niẓāmiyya. Al-Ghazālī found it necessary to "submit to his patron."[23]

ᶜAbd al-Ghāfir later says he questioned al-Ghazālī why he took up teaching again, to which the latter answered apologetically: "I did not allow according to my religion that I should withhold myself from public calling and from benefiting students with my knowledge. I felt it as a duty that I make the truth public, state it in the open and call people to it." ᶜAbd al-Ghāfir comments, "And he was telling the truth in this."[24]

The biographer tells us that when al-Ghazālī returned to teaching, he was sincere and humble and was not the haughty and conceited al-Ghazālīi

23. Al-Subkī, *Ṭabaqāt*, vol. 6, pp. 199–201.
24. Al-Dhahabī, *Siyar*, vol. 19, p. 324.

of his earlier, pre-Ṣūfī days in Baghdad. He no longer returned to what he had discarded and freed himself from seeking after glory, disputation with his peers, and arrogance against his opponents.

> [This time], no matter how much he was subjected to opposition and how much he was vilified in what he did or did not do he was exposed to jealousy and debunkment. He showed no signs of being influenced by it, nor did he react and respond to his detractors, nor did he display any disapproval of the slanders of the busybodies. I visited him several times and I remembered how he used to conduct himself in the by-gone days with maliciousness and an overbearing attitude, looking down upon people with contempt, making light of them in his opnionated conceit by being misled by his natural gifts of his thought, speech and eloquence, seeking power and glory in rank and status. All that was gone and he had become the exact reverse of all this; he became totally cleansed of all turpitude. In fact, I thought that all this change might have been deliberately cultivated by him and that he was trying to show-off that he had changed into a new state. But after long study and examination, I concluded that what I had imagined was unfounded and that the man had really recovered from his [earlier] madness.[25]

ᶜAbd al-Ghāfir continues in his characteristic and realistic manner:

> Then [i.e. after Fakhr al-Mulk's assassination by the Ismāᶜīlīs] he abandoned [his job] before he himself might be abandoned [through the mala fide activity of his slandering opponents who would certainly exploit the new change in the political situation] and returned [once again] to his house [in Tus]. In his neighborhood he constructed a madrasa for students and a khanqah for Ṣūfīs. He divided his time over the duties concerning those who were with him: Recital (and teaching) of the Qurʾān, joining Ṣūfīs in their practices and teaching sessions for students [who studied *kalām* and *fiqh*], so that not a moment of his, nor of his followers was without benefit.[26]

ᶜAbd al-Ghāfir's compact and pregnant account is truly illuminating and solves many puzzles. Although we have not quoted him on this, he states very early that al-Ghazālī was so precociously brilliant that he began writing books while he was still a student of the illustrious Imām al-

25. Ibid., vol. 19, p. 325.
26. Ibid.

Ḥaramayn al-Juwaynī (d. 478/1085), who was therefore jealous of his pupil. And although he controlled his jealousy, it remained with him until he died. This quotation also makes clear that al-Ghazālīi was pressed (not pressured, i.e., forced) by Fakhr al-Mulk to return to public teaching, which al-Ghazālī himself states he could not resist. We have found that the biographer, who was no credulous narrator but a tough critic, accepted the truth of al-Ghazālī's statement, just as he became convinced that the question of al-Ghazālī's ambivalence concerning *kalām–fiqh* vis-à-vis Ṣūfism was resolved by the fact that after his final return home he founded both a madrasa and a Ṣūfī hospice. He obviously espoused both, irrespective of how organically he integrated Ṣūfism into the kerygmatic tradition.

Besides what we have said, there was an acute need to return to law and theology at that critical juncture. The Ismāᶜīlī revolt was in full swing and their assassinations so rampant that they had become extremely dangerous to Sunnī Islam. The situation desperately required the restoration of the social order and hence a reassertion of the authority and supremacy of the Sharīᶜa. The political authority itself had become very weak and the Saljūq princes recurrently and quickly succeeded each other as rulers and were recognized as such by the shadowy caliphate authority. Perhaps this is also what al-Ghazālī means by the words "then divine decree drove me to return to public teaching," for external circumstances freed him to accept Fakhr al-Mulk's invitation to head the Niẓāmiyya at Nishapūr.

We can now fully appreciate the intellectual and spiritual odyssey of al-Ghazālī. It reveals not only a man of extraordinary caliber and attainment, but a personality of tremendous sincerity and charm, incessantly and feverishly at work and giving to the Muslims, through his works, whatever he perceived to be true and felt to be necessary. His legacy immeasurably strengthened Sunnī Islam by injecting into its intellectual shell a new spiritual life and reorienting it from being a semi-fossilized "religion" to becoming a vibrant faith.

And yet finally, we must, from the perspective of our argument in this book, face and answer the question: despite his immense performance, indubitable creativity, and incalculably influential legacy, what does al-Ghazālī's reform amount to when measured against the Qurᵓān and the Prophet's performance? To many, this question may sound simply absurd and they may well be tempted to dismiss it without further ado, by asking another question. How can one possibly compare the situation of Muḥammad in seventh-century Arabia with al-Ghazālī's situation and his *problematique* in the eleventh century? It is, of course, obvious that he was working within the context of a long-estalished tradition. And any reformer within a tradition can only work with the materials available to him at that time in that tradition. Surely al-Ghazālī's achievement in grounding the central Islamic orthodox discipline into Ṣūfī spirituality and integrating them in a meaningful way is all that any meaningful reformer can expect to achieve. Marshall Hodgson and others have observed that the Muslim community of his day remained a central point of reference for al-Ghazālī. The community guaranteed the truth for those who did not doubt; it provided guidance for those who sought it. Not the community of a past era, but the one that coexisted with him, guaranteed the truth of the entire Islamic fabric.

But, then, this is the burden of the critique of al-Ghazālī by Ibn Taymiyya, who acknowledges that of the four approaches, that of the theologians, philosophers, esoterists, and Ṣūfīs al-Ghazālī chose the last because of its fundamental spiritual and ethical merits and because "it cleanses the human heart totally from whatever is other than God."[27] Ibn Taymiyya agrees with al-Ghazālī that the basis of the Ṣūfī way is to witness that there is no God but Allāh and Muḥammad is His Messenger. Al-Ghazālī, according to Ibn Taymiyya, had made the beginning of Islam its end. This is one reason why al-Ghazālī did not, said Ibn Taymiyya, consider the method and spiritual path of the folk of the Sunna and *ḥadīth* as an option for his spiritual endeavors. Therefore al-Ghazālī did not even mention this option, he said. Then he says:

> He [al-Ghazālī] took the [Ṣūfī spiritual discoveries] to be the standard with which to judge [the veracity of] what the revelation (*sharᶜ*) provided. The reason for [this approach] was that he soon discovered by means of his intelligence and devout inquiry, that the method of the theologians and philosophers was incoherent. God had granted him faith in principle and in summary, as he himself tells us, and so he began to search for the exposition [of this faith]. Then he discovered in the discourses of Ṣūfī shaykhs that which was nearer to the truth and more reasonable than what the theologians and philosophers had to offer. And the matter was as

27. al-Ghazālī, *al-Munqidh*, p. 57.

> he found it. But, he did not gain access to the prophetic heritage, namely the sciences and spiritual states possessed by the elect of the community. Nor did he attain the proper knowledge and devotion achieved by the earliest generations and the forerunners [of the community]. [Both these groups] attained so much by way of cognitive discoveries and practical modes of service to God which those others [i.e. theologians, philosophers and Ṣūfīs] never attained. Hence, he [al-Ghazālī] began to believe that the exposition of his concise faith could be obtained only through the [Ṣūfī] way, since he knew no other path. [This happened] because the special path of the elevated prophetic example remained closed to him, since he had little knowledge in this area and also because of the doubts that he had inherited from the philosophers and the theologians.[28]

I have quoted Ibn Taymiyya at length despite the fact that he was at times not fair to al-Ghazālī. For example, he criticized al-Ghazālī for mistakenly assuming the beginning of Islam to be its end. Ibn Taymiyya's critique is nevertheless essentially correct. Al-Ghazālī studied all the Islamic disciplines that constituted the historic tradition of Islam, but he did not study and appropriate the Qur^ʾān on its own terms. Marshall Hodgson once again remarks with deep insight, although not specifically in al-Ghazālī's context, but in the general context of the religious intellectualism of those times:

> The strong kerygmatic tone of Islamic thinking, in which certain historical events were explicitly vested with ultimate values, had issued in communalism, in which the sharīʿa was reinforced by way of exclusive group loyalties – so *that the Qurʾānic event became intellectually more isolated* even then in the Qurʾān itself, where it appeared as one in a long chain of revelatory events.

The Qurʾan had, in fact, long ceased to be the direct and unique source of guidance and had been buried under its real or alleged derivatives – *fiqh*, *kalām* and now Ṣūfism.

Al-Ghazālī, as we have seen, had written a book on the Qurʾān, the *Jawāhir*. Here the Qurʾān is not viewed per se and through its own light, but through the perspective that Ṣūfism had provided al-Ghazālī. This is why the verse of the Qurʾān concerning loans seemed to him of much lower import than the verse concerning the divine throne and also these two types

28. Ibn Taymiyya, *Fatāwā*, vol. 4, p. 64.

of verses (and others like them) seemed to him isolated from each other. Al-Ghazālī, then, provided the teaching for deepening one's personal faith and rising above paltry material attachments. But his inculcation of morality was confined to personal, "soft virtues" – how to be a good person and possess all the private virtues on a strong foundation of personal faith. Although he took the then existing community as his referent – and not the Qur'ān or the real Muḥammad – he did not call for social or community virtues that would once again prepare the community as such to play the role in the world that the Qur'ān required of it. Thus a good Muslim, a good Hindu, or a good Buddhist, allowing for differences in belief, were no different from one another. The community was no longer under an obligation first to set its own house in order and then to alter the world in accordance with the Qur'ānic vision.

Conclusion

Professor Arthur Adkins, in his *Moral Values and Political Behaviours in Ancient Greece*, has distinguished "quiet virtues" from "heroic virtues" in the Greek tradition of morality, and finds, on the whole, an absence of the former there. Alisdair MacIntyre seeks the remedy for the moral decay of the present West in a re-cultivation of the values of ancient heroic societies in his *After Virtue*. In my account of al-Ghazālī, the use of the term "soft virtues" is close to that of Adkin's "quiet virtues." In al-Ghazālī's case Ṣūfī virtues include not only the "quiet virtues" of Adkins, but primarily virtues of spiritual life or inner enlightenment. But my "community virtues" have nothing to do with the "heroic virtues" of either author. By this phrase, I mean the collective effort of the community to inculcate the purity of moral orientation (*taqwā*) at the individual level and then to direct this collective effort to found an ethical, social, and political order on the earth. The Qur'ān seeks to debunk heroism. Al-Ghazālī's Ṣūfism, however, could not renovate the kerygmatic tradition and bring it in line with the Qur'ānic kerygma. His all-pervasive spiritual and intellectual influence has lasted through the centuries until today.

4

LATER MEDIEVAL REFORM

Ibn Taymiyya on the "Middle Way"

In contradistinction to al-Ghazālī's personalism, we find in Ibn Taymiyya (661–728/1263–1328) what may be called "Islamic positivism." His was a concern with the two central disciplines of the Sharīᶜa tradition in the form of theology and law, as well as the community that is the bearer of this "kerygmatic tradition" and a serious attempt to reform that tradition. While al-Ghazālī's influence was almost immediate, Ibn Taymiyya's message lay dormant through the centuries. And even when it was "discovered" by Muḥammad b. ᶜAbd al-Wahhāb and his followers in the eighteenth-century Arabian peninsula, it was miserably truncated. The Wahhābī version totally lost the vision of an integrally reconstituted Muslim community, which was at the center of Ibn Taymiyya's entire endeavor, even though, in its own right, it became seminally influential in modern Islam. We shall argue that for a genuine reconstruction of Islam to occur, the threads have to be traced back to Ibn Taymiyya with a reconsideration of certain factors. In the political field especially, the strong irjāᵓist elements in his thought need to be considered, while keeping the thrust of his overall orientation in focus, but within a more tidy and systematic framework.

First, an overall study of Ibn Taymiyya's voluminous writings leaves no doubt that his aim was to rediscover and intellectually reconstitute the early normative community of Islam which was based on the teaching of the Qurᵓān and the Sunna, as he saw it. Not that he did not find fault with even the members of the early normative community in some fundamental ways:

> Error sometimes arises by coming to regard something unlawful as lawful by [mis]interpretation; and sometimes abandoning that which is obligatory by [mis]interpretation; and, again by turning that which is unlawful into a form of worship – like those [Companions and Successors] who fought one another in the [early] civil wars, since they [mis]interpreted the obligatory and praiseworthy, or, as group of [early] jurists, ᶜAbd Allāh b. Dāwūd al-Ḥarbī (d. 213/828) said, that it is better to drink controversial *nabīdh* [a drink with a certain amount of alcohol in it generally regarded as equivalent to beer] than not to drink it.[1]

Secondly, he reminds us that in the later centuries of Islam, roughly beginning with the fourth century, Islamic developments in all fields – *fiqh* (law), *kalām* (theology), Ṣūfism, and politics – began running riot and became increasingly uncontrolled. Ibn Taymiyya terms these "neo-fiqh", "neo-*kalām*", "neo-Ṣūfism," and "neo-politics" and says that they became chaotic and irresponsible.[2] His problem therefore was first of all to discover what went wrong so that a proper reform could be undertaken. He announced his diagnosis in the opening sentences of his *Kitāb al-Istiqāma*, which he wrote during one of his three spells in Egyptian prisons between Ramadan, 705/1305 and Shawwal, 709/1309. He said:

> [This provides] a principle for the necessity of [adopting] the straight and middle road and how to follow the Qurᵓān and the Sunna [correctly] in the matter of God's names, attributes and unity in both utterance and belief; also to show that the Qurᵓān and the Sunna contain all guidance and that heretical splits and misguidance come about by abandoning part of it [i.e., guidance of the Qurᵓān and Sunna]. Further, to warn that all the corresponding innovations have occurred by excess on the negative side or the positive side and that their source lies in ambiguous language [resulting in] divergence and splits that necessarily led to mutual heresy (*takfīr*) declarations among these divergent groups. The basic cause of all of this, then, is that a part of the truth was abandoned, a part of falsehood was adopted [and, after the hardening of views] truth was deliberately concealed, and truth and falsehood were mixed up.[3]

1. Ibn Taymiyya, *al-Istiqāma*, vol. 1, p. 220.
2. Ibid., vol. 1, p. 3. The term Ibn Taymiyya uses that Fazlur Rahman translates as "neo" is "*muḥdath*." So he calls it *al-kalām al-muḥdath* (*neo-kalām*), *al-taṣawwuf al-muḥdath* (neo-*taṣawwuf*) etc.
3. Ibid.

From this we clearly understand that for Ibn Taymiyya all the disciplines mentioned above were on orthodox lines and represented one unitary Islam up to about the fourth century. After that period they were progressively corrupted, and therefore we must examine his analysis of these disciplines. Ibn Taymiyya thought that an important, if not the most important, contributing factor to this state of chaos, innovation, and radical change within Islam was the weakening of the caliphal center and the ascendancy of the Buyīds over Baghdad. This resulted in the loss of Islamic frontier lands in northern Syria and elsewhere accompanied by the spread of the Qarmatians and Bāṭinites. This shows us why Ibn Taymiyya insisted so strongly on the unity and solidarity of the community, as we shall detail in the next section. In fact, for him, the *jamāᶜa*–Sunna (community–tradition) equation is the exact reverse of the *bidᶜa–firqa* (innovation-sectarian) equation.

First of all, he reversed the position of al-Ghazālī, who had regarded *kalām* as superior to *fiqh*, and denounced the former as a sheer distortion of Islam. *Kalām*, particularly as pursued by later theologians (*mutakallimūn*), after the third century of Islam, has absolutely no basis in the Qurᵓān and the Sunna. The *mutakallimūn* regarded the proposition of their science as "certain" and those of *fiqh* as "conjectures" (*ẓunūn*).[4] The actual case is quite the reverse: the *mutakallimūn* considered their science to be true science, because it deals with the universal principles of the faith while *fiqh* only treats particular rules and cases and is liable to the pitfalls of *ijtihād* (independent thinking). One important and interesting point needs to be noted here. This opposition between theology, based on reason, and law, based on revealed authority (and called Sharīᶜa), was first formulated by the Muᶜtazila and then inherited and taken over by al-Ashᶜarī in his work on the defense of theology. Ibn Taymiyya approvingly attributed the opposite position to al-Ashᶜarī. For according to him, al-Ashᶜarī held that the assertion of the dichotomy of reason (the basis of theology) and revelation (the basis of *fiqh*) propounded by the *mutakallimūn* was, indeed, false because revelation itself contains reason. Revelation not only invites the exercise of reason, but actually has many rational principles.

Ibn Taymiyya, without providing any reference, says that according to al-Ashᶜarī in matters of the "principles of faith" (*uṣūl al-dīn*) "the Qurᵓān indicates or alerts to rational proofs (*adilla*), and its proof-value

4. Ibid., vol. 1, pp. 48–49.

[signification – *dalāla*] is not only as a revealed authority (*khabar*) as some people of theology (*kalām*) think."[5] This is precisely Ibn Taymiyya's position.

> A large number of the *ahl al-kalām* [people of theology] from among the Muᶜtazila ... like Abū ᶜAlī [al-Jubbāʾī] [d. 303/915], Abū Hāshim [al-Jubbāʾī] [d. 321/933], ᶜAbd al-Jabbār [d. 415/1024–1025], Abu ʾl-Ḥusayn [al-Baṣrī] [d. 436/1044] and others and those that followed them from among the Ashᶜarīs like Qāḍī Abū Bakr [al-Bāqillānī] [d. 403/1012], Abu ʾl-Maᶜālī [al-Juwaynī] [d. 478/1085], Abū Ḥāmid [al-Ghazālī] [d. 505/1111], [Fakhr al-Dīn] al-Rāzī [d. 606/1209] and those *fuqahāʾ* [jurists] who followed them, magnify the status of *kalām* [dialectical theology] which they title, "principles of the faith" [*uṣūl al-dīn*]. So much so that they regard its propositions as decisive (*qaṭᶜiyya*) but detract from the status of positive law (*fiqh*) which is the science of the rules regarding human acts, to the extent that they consider it to consist of "conjectures" (*ẓunūn*) and do not count it among sciences (*ᶜulūm*).[6]

Again, he says that "they assert that their discussions of *kalām*-questions are decisive and produce conviction, but the fact is that there is none among the various groups of the ᶜulamāʾ of Islam more divided and mutually divergent than these. Each group is at the throats of its opponents, claiming certainty for its own views. Indeed, each individual among them contradicts himself ... Then, with all this overwhelming confusion they excommunicate (*takfīr*) each other."[7]

Ibn Taymiyya accuses them of robbing the laws and commandments of God of all certainty and claiming it for their own pseudo-science. They assert that in matters of theology "only one of several alternative opinions can be right. As for the science concerning details [of the law – *al-furūᶜ*] everyone who asserts himself to find an answer in a given case is correct (*kullu mujtahidin muṣīb*)."[8] In the realm of juridical discretion (*ijtihād*), outside the area of the indubitable Sharīᶜa texts and consensus (*ijmāᶜ*) these people "do not provide for God any definite rule. In fact, they go so far as making a category of distinctions between a master-jurist (*mujtahid*) who is correct and one who is wrong. Rather the legal rule (*ḥukm*) for every

5. Ibn Taymiyya, *al-Istiqāma*, vol. 1, p. 6.
6. Ibid., vol. 1, pp. 47–49.
7. Ibid., vol. 1, p. 50.
8. Ibid.

person is whatever his intellectual exertion leads him to."[9] What has given rise to this disparaging view of *fiqh* as "educated conjectures," according to Ibn Taymiyya, is the growth of literature on the science of legal differences (*khilāfiyāt*) after the first three centuries of Islam. (We recall from the discussion of al-Ghazālī in the preceding chapter how he regretted having "wasted my time" in excessive pre-occupation particularly with the aspect of law dealing with differences among legal schools.) This seems to have become a popular subject with the jurists (*fuqahāʾ*), and as we saw, al-Ghazālī's analysis of this was that it gave them pomp and glory. Ibn Taymiyya thought that the first person to devote special attention to legal differences and controversial points was the Shāfiʿī scholar Abū Bakr al-Sayrafī (d. 330/941).[10] When people began to concentrate on legal differences, which became a discipline by itself called the science of legal disagreement (*ʿilm al-khilāf*), there was a flood of literature. It also become popular that *fiqh* consisted solely or mainly of controversial opinions. The fact, however, is that there is far greater uniformity and unanimity in law than disagreement, which had been blown out of proportion by the later *fuqahāʾ*. There is certainly far greater agreement and certitude in law than there is in dialectical theology.[11]

But while defending *fiqh* against *kalām*, Ibn Taymiyya also severely criticised the *fuqahāʾ* for their lack of new thinking and blind imitation of the past authorities.

> Due to the excessive blind imitation (*taqlīd*), ignorance (*jahl*) and guess-work (*ẓunūn*) on the part of those associated with the study of law, issuing juridical responsa and the judiciary, that the scholars of dialectical theology became aggressive towards the jurists. With the result that they [the theologians] excluded positive law (*fiqh*), which comprises of all the [religious] sciences, from the discourse of science itself, on the basis of what they observed in terms of following authority (*taqlīd*) and conjectural propositions.[12]

In this connection Ibn Taymiyya also notes that questions of *fiqh* have also, in fact, greatly increased, compared to the early days of Islam when life was simple, "because human actions and their categories have become more

9. Ibid., vol. 1, p. 49.
10. Ibid., vol. 1, p. 62.
11. Ibid., vol. 1, p. 59.
12. Ibid., vol. 1, p. 56.

complex."[13] But while life had become more complicated and called for greater creative interpretation (*ijtihād*), the *fuqahā*ᵓ had become more idle.

> Most [jurists] only know the school of law of his founder (*imām*). Often he would at best only have cursory knowledge. Thus he cannot make a distinction between issues that have been clearly decided upon by scriptural texts and consensus (*ijmā*ᶜ) on the one hand, and the peculiarities of that school or instances where juridical discretion (*ijtihād*) flourishes ... [Such a jurist is] like a donkey, that merely transports old books [without understanding].[14]

Ibn Taymiyya tells us that because of rampant ignorance among the *fuqahā*ᵓ, certain shocking opinions have been attributed to al-Shāfiᶜī and Mālik b. Anas to which many give credence. For example, it is argued in law that a woman irrevocably repudiated is required to marry another man, who must willingly divorce her, before she can re-marry her previous husband. Among the erroneous opinions attributed to al-Shāfiᶜī is that he said that a woman who has been irrevocably divorced may be lawfully married (to someone else) with the stipulation that she will have no sexual intercourse with her new and interim husband. This has been devised so that she may "remarry" her first husband after her second husband has divorced her without consummating the marriage. "Even children among the Shāfiᶜīs know that this a non-contentious rule in Shāfiᶜī law."[15] Similarly, it has been claimed that Mālik deemed temporary marriage (*mut*ᶜ*a*) to be lawful. In fact, Mālik and his companions were vehemently opposed to temporary marriage. He went as far as deeming the notion of a time-bound divorce to be unlawful. A time-bound divorce stipulates that the marriage will end on an agreed date six or ten months or in the future. The reason he disallowed it was because it would effectively resemble a temporary marriage in practice. Finally, Ibn Taymiyya says that a "leading authority" in Mālikī law is reported to have been told that Mālik condoned sodomy![16]

In Ibn Taymiyya's view all this happened because *fiqh* fell from its true status as the most central Islamic science in the earliest centuries of Islam. It became a degenerate body of opinion at the hands of semi-morons, who

13. Ibid., vol. 1, p. 60.
14. Ibid.
15. Ibid.
16. Ibid., vol. 1, pp. 60–61.

knew very little of their own school of law and even that superficially. Ibn Taymiyya especially targeted the Ḥanafīs, whose principles he considered to be obviously fake.[17] They had very little knowledge about issuing juridical responsa (*fatāwā*). The Ḥanafīs, therefore, were "the least beneficial to Muslims," despite the fact that "they in such large numbers are backed by official power and hold at their disposal large properties, both waqf-properties [endowments] and state properties."[18] This is because the Ḥanafīs relied excessively on speculative principles which tend to be arbitrary.[19] "I have experienced that," he says "and whoever reflects on the matter [will find out], that these jurists who rely on sharīᶜa texts (*ahl al-nuṣuṣ*) [instead of speculation] are far more capable of giving [correct] juridical responses and are more beneficial to Muslims than the people of opinion (*ahl al-raᵓy*) . . . This is because in order to solve real-life activities, Muslims need to know the source texts (*nuṣuṣ*)."[20]

Ibn Taymiyya's opposition to and disdain for traditional *kalām* was relentless. He not only regarded it as worse than degraded *fiqh* but as a singularly unfortunate development in Islam. This is not because he was a Ḥanbalī. Aḥmad b. Ḥanbal had rejected Ṣūfism with far greater decisiveness and disdain than he ever manifested towards *kalām*. In fact, Ibn Ḥanbal supported certain forms of *kalām*. We will see however, that Ibn Taymiyya much preferred non-extremist Ṣūfīs over theologians. We may also recall here that al-Ghazālī stated that out of the four paths he saw before him – theology (*kalām*), philosophy, esoterism (Bāṭinism), and mysticism (Ṣūfism), he chose the last one. Ibn Taymiyya supported him, and only regretted that al-Ghazālī did not consider another path – the true one – namely that of the Qurᵓān and the Sunna of the Prophet. One of the main charges brought by Ibn Taymiyya against mainstream Sunnī kalām, Ashᶜarism, was that it declared humankind to be impotent in the interest of "saving" God's omnipotence and absoluteness. He held that any law worthy of the name requires that when an accused is brought before a judge, he/she is assumed to have the power to act, and it is for this reason that human beings are regarded as responsible.

Ibn Taymiyya not only denounced *kalām* – the "science of the principles of the faith" (*ᶜilm uṣūl al-dīn*) – but also assailed the "science of the

17. Ibid., vol. 1, p. 10.
18. Ibid., vol. 1, p. 12.
19. Ibid., vol. 1, pp. 9, 12.
20. Ibid., vol 1, p..12.

principles of law" (*ᶜilm uṣūl al-fiqh*). Now, the first person to have formulated the principles of law was, of course, al-Shāfiᶜī, for whom Ibn Taymiyya had nothing but praise. It is not the science of the principles of law per se of which he disapproved. Rather, it is its later development, *kalām*, that he resented. Similarly, he did not disapprove of the *kalām* of the *salaf* or early authorities, but that of the later generations when it became infected by the views of the Murjiʾa, the philosophers, and later by Ṣūfism. His attitude to Ṣūfism was similar: he wholeheartedly approved of the early orthodox Ṣūfīs such as al-Junayd, but denounced certain later developments in some Ṣūfī circles. Indeed, at the beginning of his *Kitāb al-Istiqāma*, he tells us: "The innovated opinion in fundamentals of belief is deemed to be the new theology (*kalām*); in matters of positive law, the innovated opinion in law is considered new; new forms of worship are considered tantamount to innovated Ṣūfism; and so is the case with political theory. Many groups think that the practice of faith is in need of these innovations, especially those that pursue their own method. But it not so."[21]

Ibn Taymiyya distinguishes sharply between the earlier and later Ṣūfīs. The former are characterized by moral and ascetic concerns, while the latter were preoccupied by indulgence in ecstasies that yield pleasure. Ibn Taymiyya points out that an excessive preoccupation with acts of worship that alienate a person from the social world is the hallmark of Christian monks and many Ṣūfīs. Both are wrong since this kind of "spiritual exercise" actually yields pleasure and is a form of self-indulgence. With the advent of "innovated" *kalām* and innovated Ṣūfism, the two became polarized, and often mortal enemies. The *mutakallimūn* came to resemble the hard-hearted Jewish learned men, while the new Ṣūfīs increasingly resembled Christian devotees to excessive worship.[22] He says:

> It should be noted that the ascetics and pious devotees became excessive in their indulgence in [matters of enjoying] sweet voices [music] and lovely sights [human beauty]. The rationalist scholars and intellectual theologians became indulgent in theorizing and speculation. Thus, the one side became guilty of innovated *kalām* and the other side guilty of innovated music. The one indulges in letters and the other in sounds. You will find those devoted to music [Ṣūfīs] excessively critical of the people

21. Ibid., vol. 1, p. 3.
22. Ibid., vol. 1, pp. 220–221.

> of *kalām*, in the manner that Abū ᶜAbd al-Raḥmān al-Sulamī (d. 412/1021) wrote a book in condemnation of scholastic theology and theologians, he [and others] being among the people of Ṣūfī music. On the other hand, you will find scholars and theologians going to extremes in denouncing Ṣūfīs who are fond of music, as in the case of Abū Bakr b. Furak (d. 406/1015) and the writings of dialectical theologians in condemnation of those fond of music and Ṣūfīs are too numerous to be counted. The reason is that the scholars suffer from the deviancy common in Jewish intellectuals and scholars, while the Ṣūfīs suffer from the deviationism of Christians given to excessive worship and devotionalism ... The [true] Muslim, therefore strives for the realization of the [Qurʾānic] prayer, "[O Lord!] lead us along the straight [i.e. the middle] path.[23]

In an extensive and detailed critique of the Ṣūfī theologian, ᶜAbd al-Karīm al-Qushayrī (d. 465/1072) and his defense of music in Ṣūfism, Ibn Taymiyya adopts the view that "at best music can be regarded as permitted."

> His [al-Qushayrī's] discourse contains two theses. Firstly, that it is permissible [in religion] to listen to pleasurable voices and tunes, provided that the listener entertains nothing objectionable in his mind and that the music he listens to contains nothing blameworthy in the sharīᶜa and that he [does not lose his self-control and] follows his uncontrolled desires. Secondly, the music that incites the listener to incline to God's obedience and avoidance of sins, makes him mindful of God's true promise and creates praiseworthy states in his mind is [not only permissible but] positively recommended [in the Sharīᶜa]. On these two premises those who [not only] consider music [permissible but] positively recommend it, like Abū ᶜAbd al-Raḥmān al-Sulamī and Abū Ḥāmid al-Ghazālī, base their arguments. Some of them sometimes even regard music as obligatory [in religion] when they see that religious obligations cannot be [properly] performed except by music.[24]

Sometimes these people prefer music even to the recitation of the Qurʾān,"[25] says Ibn Taymiyya, probably referring to al-Ghazālī who, in his *Iḥyāʾ*, advances seven reasons why music can be more potent in arousing ecstasy than Qurʾān recitation.[26] Ibn Taymiyya continues:

23. Ibid.
24. Ibid., vol. 1, pp. 235–236.
25. Ibid., vol. 1, p. 236.
26. al-Ghazālī, *Iḥyā*, vol. 2, pp. 346–360.

In this respect they resemble those who make the acquisition of neo-*kalām* an obligation [in religion], and are similar to those who prefer knowledge of *kalām* above the benefit of learning derived from the Qurʾān and reports of the Prophet (*ḥadīth*). In fact, among the latter, are people who even think that [a Muslim's] faith (*īmān*) cannot be complete without the *kalām* they had invented, calling the opponent of *kalām* an infidel (*kāfir*) and sinner (*fāsiq*)...[27]

Also among the lovers of music [i.e., Ṣūfīs] there are those who think that *īmān* remains incomplete without it. Some of them use strong language against the opponents of music, even on occasion trying to assassinate them. However, as a group the Ṣūfīs are better than the proponents of dialectical theology (*ahl al-kalām*), because these latter commit other kinds of sin as well [such as preferring dialectical theology and declaring its learning an obligation]. For this reason, between the lovers of music and their detractors there has come to exist such a polarization that it has sown discord, enmity and rancor [among Muslims].[28]

After a few lines Ibn Taymiyya continues:

Because of this [development] there arose from these two premises [stated by al-Qushayrī], wherein truth has been mixed up with falsehood, an opinion not held by the early fathers (*salaf*) and religious leaders (*aʾimma*, sing. *imām*) of the Community. Although it has been related from some of the [early] Medinese [religious personalities] and others that they used to listen to music, none of them ever said that this was a meritorious and commendable practice in terms of revelation (*sharᶜ*). Those among them who did listen to music thought it to be something reprobate, preferably to be abandoned, or viewed it to be among the sinful practices. The goal was to be absolved from sin or to view it as permissible, just as it would be permissible to extend the meaning of food and drink [as necessities] to include pleasurable food and drink; just as it would be permitted to extend the meaning of clothing [as a necessity] to include attractive clothes, and so it can also be with regard to housing. To anticipate reward for this kind of act and gain nearness to God has not been recorded from any of the early fathers and religious leaders of the Community. Further, what has been recorded from them is that they

27. Ibn Taymiyya, Istiqāma, vol. 1, p. 236.
28. Ibid., vol. 1, pp. 236–237.

> thought of this [music] as something introduced by heretics who posed as Muslims (*zanādiqa*, sing. *zindīq*). Al-Shāfiʿī said [upon his return from ʿIrāq]: "I have left behind in Baghdad something the heretics have innovated called *taghbīr*, whereby they divert people from [listening to the recitation of] the Qurʾān." *Taghbīr* is striking [a musical instrument] with a stick which sets off a cloud of dust. It is one of the musical instruments that accompany the melody of music. Al-Shāfiʿī with the perfection of his knowledge and faith was perceptive enough to see that this [the introduction of music into Islamic Ṣūfī] practices was designed to displace the Qurʾān.[29]

The above account of Ibn Taymiyya provides a basic outline of both his methodology and approach to understanding Islam and the major developments that occurred in Islam up until his time as well as his reformist orientation. This account is almost exclusively based on his *Kitāb al-Istiqāma*, the explicit purpose is to show that both Islam and Islamic reform require an approach that is synthetic and middle of the road. In fact, the middle of the road must be syntheses of various and, indeed, divergent developments within Islam. None of these developments are without a genuine basis in the Qurʾān and the Sunna of the Prophet. And yet all have erred in varying degrees once they abandoned the Qurʾān–Sunna anchoring point and became undisciplined by becoming a law unto themselves. Even the Muslim philosophers at certain crucial points performed excellently in Islamic terms: their argument from contingency to establish the Necessary Being God (*wājib al-wujūd*) is impeccable. In most of their remaining doctrines that have a bearing on religion, they go wrong in varying degrees. As for the disciplines regarded as Islamic such as *kalām*, *fiqh*, and Ṣūfism, Ibn Taymiyya genuinely accepted all of them in their early stages when they were close to the Qurʾān. But he condemned them, particularly *kalām* and Ṣūfism, in their later development. His denunciation of later *kalām* is harsher, as we have seen, than that of Ṣūfism. *Fiqh*, despite its vagaries, noted earlier, is the most reformable since it is tied to action. Here is a highly illustrative passage on the relative value of *kalām* and *fiqh* taken from his *Majmūʿ Fatāwā* (Collected Responsa). After describing in detail the mutual disagreements and agreements of Muslim sects, he says:

29. Ibid., vol. 1, pp. 237–238.

The basis of this, that I have mentioned elsewhere, is that [theological] questions based on transmitted reports (*khabar*) [i.e., Qurʾān and Sunna] can be treated as practical questions [of law], even though the former are called "questions of principles" (*masāʾil uṣūl*), while the latter are called "questions of details" (*masāʾil furūʿ*). These are terms invented by certain jurists (*fuqahāʾ*) and dialectical theologians (*mutakallimūn*). [These terms] are particularly associated with the dialectical theologians (*uṣūliyyūn*), especially when they discuss questions [that involve a judgment] of right and wrong. As for the majority of genuine jurists and Ṣūfīs, they hold issues affecting practices to be more important than disputed statements [of theology]. This is because the *fuqahāʾ* are concerned only with matters of practice. For the most part they dislike discussing questions unrelated to action, as was held by Mālik and other Medinese scholars. The truth of the matter is that [between theology (*uṣūl*) and law (*furūʿ*)], the basic issues are "questions of principles" (*masāʾil uṣūl*), while derivative ones are "questions of detail" (*masāʾil furūʿ*). Thus, knowledge about the mandatory nature of basic duties, like the five pillars of Islam and those prohibitions that are obvious and unequivocally transmitted [with certainty] is similar to the knowledge [of theological beliefs] that God has power over all things and that He knows everything, that He is hearing, seeing; that the Qurʾān is God's speech and other obvious reports that are consecutively transmitted. Therefore, just as a person perpetrates unbelief (*kufr*) by rejecting those practical rules on which there is consensual agreement, so would the rejection of these [theological beliefs] be tantamount to the same.[30]

Our statement [that some theological beliefs can be treated on a par with practical legal issues] comprises more than one point. [One] is that each science is divisible into that which is certain (*qaṭʿī*) and that which is conjectural (*ẓannī*). [Another point] is that [in the field of theology] only one opinion [among several alternatives] is true. Thus a person who errs [in discovering the truth] may either be pardoned [by God] or may incur a [punishable] sin (*mudhnib*), or may be deemed a sinner (*fāsiq*). Actually, the one [who errs in theological matters] may be on par with the person who errs in practical legal matters. In the case of the latter [legal matters] due to the volume of substantive law and the need for such detail, in these matters people are comfortable in expecting controversy (*tanāzuʿ*) and dispute (*ikhtilāf*). Dispute in [theological

30. Ibn Taymiyya, *Fatāwā*, vol. 6, pp. 56–57.

matters] leads to harm and cannot be tolerated, except of course if it is in order to ward off a greater mischief.[31]

Thus, when it became necessary to provide elaborate detail for practices and its multiplicity of derivatives, the occurrence of disputes in these were somehow automatic. People were content about such disputes [regarding details], as opposed to matters related to reports (*al-umūr al-khabariyya*). In the case of the latter, if there was agreement in summary form, and these could be elaborated without disagreement, then it was fine. Should disputes occur in their elaboration, this becomes an occasion for mischief, without there being any such necessity ... With regard to [theological issues], if discussion was pursued on the basis of sure knowledge (*ᶜilm*) that did not lead to mischief, unless of course genuine grounds for excommunication existed, there was otherwise no need to excommunicate each other (*takfīr*). The latter [excommunication] by God, would only occur when real contradictory positions were adopted in a dispute! As to all other forms of dispute, such as disagreement generated by typology, perspective, and wording, these were less significant. Yet these [latter kind] were many, or dominate the character of disputes in matters related to reports.[32]

As for the Ṣūfīs and devotees of God, in fact, most of the common people, for them the consideration is primarily the performance or neglect of good deeds. If pious acts are evident, then a person can enter their ranks, even if he errs in matters of reported authority [*masāʾil khabariyya* – Qurʾān and *ḥadīth*]. If [pious acts are not evident] one will not enter their ranks, even though one may be correct in questions of reported authority. They are, indeed, indifferent to the latter [reported authority]. "Principles" (*uṣūl*) for them are matters of practical conduct, they call these *uṣūl*.[33]

Īmān, *Islam, and Good Acts*

The problem of *īmān* (faith) and the definition of a *muʾmin* (person of faith) was the first fundamental theological question that arose in Islam after the assassination of the caliph ᶜUthmān, as discussed in chapter 1. The early answers to this question, and to the question of free will that arose as a result, were also discussed previously. These questions and those of God's

31. Ibid., vol. 6, pp. 57–58.
32. Ibid., vol. 6, p. 58.
33. Ibid., vol. 6, pp. 58–59.

attributes remained the stock-in-trade of Islamic theology throughout the medieval period. Ibn Taymiyya has widely and repeatedly discussed these questions in the vast corpus of his writings. His work is highly repetitive because he wrote mostly in the form of authoritative answers (*fatwā*, pl. *fatāwā*) to questions put to him or as views solicited from him. But on every question he touched, Ibn Taymiyya brought a freshness of perspective that is gratifying in view of the sickening repetitiveness of his predecessors who had pretty much become hide-bound within their schools of thought. The greater the importance of a problem for the reformation of Islamic doctrine and practice, the more refreshingly original Ibn Taymiyya appears. True, he is far from al-Ghazālī's sophistication and the latter's gift for finding "inner meanings" and discovering subtle points. But Ibn Taymiyya's purpose was also very different. He saw it as his task to "put things right" and reorient the Muslim Community (*umma*) in the proper direction, which he saw as having been in increasing error over the long centuries since the very early generations of Islam (*salaf*), rather than to give a prescription for the salvation of the individual soul. We have already had some flavor of this task of reorienting by looking closely at his judgments on major Islamic groups and divisions. It is in this overall context that his contribution to the topic of the present section assumes such great significance. We shall also see later, in this connection, Ibn Taymiyya's reevaluation of the nature and function of the community.

We tried to show in the first chapter that the positions taken on *īmān* by the (Khawārij) Muᶜtazila and the (Jahmiyya) Murjiᵓa were mutually contradictory. The former held that good acts are integral to *īmān* and that hence a person guilty of heinous acts becomes devoid of faith. The latter maintained that good acts lie outside *īmān* and that hence the perpetrator of heinous acts keeps his/her faith unscathed. The two agree, of course, that *īmān* is indivisible, that a person cannot have part of *īmān* and lose part of it: he/she must either have full *īmān* or no *īmān* at all. There were many religious leaders who held that *īmān* increases with good acts, but does not decrease with bad ones or that it both increases with good acts and decreases with evil acts, but that it never reaches a zero point. A Muslim cannot be characterized as a *kāfir* simply for questioning the values of Islam or violently rejecting a clear revealed text, unless they have indulged in interpretation of the text (*taᵓwīl*). These were all variations on the Murji'a theme, i.e., none of the holders of these variants held that *īmān* and *kufr* or *nifāq* (hypocrisy) can exist side-by-side in the same person. A *muʾmin–kāfir* (believer–unbeliever) or a *muʾmin–munāfiq* (believer–hypocrite) was an unheard-of expression in the period before Ibn Taymiyya.

Now, this is precisely what Ibn Taymiyya holds:

> Hence, in one person both faith (*īmān*) and hypocrisy (*nifāq*) come together; just as certain factors of faith and unbelief can converge. As we find in the two authentic books of Muslim and al-Bukhārī material related from the Prophet (peace be upon him) that he said: "Four characteristics are such that if they are present in a person, he/she is a pure hypocrite. And whosoever has one of those characteristics then such a person has one characteristic of hypocrisy, until they abandon it. [These characteristics are] that when the person talks, he/she lies; when entrusted [with something] then the person cheats; when making a promise, the person breaks it and when quarrelling [with anyone] employs obscene language.[34]

It must be noted that although the identification of faith with good works and its reverse can often be found in the Qurʾān – "those who believe and do good deeds" (Q. 103:3) – this is very palpably the case with *ḥadīth* materials. Similarly, and as a corollary, faith is regarded as indivisible and sometimes conjoined to unbelief. The Qurʾān illustrates this: "So that God may discernibly set those apart who are hypocrites [by calling upon them to join battle at Uhud], when they were told: 'come and fight in the cause of God and in defence [of Madīna].' They replied: 'If we were sure that fighting would take place, we would have followed you [Muslims].' On that day they were nearer to unbelief than to faith. They say with their mouths what is not in their hearts" (Q. 3:167).

Ibn Taymiyya used verses such as this and a great deal of *ḥadīth* to prove that *īmān* is not a monolithic construct. It is a veritable mosaic made up of faith and all sorts of good acts; and it can and mostly does cohabit with hypocrisy (*nifāq*) and unbelief (*kufr*). Here is another well-known *ḥadīth* frequently quoted by Ibn Taymiyya: "The Prophet (on whom be peace and salutations) said: 'Faith comprises seventy plus factors: the highest being the profession that there is no God but God. The lowest [factor in faith] being that one should remove a hurtful thing [like stones,

34. Ibid., vol. 7, p. 520.

thorns] from the path [of passers-by], and modesty is one factor of faith (*īmān*) as well)'".[35]

For Ibn Taymiyya, *īmān*, *nifāq*, and *kufr* come in degrees of strength. The essence of the matter is that a person has one factor of faith and one of hypocrisy. Someone who is a Muslim can simultaneously suffer from a factor of unbelief which is less than the amount that might take him outside the pale of Islam. Ibn Taymiyya's thinking is undoubtedly in tune with the Qurʾān. One type of unbelief, as we have seen, exists in a believer (*muʾmin*), but such a person is not considered to be a full unbeliever. This is due to the fact that unbelief (*kufr*), like faith (*īmān*), also occurs in degrees of intensity or the lack thereof. Part of a *ḥadīth* quoted by Ibn Taymiyya talks of a believer (*muʾmin*) who has "but an atom's worth of faith (*īmān*), while the rest of this person's being is unbelief (*kufr*) and hypocrisy (*nifāq*)."[36] Such unbelief exists in an ordinary Muslim who understands and practices little of Islam. It is also found in learned men and intellectuals who gravely misinterpret Islam at certain crucial points, sometimes mistakenly, but more often deliberately. Such a person is called either a *fāsiq millī* or *kāfir millī*, meaning a "grave sinner" or "unbeliever" respectively, who nevertheless remains within the pale of the religion (*milla*).[37] Intellectuals are often in grave danger of passing beyond this into absolute unbelief (*kufr muṭlaq*) when they are victims of desires such as fame and money. Such people have to re-convert to Islam after repentance, as happened to Fakhr al-Dīn al-Rāzī. He, apparently at the request of the mother of one of the Khwārazm-Shāhs, who probably was a pagan, wrote a book explaining the reasons why people worship stars. But, not stopping at this, al-Rāzī recommended star-worship and thus became an (absolute) *kāfir* until he repented and "returned to Islam" once again.[38] Then there is the *kāfir kitābī*, like Jews and Christians, who have revealed books wherein they believe, but reject other prophets and books. They are *kāfir*, no doubt, but since they do believe in some revelation(s), they are not like pagans and idolators, and Muslims must refrain from deciding their fate in the hereafter.

From *īmān* to total *kufr*, then, there is an infinite gradation both within and outside Islam. The Murjiʾites refused to include acts as an essential

35. Ibid., vol. 7, p. 517.
36. Ibid.
37. Ibid., vol. 7, p. 524.
38. Ibid., vol. 4, p. 55.

part of faith (*īmān*) because they wished to preserve the Muslim community (*umma*) and its function. As we shall see below, this position resulted in them being compared unfavorably, not only to Jews and Christians, but also to Zoroastrians. Back to the question of *īmān* – just as *kufr* has gradations, so has *īmān*. When *īmān* becomes strong, each of its parts necessarily implies others, but in a weak state it may not imply them all. Thus when a person's heart comes to assent (*taṣdīq*), recognition or knowledge (*maʿrifa*) of God and love for Him and His Messenger, it necessarily implies hate for and hostility against God's enemies.[39] Thus, for Ibn Taymiyya, love for God directly entails hostility (*jihād*) towards His enemies. He also supported his stand via the *ḥadīth*, "Whosoever should die without fighting [in Allāh's cause] and without even thinking of doing so all his life, cannot be a [full] *muʾmin*,"[40] since true love for someone entails enmity against his/her enemies.

When *īmān* alone is mentioned in the revealed texts as characterizing a person or a group, *islām*, namely the performance of external acts, is definitely assumed to be an integral part of it. But sometimes *īmān* and *islām* or *īmān* and good acts are juxtaposed; in such cases *īmān* may be taken to refer to the inner state of faith (which, however, as said just now, includes assent, knowledge, and love of God) while *islām* and good acts refer to outer behavior, provided it is understood that both are organically related to each other. The Murjiʾa, we recall, believed that *īmān* only invites to good deeds but does not necessarily entail them.

Free Will and Determinism

Since true faith and works go together and since works require effective free will, the question of divine determinism of human acts comes to the fore at this point of the development of Ibn Taymiyya's argument. It also, of course, centrally concerns the attributes of God in terms particularly of His will, power, and command. The Sharīʿa is the command of God for humanity, which implies an "ought," while the will and power of God is effective and implies only an "is." In the previous chapters we raised the dilemmas that the doctrine of *irjāʾ* raised. Ibn Taymiyya could neither side with the Muʿtazilites and accept that God's will, in the case of human actions, meant only His command, nor could he side with the Murjiʾa and

39. Ibid., vol. 7, p. 538.
40. Ibn Taymiyya, Istiqāma, vol. 2, p. 36.

accept that God's command is only His will and power. He did, however, denounce the latter far more vehemently than the former, since the Murjiʾa deprived religion of the distinction between good and evil, rendered it ineffective, and opened the door to all evil, particularly when Murjiʾism resulted in or was combined with monism/pantheism among the Ṣūfīs. Ibn Taymiyya's strategy was to distinguish between God's universal creative will and His command which is the Sharīʿa:

> So the majority of Muslims and others, like the leaders (*imāms*) of the four schools of law and others among the pious ancestors (*salaf*) and other scholars, all affirm God's wisdom and purpose (*ḥikam*) [in His creation and legislation]. They do not deny [His wisdom and purpose] like the Ashʿarites and others [such as the philosophers] do. [The latter] only affirm a [divine] will (*irāda*), but do not [affirm] wisdom; and [affirm] only [God's] all-compelling will (*mashīʾa*) without affirming mercy (*raḥma*), love (*maḥabba*) and no gratitude (*riḍā*). In so doing they make all creatures equal vis-à-vis Him, failing to distinguish between [the characteristics of] will, love, and gratitude. [And so, they fail to distinguish] between what occurs as unbelief (*kufr*), unrighteousness (*fusūq*) and disobedience (*ʿiṣyān*). The leaders of the majority of Muslims say: "God loves [faith (*īmān*) and good acts] and these gratify Him, even as He wills them." And when they say: "He does not love, nor is He gratified [by unbelief and disobedience] in His Command [as distinguished from His Creative will]," they are saying: "He does not will something as His command or religion [as distinguished from His creative will] . . ." Nor do the [leadership of the majority] agree with the Muʿtazila who deny the power of God the Sublime, His universal creative will (*ʿumūm khalqihi*), His all-compelling will [that creates both good and evil], and His power. Nor do they compare Him [anthropomorphism] to His creation in those matters that are declared to be obligatory and prohibited [for humankind: i.e., they do not use human reason to measure God's nature] as do they [the Muʿtazilites] . . . Indeed, they say God is the creator and owner of everything: whatever He willed happens, and whatever He did not will, does not occur. And He is, indeed, powerful over all things. And He loves those who perform good acts (*muḥsinīn*), those who espouse reverential fear (*muttaqīn*) and those who are just (*muqsiṭīn*) . . . But they [the majority, unlike the Ashʿarites] also state: "notwithstanding the fact that God is the creator, lord and owner of all

things, in His creation He distinguishes between their substances and their actions [by setting up standards of His commandments]. It is in accord with what He had said: 'Shall we make those who surrender on par with those who are criminals?' (Q. 68:35)."[41]

It must be pointed out that on this [crucial and delicate point], many sections among the folk of theology and mysticism (*ahl ᵓl-kalām wa ᵓl-taṣawwuf*) have [seriously] erred. They have actually adopted a position that is far worse than that of the Muᶜtazila and others who espouse free will. For surely the latter attach great importance to [divine] commands and prohibitions; promise [of reward] and threat [of punishment]; and obedience to God and His Messenger; and they command the performance of good deeds and prohibit the performance of evil. But they [the Muᶜtazila et al.] went astray in the matter of free will (*qadar*). They wrongly believed that if they affirmed God's universal creative will, His all-inclusive power and all-comprehensive creativity of everything [both good and evil], it would result in an objectionable affront to His justice and wisdom. They erred in this belief.

In opposition [to the last-mentioned group] were a party of scholars, devout worshippers, some folk among the proponents of theology and mysticism, all of whom affirmed God's omnipotence. And they truly believed that God is the lord of everything and its owner and that whatever He willed happened and whatever He did not will did not occur. Now, all this is good and correct. But they fell short of [recognizing] the divine command and prohibition; promise and threat. Some became excessive, to become extremists and heretics. In fact, they became similar to those polytheists (*mushrikūn*), who said: "If God had so willed we would have committed no association (*shirk*), nor would have our forefathers have [done so], nor would we have tabooed anything" (Q. 6:148). Now, the proponents of free will (*qadarīyya*), even if they did resemble the Magians in the sense that they affirmed an [ultimate] actor [a human being], other than God to be the [cause] of evil, this group [their opponents], came to resemble the polytheists ... Surely, the polytheists are more evil than the Magians! All Muslims agree that the Magians are acknowledged [as a religion] on their payment of a poll-tax [and are therefore not killed]. Some scholars have even held that it is permissible for Muslims to marry their women and partake of their food [similar to Jews and Christians]. As for the polytheists (*mushrikūn*), the community is unanimous in their belief that one cannot marry their women and may

41. Ibn Taymiyya, *Fatāwā*, vol. 8, pp. 97–98.

not eat their food. The view of al-Shāfiᶜī and the more well-known opinion of Aḥmad [Ibn Ḥanbal] and that of other scholars besides these two, is that the [polytheists] are not acknowledged by their payment of poll-tax [in order to survive]. The vast majority of ᶜulamāᵓ are of the view that Arab polytheists in particular cannot be allowed to pay poll tax, although the Magians are [allowed to do this]. . . .[42]

The essential point here is [the following]. A person who after having affirmed God's omnipotence (*qadar*) thereafter produces it as an argument to nullify God's commands and prohibitions (*al-amr wa ᵓl-nahy*) is more evil than the one who only affirms divine commands and prohibitions, but does not affirm God's omnipotence [but does so in order to affirm humankind as an ultimate, free actor]. Not only Muslims, but also followers of other [revealed] religions agree upon this [view], as in fact all humanity does. For indeed [it means] that despite affirming God's omnipotent will and bearing witness to His universal lordship over all creation, one still does not distinguish between what is commanded and what is forbidden; and [does not distinguish] between those who have faith and those who reject truth; and [does not distinguish] between God's servants and His rebels. Such a person cannot claim to believe in any of the messengers or in any revealed Book. In such a person's view Adam and the devil are equal; Noah and his people are equal; Moses and the Pharaoh are equal; and the early converts to Islam [who perceived its truth without delay] and the Makkan pagans – are all equal.[43]

This deviance has become rampant among the mystics, ascetics, and devout worshippers. This is especially true when they combine with it the monotheism (*tawḥīd*) of the theologians [such as the Ashᶜarīs] who affirm God's omnipotence and universally compelling will, without affirming God's love and gratitude [for good] and enmity and dislike [toward evil]. These people say: "Monotheism (*tawḥīd*) is the monotheism of lordship" [i.e., as the sole creator-sustainer, but not as the guide who is the source of guidance and hence of reward and punishment]. As for the "[monotheism] of divinity," they reduce this to the mere power to create. [In saying this] they do not know [anything about] the monotheism of divinity [*tawḥīd al-ilāhiyya*]. They do not perceive that the divinity is the one who is godlike and worshiped (*anna ᵓl-ilāh huwa ᵓl-maᵓlūh al-maᶜbūd*). [Such people] do not realize that their mere professing that God is the lord of everything does not mean one has realized true monotheism

42. Ibid., vol. 8, pp. 99–100.
43. Ibid., vol. 8, p. 100.

(*tawḥīd*), unless one also witnesses that there is no deity (*ilāh*) [one worthy of worship] except God. As God says: "And most of them do not believe in God, but that they commit shirk as well ..." (Q. 2:106).[44]

What a delicate point this is! So many feet slipped in it! So many minds have been lost in it, where, indeed, the very religion of Muslims has been distorted. Because of this monotheists have been confused with idol-worshippers in the sight of those who claim to have attained to the pinnacle of monotheism, and finally found the spiritual and theological truth. It is obvious to all who believe in God and His messenger, that the Muᶜtazila and Shīᶜite Qadarites [advocates of free will] who affirm God's command and prohibition; [affirm] threat and promise, are much better than those who equate between believers and unbelievers; and [claim that] the righteous and the unrighteous ... are all equal, and who regard [this confusion] to be the most profound truth and the pinnacle of monotheism...[45]

It has been related on the authority of ᶜAbd al-Raḥmān b. Mahdī [d. 198/813–814], [a contemporary of the jurist Abū Ḥanīfa] that Sufyān al-Thawrī disapproved of the term "predetermined" (*jabara*). [Instead] he said: "God 'molded' or 'formed' (*jabala*) the bondsmen [God formed the nature of humans rather than predetermined their acts]." My purpose [in stating all these traditions] is that al-Khallāl [d. 311/923] and others among the people of learning included the advocates of predeterminism (*jabar*) under the rubric of "qadarites" (*qadarīyya*). [They were so categorized] even though they did not use predeterminism to justify sins. Then [imagine the verdict] on those who justify their sins on the basis of determinism? It is apparent that those Qadarīs who promote determinism to justify the nullification of divine commands and prohibitions are far more blameworthy in the sight of God than those who utterly deny divine determinism. [This is because] the formers' deviance is much more serious. For this reason the Qadarīs have been associated with the Murjiᵓites in the discourse of several of the pious ancestors (*salaf*). Indeed, even a prophetic report (*ḥadīth marfūᶜ*) is cited to this effect. The reason being that both of these innovations [Qadarī and Murjiᵓī predeterminism] destroy the divine command and prohibition, as well as the promise and threat of chastisement. *Irjāᵓ* weakens one's faith in divine chastisement and reduces obligations and prohibitions to a triviality. As for the Qadarī [predeterminist], he becomes a supporter of

44. Ibid., vol. 8, pp. 100–101.
45. Ibid., vol. 8, p. 103.

> the Murjiʾa, [if he justifies sins on the basis of his determinism]. And if he denies [determinism] then he and the Murjiʾī are at loggerheads.[46]

Ibn Taymiyya undoubtedly blamed the Muʿtazila for upholding human freedom at the expense of divine omnipotence. He does so not only in the lengthy passage just cited, but in numerous other places. Yet he invariably prefers them over the Murjiʾa and other determinists, in particular over all monists/pantheists à la Ibn ʿArabī, who obliterated or at least rendered ineffective the all-important moral distinction between God and evil without which no religion can survive, especially one such as Islam which is so action oriented. In this context he often cited and interpreted the *ḥadith* about the dispute of Moses with Adam. Moses, upon an encounter with Adam, said to him: "Are you the Adam, the father of all humanity, whom He created with His own hands, then breathed of His own spirit into him and taught him the names of all things? Why did you get us and yourself expelled from the garden?" Adam replied to him: "Are you the Moses whom God chose for His messengership, distinguished him by speaking to him and wrote the Torah for him with His own hand? How long before my creation did you find the words pre-written [i.e., in the divine plan]: 'Adam disobeyed His Lord and went astray (Q. 20:121)?'" Moses said: "This was [pre-written] so much time before [your creation]." Adam thus argued down Moses.[47] This *ḥadith*, found in both Muslim and al-Bukhārī, is characteristic of Sunnī predeterministic teaching and it is through such *ḥadīths*, as we saw in the first chapter, that the Sunnīs, and particularly the Ashʿarīs, won a decisive victory over the Muʿtazila. Ibn Taymiyya, who, of course, accepted all Sunnī predeterministic teaching, nevertheless interpreted this *ḥadīth* in the light of his own free-will doctrine: predeterminism, yes; employing it as an argument to explain away or cover up sins, no. In the case under discussion, Adam's victory over Moses does not consist in the former's invocation of predeterminism to justify his own errancy, but rather in telling Moses that he (Moses) must not blame Adam for an affliction that came to him (Moses) from God. Indeed, says, Ibn Taymiyya, Adam had been forgiven by God after he repented, as the Qurʾan says at Q. 2:37. Therefore, blame could attach to him no longer. Ibn Taymiyya's set doctrine is that to accept God's determinism is an

46. Ibid., vol. 8, pp. 105–106.
47. Ibid., vol. 10, p. 505.

essential part of the Islamic faith – and he constantly scolds the Muᶜtazila for denying this – but to put determinism forward as excuse for one's errors is a cardinal sin. How does that work?

This aspect constitutes the political determinism (irjāᵓism) of Ibn Taymiyya. So far as human action is concerned with religio-moral issues he was no determinist, but was probably more aligned with Muᶜtazilism. Yet, for him, divine will overarches everything. All activities in the universe, including those of humans, is governed by divine will as the Qurᵓān repeatedly asserts as it invites humans to voluntary action. We have seen that, on the question of faith, Ibn Taymiyya rejected the "take it all, or leave it all" attitude of both the Muᶜtazila and the Murjiᵓa, who insisted that a person either has the whole of faith or none of it. He affirmed that, in varying degrees, people combine faith with unbelief; he now had to find a way to preserve both free will and determinism in such a way that they do not contradict each other. On the present issue, again, the Muᶜtazila and the Murjiᵓa were opposed in a mutually exclusive manner.

Ibn Taymiyya treated this question from several approaches and used different tools and strategies. This problem has defied an intellectual solution in the entire history of human thought. However, religious consciousness and more particularly, Qurᵓānic consciousness, must find room for both. The present writer has offered his own answer on the basis of treating both determinism and "free will" as clearly given data in both the common human experience and in the Qurᵓānic revelation. In the light of our lengthy quotation from Ibn Taymiyya, a view repeated throughout his writing, one answer is that God's will is of two kinds or, rather, at two different levels. These two must never be confused. If they are confused then this can only occur at the expense of a moral–religious consciousness and in favor of an intellectual–aesthetic kind of religious consciousness. An intellectual religious consciousness must in the end opt for monism and its destructive ethical consequences, while a consciousness based on religious morality must accept a fundamental moral dualism, in order to realize a living and functional religion. Premised on the Qurᵓān, Ibn Taymiyya accepts the universal creative will of God. It is a will that creates everything both good and evil, on the one hand, and a divine command whereby good and evil stand clearly distinguished, indeed, antithetically opposed. The first he calls creative will (*irāda kawniyya*). The second is a religious (moral) will or command (*irāda dīniyya*). These two aspects of the divine will are not just mechanically juxtaposed, but integrated and subsumed under the purposive activity of God, which both philosophers and Murjiʾa denies, the Ashʿarīs included under the last mentioned, and against whom Ibn Taymiyya strongly inveighs. His explanation for the presence of evil is that it is necessary to attain the greater good. Evil is only incidental to the good and it is relatively small compared to the abundance of good.

Ibn Taymiyya's second strategy, which seems to perfect the first described above, is that determinism, as the all-comprehensive determinism of God, is an object of faith and not a principle of action. In view of a Muslim's belief that nothing happens without God's omnipotent will, it is a tautology to say for example that my writing these lines occurs by God's will. But until my writing actually occurs, I do not know what God's will was with regard to my writing. Therefore, my attribution of my act or any act cannot be properly attributed to God until it is a matter of the past. For we can never know, at least for certain, what the will of God is going to be for the future. It is in this connection that, as we shall observe particularly in the context of political action, Ibn Taymiyya advocated a strange passive acceptance of political tyranny. Here it should be noted that he advocated acceptance of whatever calamity occurs to one as a "misfortune sent by God" even if it be aggression committed by fellow humans. One must pray to God for relief, but accept the misfortune, not only passively, but even gladly. We have already seen this in connection with the story of Moses and Adam. Adam did not blame Moses for doubting the divine predetermination by God of his fall, but rather because Moses blamed Adam for his (Moses') own affliction by taking recourse to the fall, instead of accepting the tragedy cheerfully. This is also in keeping with Ibn Taymiyya's practical life. Indeed, his life was a mirror of what he believed. At his trial in Damascus, he said to his inquisitors: "If you beat me, I will accept this as a decision of God about me. And if you send me to jail, I will be only too happy at my incarceration, for I have nothing to lose, having no wife or children!" He was a celibate. This most certainly does not mean that Ibn Taymiyya advocated passivity or non-action: far from it. But he held that if, after all one's struggle, or if unawares and suddenly, a misfortune descends upon one that can no longer be resisted, one should accept it both with patience and praise to God.

'The third phase of the argument, which has a strong internal cohesion with the previous two, is Ibn Taymiyya's uses of the Aristotelian concept of the efficient and the teleological causes to explain the respective roles of determinism and freedom. Determinism is God's will which makes all things happen and is the efficient cause of all. In turn God's command, while it presupposes that will, is exclusively concerned with the future, not what has happened, but what ought to happen. It is, therefore, exclusively addressed to the human will in terms of what it is expected to bring about in the world. This command is the Sharīᶜa. A human being, as a thinking and active agent in this world, is therefore asked to implement the Sharīᶜa in a historic context. Humans are allowed to use and interfere with the workings of nature, although belief in the omnipotent but purposeful will of God must always remain in the background of their minds.

This is, once again, a highly original construct of a solution to a notorious problem. Whether or not it satisfies the philosophical demand, I do not know. To be quite frank I do not know what that demand is. As a religious prescription, it is superb and perfectly in accord with the Qurᵓān. On the one hand, it does away with that superficial Muᶜtazilite doctrine which in effect reduced God to human status by imposing upon the divine the requirements of justice formulated in human terms. On the other hand, it does away with the phony and arbitrary will of God, whereby if God so decided He could declare both lying and murder to be good, as maintained by the Ashᶜarites and Murjiᵓis. Ibn Taymiyya's repeated statements that the Muᶜtazila are preferable to the Ashᶜarites, the Murjiᵓa, and the monistic, pantheist Ṣūfīs are to be understood in this context.[48] All of them do away with the distinction between good and evil and in principle render the Sharīᶜa totally anomalous.

Ibn Taymiyya's Political Doctrine

> The mainspring [of political life] is knowledge. This is because the sense of the just and the unjust depends on knowledge. Hence all religion is nothing but knowledge and justice, while its opposite is but injustice and ignorance. God the exalted has said: "And man bore it [the burden of moral responsibility refused by the entire creation]; man is, indeed,

48. Ibid., vol. 16, p. 242.

unjust and ignorant" (Q. 33:72). Now, since man is prone to injustice and ignorance – and this happens sometimes on the part of rulers, sometimes on the part of subjects, and sometimes on the part of a third party – the requisite knowledge and justice demand (bearing with) patience the injustice and tyranny of rulers, as is the principle of the *ahl al-Sunna wa᾽l-jamāᶜa*. The Prophet, on whom be peace and salutations, also commanded this through well-known reports. He said: "After me, you will encounter egotistic rulers, but you must bear them with patience until you meet me at the pond [of Kawthar]." The Prophet also said: "Whoever encounters on the part of his ruler something that he does not like, then he must bear it with patience." There are other examples too. For instance, the Prophet said: "Give them [the rulers] their due, while you ask from God your due." Muslims have been forbidden to fight their rulers so long as these continue to perform the [daily] prayers. This is because they have with them the requisite basis of faith [belief in] the unity of God and His worship [alone]. They also have several good points of conduct and abstinence from many evil deeds.

As for what transpires by way of injustice and tyranny at their hands on the basis of reasonable or unreasonable interpretation (*ta᾽wīl*), they may not be violently removed on the claim that [their interpretative act] is unjust and tyrannical – as many people are wont to do. [They wish to] remove an evil and then substitute it for what is a greater evil and remove one transgression and replace it with a greater transgression. Thus, rebellion against them [rulers] brings about injustice. The latter must, therefore, be endured just as one often endures the aggression of those who are commanded to do good and prohibited from evil. Witness God's statements: "Command the good (O Prophet!) and prohibit evil and bear patiently the harm caused to you [as a consequence]" [Q. 31:17]; "You must be steadfast (O Muhammad! against opposition) as Messengers firm of heart have done [before you]" [Q. 46:35]; "Be patient, then, (O Muhammad!) with the judgement of your Lord – for you are right beneath Our eyes" (Q. 52:48).

This is a general rule applicable to the rulers and the subjects: When they [the rulers] command good and prohibit evil, then it is their [the subjects'] duty to steadfastly bear the applications that come to them due to the person of God (*dhāt Allāh*), in the same way that those who undertake *jihād* bear with patience what affects their lives and properties. Steadfastness in the face of affliction to one's honor deserves

> even greater merit. The reason being that the purpose or salutary end (*maṣlaḥa*) of commanding the good and prohibiting evil cannot be fulfilled except through these means. Now, the *means* whereby an obligatory end has to be fulfilled also becomes obligatory. Rulers and administrators fall into this category. They must, therefore, display extraordinary patience and forbearance, just as they must exercise extraordinary bravery and generosity. That is because the purpose (*maṣlaḥa*) of governance cannot be properly served without these [extraordinary means]. Similarly, it is the duty (*wājib*) of the rulers to bear with patience the excesses and tyranny of their subjects, if the interest [of governance] can only be served in this way. Especially if abandoning this policy could lead to greater disorder, than what already exists. In a like manner it is the duty of the subjects to bear the excesses and tyranny of their rulers, provided that in abandoning patience there is a greater evil.
>
> Thus, both the rulers and the ruled have claims upon each other which must be satisfied, some of which was mentioned in my own work *The Book of Jihād and Justice*. Each party must be patient with the other and exercise forbearance with the other on many issues. Tolerance and patience is imperative on both parties. God the Exalted has said "Those [are people of faith] who enjoin upon one another patience and merciful treatment" (Q. 89:17) . . . As for the fact that Muslims must desist from injustice and do justice to each other, well its religious obligation is far more obvious. Therefore, there is no need to elaborate upon it here.[49]

This passage gives the essence of Ibn Taymiyya's political thought. He did not envisage discord and conflict among Muslims. As we also pointed out in the first section of this chapter, under no condition did Ibn Taymiyya condone in-fighting among Muslims. Earlier we came to learn that he regarded the in-fighting among the Companions and the Successors of the Prophet as an "error based on misinterpretation." The normal view adopted by the Sunnīs about early Muslim civil wars is that those who fought each other made an error in their intellectual judgment (*ijtihād*) of the moral, juridical, and political issues at hand. This error is then justified in terms of the doctrine of the infallibility of ethical judgment. This doctrine says that even if a master jurist (*mujtahid*) erred in his legal judgment he would still get one reward, and if a *mujtahid* hits the correct answer he gets a double reward. The Companions and the Successors, therefore, get one reward

49. Ibid., vol. 28, pp. 179–181.

each for fighting each other! Ibn Taymiyya, however, did not use the term *ijtihād* at all in this connection. Instead he called it a "misinterpretation" which far from resulting in a reward may at best be forgiven. Misinterpretation, according to Ibn Taymiyya, may either be forgivable or may constitute a grave sin or, indeed, may constitute unbelief (*kufr*). Ibn Taymiyya had no doubt that participants in early civil wars committed a grave sin. Nevertheless, he stated that their services to Islam are so great that God will forgive them.

Ibn Taymiyya's unique political attitude, which borders upon political determinism (irjāʾism) arose from his own career and experience. The primary existential value in religion was the Muslim community (*umma*). In the first chapter we saw that Murjiʾism, when it first arose as a reaction against Khārijism–Muʿtazilism, began with the aim of promoting the solidarity of the community. It was a kind of manifesto for instituting an integral community, divided into sects and subjects, at the expense of moral concerns. The preceding pages have disclosed that Ibn Taymiyya raised the moral concerns to a central place. The Qurʾān itself raises moral concerns and sets them as tasks that believers should self-consciously adopt. It may be that because the political unity of Islam had been shattered after the Mongols, Ibn Taymiyya's concern for the solidarity of the community became even stronger. However, historical developments apart, this is also the logic of the Qurʾān, whose emphasis on the unity and solidarity of the community is as strong as it is on monotheism and socio-economic justice.

It is in this stance, a combination of moral concern with those of the existential values of the community, that Ibn Taymiyya's determinism (*irjāʾ*) is different from earlier forms. Whereas earlier *irjāʾ* had one-sidedly stressed unconditional obedience to the ruler at all cost, Ibn Taymiyya formulated a theory of mutuality, centered around the concept of the *umma* as a whole, under which both the ruler and the ruled have their being. First of all, Ibn Taymiyya held that rule is a "trusteeship" (*amāna*) and he quoted the Qurʾānic verse: "God commands you to deliver the trusts to those to whom they are due and that when you judge among people, judge with fairness" (4:58). This verse is said to have been revealed on the occasion of the fall of Makka to the Muslims. The Prophet had received the keys of the Kaʿba from the Banū Shayba. The Prophet's uncle ʿAbbās requested that he be given those keys so that he could combine the offices of the custodianship of the Kaᶜba and of supplying water to the pilgrims. When this verse was revealed, the Prophet gave the keys back to the Banū Shayba. This message underlined the importance of justice and goodwill towards the subjects on part of the ruler.[50]

The second verse of the Qurᵓān, which Ibn Taymiyya regarded as the second pillar of his political doctrine, is the one immediately succeeding the above verse, which says: "O believers! Obey God, obey the Messenger and those in authority over you. And if you dispute with each other concerning something, have recourse to [the decision of] God and the Messenger" (Q. 4:59). This verse asks the Muslims to obey their rulers and not rebel against them. Ibn Taymiyya concluded that these two verses imply the reciprocity between subject and ruler discussed above. But since Ibn Taymiyya had accepted pretty well all the deterministic Sunnī political *ḥadīth*, he insisted that Muslims must continue to obey their rulers, even if they were tyrants. He then stated the standard Sunnī political view that Muslims must obey tyrants, rather than rebel against them, unless the rulers command them to do something against the Sharīᶜa.[51]

Nevertheless, at this level Ibn Taymiyya's concept of reciprocity surfaces again. Although he did not condone rebellion, he said that should the subjects rebel, as indeed frequently happened, rulers must be lenient to such rebels and not kill or severely punish them. This mutuality is of course the application of Ibn Taymiyya's basic doctrine stated earlier in the political context: that under no condition may a Muslim kill another Muslim, or accuse him/her of absolute unbelief (*kufr ᶜala ᵓl-iṭlāq*). Neither, therefore, may Muslims rebel against the Muslim government, nor may the government severely punish rebel Muslim subjects. For people who rebel, not against the government, but against the state and/or the community and disrupt law and order and resort to beating and killing, harsh punishments do apply, which are mentioned in Qurᵓān 5:33.

It is this crucial point, Ibn Taymiyya's concept of "Islamic reciprocity," that Ibn ᶜAbd al-Wahhāb, the eighteenth-century founder of the "Wahhābī" movement, either misunderstood or ignored. For Ibn ᶜAbd al-Wahhāb acted in double violation of this principle. He rebelled with armed forces against Muslims, whom he castigated as unbelievers, against Ibn Taymiyya's

50. Ibid., vol. 28, p. 245.
51. Ibid.

teachings. It is, of course, possible that he was not thoroughly acquainted with Ibn Taymiyya's doctrine. More likely though is that he acted more in conformity with the Bedouin character of his environment than as a self-proclaimed follower of Ibn Taymiyya. Ibn Taymiyya's excessive emphasis on political obedience is questionable since it rests squarely on determinist Sunnī doctrine, based on *ḥadīth* materials discussed above. But then there is also no reason to believe that Ibn ᶜAbd al-Wahhāb ever questioned Ibn Taymiyya's reliance on such *ḥadīth* or questioned such reports.

Ibn Taymiyya, however, does go far beyond the concept of reciprocity between subject and ruler. He advocated a form of implied equality between ruler and the ruled. He described the ruler as a "hireling" (*ajīr*) or servant of the people. He recounts that Abū Muslim al-Khawlānī once came to the Umayyad ruler Muᶜāwiya b. Abī Sufyān and said to him: "Peace be upon you, hireling (*ayyuha ʾl-ajīr*)!"[52] The people attending the court corrected him, and told him to say: "Peace be upon you, ruler/prince (*amīr*)." (This story contains a play on the words *ajīr* and *amīr.*) But al-Khawlānī repeated the word "hireling" three times. Upon this Muᶜāwiya then said to those present: "Leave Abū Muslim alone. He knows best what he said."[53] Abū Muslim then addressed Muᶜāwiya in the following words: "You have been hired by the owner of this herd [your subjects] to look after them. If you treat the mangy ones back to health, heal the sick ones and can show preference to their lowest ones over their highest, the Owner of the herd will give you your due reward. But if you do not heal the mangy, nor treat the sick, or do not show preference for their lowest over the highest, then the Master of the herd will punish you."[54] In his commentary upon this event, Ibn Taymiyya combines the concept of reciprocity with that of an agent in a business partnership, called *sharika*. In such a partnership, each partner contributes capital and each also works both for himself and also acts as an agent for his partner in buying and selling stock. At the end of the year, they share their profit or loss in proportion to their capital invested and work contributed. The relationship between the ruler and subjects is such a partnership. Ibn Taymiyya says:

52. Ibid., vol. 28, p. 251.
53. Ibid.
54. Ibid.

> And this fact [that the ruler has the duty to look after all his subjects] is obvious when considered well. Creation are, indeed, the servants of God and the rulers are God's deputies appointed over His servants. In fact, rulers are "agents" (*wukalāʾ*) appointed by people on their behalf. This is analogous to the relationship of one partner to the other [in a business]. Therefore, they [the rulers] carry in themselves the functions both of guardians [of the interests of the other party] and agents [on their behalf]. Now, if a guardian or an agent appoints a deputy who is not the best person for commerce and [buying and selling] real estate; or he sells a certain commodity for a certain price while there is someone ready to pay a higher price for it, then he has committed treachery against his partner [or his agent]. This is especially true if the beneficiary of the favoritism was a friend or relative, since the other partner will despise and condemn [his actions] for being betrayed and for making the relative or friend of the partner a beneficiary [at the other partner's expense].[55]

Ibn Taymiyya, of course, was well aware that for deceit in business there are legal remedies. In spite of that, he never formulated any legal remedies for treachery within a political partnership. He could not – with the demise of the Khawārij and the onset of determinism, coupled with the temper of practical politics and political theory, it became almost impossible to devise any legal machinery for bringing rulers to account for their actions. Ibn Taymiyya could have done this if he had brought the Qurʾānic concept of consultation (*shūra*) to its proper place at the center of Islamic political thought. It prescribes that Muslims must decide "their affairs by mutual discussion and consultation" (Q. 42:38), which could only be done by the participation of the community in the affairs of government. This could be achieved through the election of representatives. However, the concept had been distorted into consultation by the ruler of such people as he thought worthy. This distortion occurred at the advent of the Khawārij, and as a reaction to their ultra-democratic stand. With Islamic history being so conditioned, it would have been radical, even beyond imagination, in Ibn Taymiyya's time for someone to come up with such a revolutionary idea.

As we have indicated earlier, Ibn Taymiyya had accepted practically all the deterministic reports that the Muslim tradition had invented and made its own. He regarded all the Sunnī *ḥadīth* demanding unconditional obedience to the political authority as genuine. Although he did severely

55. Ibid., vol. 28, pp. 251–252.

criticize certain "people of the *ḥadīth*" who "despite their ignorance of *ḥadīth*, attack other people," he himself pretty much accepted all *ḥadīth*. He accepted the *ḥadīth* according to which any person who professes "there is no God but God" goes to paradise. He accepted all *ḥadīth* on the Prophet's intercession on the Day of Judgment. He even accepted *ḥadīth* that prognisticated and anticipated the rise of the Muᶜtazilites and which condemned them as the Qadarīyya, namely, that the Prophet said: "The Qadarīyya are the Magians of this Community." This *ḥadīth* advocates their total excommunication. Ibn Taymiyya did not realize that by citing this *ḥadīth* he contradicted himself, since earlier he had declared himself against the excommunication of any Muslim or Muslim group on the grounds of an error in interpretation (*taʾwīl*). He also forgot that he had praised the Muᶜtazila for their relative correctness compared to the Murjiʾa and other sects. Finally, he accepted the obviously Ṣūfī *ḥadīth*: "God is beautiful and love beauty." It is this uncritical acceptance of *ḥadīth* that distorts his concept of the Sunna and shackles him.

However, from what has been said about his views on the various central subjects of Islamic theology and religion, particularly the baffling question of faith and unbelief, the relationship of faith to acts, there is no doubt that he brought new and refreshing solutions to all these. Above all, this creative approach to the understanding of Islam is uniquely correct among all Muslim thinkers of medieval Islam, including the illustrious al-Ghazālī who certainly far outstrips Ibn Taymiyya in subtlety and profundity. However, these qualities do not avail much when it comes to the fundamental problem of formulating the proper approach to Islam – the Qurʾān and the genuine model behavior of the Prophet. Ibn Taymiyya's knowledge of the complicated webs and entanglements of the sectarian views of Muslims that developed over the centuries is so highly nuanced that it defies description. To a person not intimately conversant with his work, his language appears harsh and may sometimes shock. A closer examination reveals it to be literally correct, and I hope that the foregoing account may have helped clarify this.

Conclusion

To complete Ibn Taymiyya's account of politics, his statements on Islam and the state are again unique. He stated the relationship of the two in such modern, indeed contemporary terms, that one would think that the poet-philosopher Muḥammad Iqbāl literally wrested the very words from him. With all his idealism, his hard realism shines through the statements as well. "Power and honesty," says Iqbāl, "are but rarely found together." Yet religion and state are inseparable. "When political authority is divorced from religion or religion from political authority, people's affairs get corrupted." It is, therefore, absolutely essential that political power must not be left to go its own way, but must be oriented in a moral direction. There are men who are so pious that they do not want to have anything to do with political power because they think that political power is inevitably corrupt. However, sometimes it is not just piety that keeps them away from politics, but they suffer from cowardice or narrowmindedness as well.

For Ibn Taymiyya it is necessary that governance be used as a means of attaining the goals of religion and to draw nearer to God. This is the best way of attaining proximity to God, because it at the same time also improves and reforms the condition of the people. Ibn Taymiyya then explains that those who seek ascendancy to power are four types.

> First, there are those who want access to power in order to promote corruption on earth, which is a sin against God. These are kings and political leaders who sow mischief on the earth, like Pharaoh and his party. They are the most evil of God's creatures.[56] ... The second group are those who want to sow mischief on earth without seeking access to power, like thieves and other criminals among low-life persons. The third group consists of those who seek access to power without employing corruption, like men of religion who use it to gain power over people.[57] As for the fourth category, these are the people of paradise who neither want power, nor do they spread corruption on earth even though they are really higher than others ... How many a person is there not who seeks ascendence to power but it only accelerates his decline? And, how many are there not who have been made really powerful, but they seek neither power, nor do they spread corruption. The reason is that the intention to seek dominance over people is tyranny (*ẓulm*). Given the fact that all humans are one race, the desire to seek dominance over one's own species and making fellow human beings subservient is tyranny. Add to this tyranny the fact that people hate such a dominating person and

56. Ibid., vol. 28, p. 392.
57. Ibid., vol. 28, p. 393.

become his enemies. The just (*ᶜādil*) among people do not like to be subjugated by someone who is their equal, while the unjust person would prefer to be the dominant one himself. It is [a fact] – in terms of reason and religion – that some humans will be elevated above others in command, as we had already mentioned ... Hence, the Sharīᶜa was provided in order to regulate power (*sulṭān*) and wealth (*māl*) in causes that are approved by God.[58]

When the desire for wealth and grandeur became the dominant motives of those in political authority, then they had effectively abandoned [the imperative] of genuine faith in matters of governance. This resulted in many people coming to view governance to be the very opposite of faith and the antithesis to the completion of religion. So among people you may find those who are motivated by faith and therefore they would turn away from everything, except those things with which faith can be improved. Then there are also those who see only the need to acquire political power and pursue it while abandoning religion, assuming it to be antithetical to political power. In the eyes of this kind of person, religion signifies compassion and despair, not domination and power. Similarly, religious persons in pursuit of establishing religion are afflicted with challenges and fail to complete their religious obligations and then begin to panic. This makes the non-religious person consider the path of religion to be a weak and humiliating one that cannot serve the interest (*maṣlaḥa*) [of the religious person] and is incapable of serving the interests of others.

Now, these two corrupt ways: [first] the way of the [so-called] religious person who cannot get his religion to perfection for the lack of political authority, military power and financial support; and, [second] the way of the person who acquires political power, wealth and military power, but has no intention to establish religion; both are tantamount to the paths of "those who have earned the wrath of God and of those who have lost the path" [Q. 1:7]. Those who have lost the path are the Jews and those who have earned the wrath of God are the Christians.[59]

58. Ibid., vol. 28, pp. 393–394.
59. Ibid., vol. 28, pp. 394–395.

5

INDIAN REFORMIST THOUGHT

Shaykh Aḥmad Sirhindī

Shaykh Aḥmad Sirhindī (1564–1624), known as "Renovator of the Second Millennium" *(mujaddid-i-alf-i-thānī)* of Islam – a title he himself proclaimed – belonged to Sirhind in east Punjab (India) where his tomb is still an object of popular veneration. His contribution to Islamic reform lies in his efforts to bring Ṣūfī doctrine and practice under the aegis of the Sharīᶜa and to vindicate the status of prophethood against that of sainthood (*wilāya*), which had pretty well replaced the former in popular Ṣūfism. He belonged to the most orthodox of all great Ṣūfī orders, the Naqshbandiyya, which had come to India from its home of origin in Central Asia. Besides its orthodoxy, the Naqshbandiyya had a tradition of association with the courts of rulers since the time of Khwāja ᶜUbayd Allāh Aḥrār (d. 1491), and developed the ideology of influencing government policies. Sirhindī's immediate preceptor was Khwāja Bāqī Billāh (d. 1603). While he stressed the observance of Sharīᶜa law he did not court any government or prince, but was rather an ascetic recluse. Many prominent notables of Akbar's court did become his disciples at their own request. After his death, they shifted to Shaykh Sirhindī.

Shaykh Aḥmad, who had left home in 1600 with the intention of going on the pilgrimage, went to Delhi instead on hearing of the spiritual powers of Bāqī Billāh. Through the latter, Sirhindī thus joined the Naqshbandī order. Although Bāqī Billāh died only three years later, they had formed an immediate attachment, which had an inspirational effect on Sirhindī. We are told that indeed a few weeks into his discipleship, Sirhindī reached the heights of spiritual perfection. He changed his plans for going on pilgrimage, returned to Sirhind, and occupied himself with teaching and guiding disciples. From then on to just before his death in 1624, Shaykh Aḥmad was an activist spiritualist, unlike his preceptor.

Shaykh Aḥmad's dynamic inner personality had been directed into a spiritual path by his preceptor's magical touch, as it were. Soon after his return to Sirhind from his relatively brief first visit of discipleship to Bāqi Billāh, Shaykh Sirhindī began to write letters in quick succession to his master, recounting his spiritual experiences. The letters, however, both in tone and tenor, give the impression of being addressed by a master to his pupil, and not by a pupil to his master. From the beginning, Sirhindī assumed, unconsciously as it were, the role of a militant reformer in the spiritual milieu of India. As time went on, his attitude became self-conscious and he claimed to be the "Renovator of the Second Millennium" of Islam. To him this was a kind of critical epoch when among pre-Islamic peoples "a prophet of unusual capacity for determination" (*az anbiyā-i ulul ᶜaẓm*) may have been raised up by God.

Several factors contribute to the critical nature of Shaykh Sirhindī's times for Islam. At the center of it all stood popular Ṣūfism, latitudinarism, and quasi-pantheistic Ṣūfī beliefs and practices (which became mixed with similar Hindu trends) advocated by spiritual developments in India under the impact of Ibn ᶜArabī's teachings. At the political level it culminated in the heavily addictive religion of the emperor Akbar and his ideologically motivated associates. Akbar had legislated against the slaughter of cows, presumably to satisfy the Hindus. He had adopted certain clearly old Zoroastrian practices such as the veneration of the sun and fire. He flirted with Catholic emissaries of the Pope, and in fact left them with the distinct impression that his conversion to Christianity was imminent. Hindus had been sufficiently encouraged sometimes to block the building of mosques, and to erect a temple with the very materials that had been collected to build a mosque.

Unfortunately, most of the recent literature on Shaykh Sirhindī is colored by biases of different kinds. Separate Pakistani and Indian viewpoints of him, his role, and achievements have also crystallized. Of course, if one wants to push back the sharp Muslim–Hindu division in the subcontinent, and hence trace back the seeds of the India-Pakistan partition, one can logically go back to the Mujaddid's teaching. But there is also the sectarian factor, no less significant than the Hindu–Muslim division. The Mujaddid instituted polemics against the Shīᶜī, whose influence in India increased during Akbar's reign. Sayyid Athar Abbas Rizvi's otherwise remarkable work, containing much rich and precious informative detail, is, in its evaluation and assessment, unreliable and obtuse at certain crucial points.[1]

Leaving aside his fiery temperament and certain scandalous claims (which abound in the careers of so many Ṣūfīs anyway) about the Mujaddid, there is sufficient material that deserves examination. There are, for example, his practical letters to various nobles, courtiers, and potentates aimed at influencing their policies toward reviving orthodox Islam in public life, as well as his criticisms directed at Hinduism and Hindus. Leaving aside the question of the extent of his success, our immediate task is briefly to state and assess his originality in relating the Ṣūfī path to the Sharīᶜa and bringing the former under the aegis of the latter. That is the basis of the quality of his contribution to Islamic reform. Let it be said at the outset that Sirhindī was not a reformer or a savant of the order of al-Ghazālī or Ibn Taymiyya before him, or Shāh Walī Allāh after him. His is not a synthesis or an attempted synthesis of the traditional Islamic discipline. Nevertheless, his focus, though narrow, is sharp, intense, and profound and highly consequential for the subsequent orientation of the Muslim community in India.[2] In some fundamental sense, one can pair him with Ibn Taymiyya. The standpoint of both on important issues is very clear. Both expressed acceptance or rejection without mincing their words. But the resemblance goes further. Both were centrally concerned with resurrecting and rehabilitating the Prophet and his Sharīᶜa, and causing them to prevail over the morass of amorphous spiritualities and ideologies of Ṣūfism. This was also Ibn Taymiyya's aim regarding *kalām*, while Sirhindī operated purely within the Ṣūfī fold.

The essence of Sirhindī's doctrine, elaborated in my above-mentioned work [*Selected Letters*], is that he was the first to reformulate Ibn ᶜArabī's scheme of emanation or self-redemption of the Absolute. Ibn ᶜArabī held

1. Rizvi, *Muslim Revivalist Movements*.
2. [Fazlur Rahman argues in his *Selected Letters of Shaikh Aḥmad of Sirhind* that Sirhindī's contribution to mysticisim was orginal, but that he also made some original interventions in matters of dialectical theology (*kalām*), see pp. 31–68.]

that at the level of the descent (*tanazzul*) of the Absolute there are divine names and attributes that appear in details such as existence, life, knowledge, will, power, etc. In the chamber of God's mind there are also "fixed essences' (*aᶜyān thābita*) or "essences of contingents" (*aᶜyān mumkinat*) which are generated by various combinations and continuations of the divine attributes. These fixed essences of the contingents do not exist – they are only in God's mind. In the now classic words of Ibn ᶜArabī: "The essences have not [even] smelt of [positive] existence." These essences represent all particular beings, both capable and incapable, all positive spatio-temporal existence. God gives existence to such among them as are capable of existence. These essences represent the ideals of all particular existence, which develop after them by unfolding their potentiality. No point can ever be actually reached. No spatio-temporal being can ever "catch up with" and thus become identical with its ideal. This ideal is the law that develops the potentialities of existences, in its role as a functioning god (*rabb*). The distinction between the "functioning god" (*rabb*) and the "one" (*aḥad*) can never evaporate: otherwise, the entire world-process would come to a halt. When these essences (the highest of which is that of Muḥammad) are reflected into the mirror of the divine attribute of existence, then what we call the spatio-temporal world comes into existence. This occurs as a result of the self-unfolding nature of being (*al-wujūd al-munbasiṭ*).

There is little doubt for a careful reader of the work of Ibn ᶜArabī that his purpose was to introduce a radical humanism into Islam: God and humanity are absolutely interdependent; humankind is the "pupil (*insān*) of God's eye" through which alone He can see. The perfect person is the mirror through which God sees Himself, and God is the mirror through which people see themselves. True followers of Muḥammad (*muḥammadī al-mashraᶜī*) are people who combine in themselves and believe in all the creeds; otherwise, they are not true *muwaḥḥidūn* (monotheists) but *mushriksūn* (polytheists). This last statement, although it appears shocking to most Muslims, is in reality not far from what the Qurʾān holds; for it repeatedly states that God's guidance has been universal and is not confined to Muslims, Jews, and Christians and that no community may lay propriety claims on God. Nevertheless, the Qurʾān does claim that there has been religious evolution in history and that Islam is the most consummate religion, and that the

Qurʾān is the most consummate revelation. Further, it frequently reiterates that the votaries of previous religions have, largely through sheer willfulness, distorted their revelations and misinterpreted their doctrines, and thus promises that the Qurʾān alone shall remain intact and textually uncorrupted. Nevertheless, there does remain some truth in religions.

In the aggressive optimism of Ibn ʿArabī there is no room for real evil. Evil is only apparent, not ultimate. Satan, indeed, is ultimately good, for he is faithfully performing the function assigned to him in the scheme of things and the divine plans. He explained the conflict of good and evil in terms of the waves that arise from the sea, collide with each other, and then fall back into the same sea. Sirhindī sought to rehabilitate the ultimacy of the struggle between good and evil. The theory of God's descent (*tanazzul*) is adopted from Ibn ʿArabī. However, instead of essences of contingents as reflections of the divine attributes he proposes an alternative explanation: the essences of contingents are really the opposites of divine attributes. Sirhindī considered these to be the negations or non-beings (*aʿdām*). Thus most beings, of which the highest is the devil, are invested with the shades of divine attributes and thus our spatio-temporal world comes into being. Why does this drama occur? By casting the shadows of His attributes upon these non-beings, God wants to transform them from non-being to being, and evil to good. It is not the destruction of evil, but its transformation into positive good, that is the divine plan.

From this doctrine directly flows the inevitability of the basic importance of the moral struggle and the primacy of the Sharīʿa over the Ṣūfī *ḥaqīqa*. The *ḥaqīqa* cannot be anything but the *ḥaqīqa* of the Sharīʿa. The Ṣūfī, who flees from this world thinking of it to be evil and ostensibly "goes to God" can achieve nothing but a delusion. For it was God who in the first instance ordained the moral struggle through the Sharīʿa which the Ṣūfī abandons and from which he or she escapes. In the realm of the angels there is no struggle, but quiescence and repose. It is down here on earth that there is sweat, labor, and struggle. This is why when Ṣūfīs leave the earth they shed it eternally and think they have attained to salvation. The Prophet, on the other hand, when he ascends to God, he keeps his "earth" intact and therefore returns to the earth to act and struggle. The test of a person's true ascent "is that he must come down to the society and work." Having been enriched by his ascent, he cannot just have "gone up there," either.

This, then, is the essence of the Mujaddid's message. There is no doubt that he said something new, something fundamentally meaningful, and something highly consequential. I have yet to see any modern treatment of Shaykh Sirhindī that has grasped the central message of his thought, which has been repeated in our own age by Muḥammad Iqbāl. Indo-Pakistani scholarship on Sirhindī has been the victim of externalities and sadly superficial thinking.

Shāh Walī Allāh of Delhi

Aḥmad b. ᶜAbd al-Raḥīm (1702–1762), known as Shāh Walī Allāh, was a prolific writer and influential thinker both within the Indian subcontinent and the Arab world. In the subcontinent, the chain of *ḥadīth* instruction of the majority of *ḥadīth* scholars can be traced back to him. His most famous work, *Ḥujjat Allāh al-Bāligha* (God's Decisive Argument), a sort of philosophy of religion, was taught at al-Azhar University in Cairo for a considerable period of time. Murtaḍā al-Zabīdī (d. 1791), author of the famous Arabic dictionary *Tāj al-ᶜArūs* and a massive commentary on al-Ghazālī, was a student of Shāh Walī Allāh in Delhi, before he finally settled in Cairo in the later eighteenth century. Walī Allāh, from the point of view of the content and quality of his thought, is certainly one of the top-ranking personages of Islam, though he is as yet not well known.

The methods of Shāh Walī Allāh and al-Ghazālī make an interesting comparison: both were temperamentally and consciously synthetic spirits, appropriating rather than rejecting, absorbing rather than exchanging. While al-Ghazālī moved from problem to problem, absorbing and appropriating material as he went, Shāh Walī Allāh used and adapted data from all directions simultaneously to produce a system that was, despite its difficulties, whole and synthesized.

Shāh Walī Allāh presents a synthesis of all the disciplines traditionally cultivated by Muslims such as philosophy, theology, psychology, sociology, law, Ṣūfism, and, indeed, history. He himself tells us:

> You should know, Brethren, may God have mercy on you, that every age is characterised by a special kind of knowledge in the distribution of the mercies of God, the Almighty. If you consider the condition of the early phase of this blessed Community when none of the Sharīᶜa-sciences had

> been systematised and compiled, nor the various branches of literature, nor yet much discussion about them had taken place, but divine inspiration continued to appear in their minds. One kind of knowledge after another in accordance with His wisdom for each age, this point should become clear to you. My lot, in this particular age, in the distribution of God's mercy is that in my mind come together all the branches of knowledge [cultivated by] this Community – its rational sciences, traditional sciences and spiritual sciences, and that all of them be synthesised and their sharp edges of differences become smooth in such a way that each science falls into its proper place. All praise to God.[3]

One might get the immediate impression, even after a haphazard and cursory reading of him, that one is dealing with a dilettante in Walī Allāh or some kind of an artificial construct in his system. But this notion is proved totally wrong on a careful study of his writings after one has got hold of his central ideas, which are the linchpin of his system of thought. Even certain obvious facts point to his originality. For example, he had a preference for the *Kitāb al-Muwaṭṭā* of Mālik over the most celebrated works of *ḥadīth* such as those of al-Bukhārī and Muslim. And the fact that he wrote two different commentaries on Mālik's work, one in Arabic and one in Persian, although he himself was a Ḥanafī and not a Mālikī in itself speaks volumes. Again, despite his insistence on the importance of and spreading of Arabic, he pioneered a translation of the Qurʾān into Persian, for which he is said to have endangered his life at the hands of some fanatics.

First of all, Shāh Walī Allāh carves out a metaphysics from the philosophico-mystical tradition of Islam which he interprets and formulates into a new structure with a view to bringing the orthodox religion, the Sharīʿa of Islam, into full focus. Around this, then, he weaves all his theories in the various fields. One salient feature of this metaphysical system may be noted before we actually attempt to delineate it. This is that, like neo-Platonism in general, it cannot recognize any sharp distinction between the material and spiritual. There are spiritual agencies in the world, but they act on matter. Walī Allāh naturalizes the so-called

3. Shāh Walī Allāh, "al-Juzʾ." [Fazlur Rahman noted that this quotation was from Shāh Walī Allāh's autobiographical note, "*al-Juzʾ al-Laṭif*." However, this source does not present the material in this sequence, although it does paraphrase the content. Shāh Walī Allāh made very similar statements in his other works *Tafhīmāt Ilāhiyya* and al-Budūr al-Bāzigha.]

supranatural and, conversely, supranaturalizes the natural. In fact, this distinction cannot exist for him in the final analysis. In a way, everything is natural, insofar as nothing occurs without a cause. The universe, *shakhṣ akbar*, is literally the "greatest person," an authentically Stoic–neo-Plotinian idea – for example, where emotions cause physical changes and physical changes entail spiritual effects. Yet, the overall picture of the universe and accounts of whatever happens therein is thoroughly rational, as, indeed it is natural.

God is Absolute Being or Existence. This does not mean that there is a concept or category of existence under which God falls as all particular beings fall under a general concept. Rather, God as Absolute Being in the sense that the category of being in general is itself in His titanic grasp and derived directly or indirectly from Him.[4] This is Ibn Sīnā's doctrine of God as Necessary Being upon whom all contingent being depends. Whenever one therefore considers any contingent being, one is inevitably led to the Necessary Being. Being as an abstract concept therefore exists only in the mind. However, contrary to Aristotle and all his Muslim followers, Shāh Walī Allāh asserts that being (or existence) is the highest genus. (Peripatetics hold that if being is regarded as genus, it will become part of the essence of a thing, which is unacceptable.) But since things can be properly known and defined by their contradictories and being has no contradictory, the philosopher's custom has been not to regard being as genus. It is because of this limitlessness of being that even non-existence can be invested with some sort of "mental" existence and correct propositions can be asserted of them. Indeed, Walī Allāh tells us that in the Divine Realm, terms such as "existence in the external world" can be applied by a loose linguistic usage. If someone wants to connect the Divine Realm with the lower world (*shakhṣ akbar*) through applying terms such as existence, hearing, seeing, power, etc., they exceed the bounds of reasonableness. Of course, reason can make certain concessions when it is forced to, just as the Sharīᶜa does the same based upon the inability of people to carry out the Sharīᶜa obligations strictly. Thus, among the concessions of reason is the permission to use the word "existence" of the Divine Realm, while among the concessions of the Sharīᶜa is to permit one to say that God is "on His Throne" and that He has hearing, sight, hand, face, anger, and mercy. "There is nothing the like of Him and He is hearing and seeing" (Q. 42:11).

4. Fazlur Rahman, *Selected Letters*, pp. 5–7.

God, the Absolute, becomes characterized by attributes. Shāh Walī Allāh says that this naming takes place by means of descent (*tanazzul* or *tadallī*), or more usually by self-manifestation (*tajallī*). These attributes or names can be broadly divided into two categories, those that characterize the creation or the beginning (*mabdaʾ*) of the world from Him and those that describe the return (*ᶜawd*) of the world to Him. In the middle lie those names that relate the world to Him in terms of the governance of the universe and its management by Him. Walī Allāh believed in an infinite number of cyclic universes, and he tried to refute the philosophical argument against an infinity of actualized universes. Although addition and subtraction are inconceivable on the side of infinitude, on the side of finitude it is always possible, since on the latter side there will always remain one that can be added.

According to Walī Allāh, the First Emanant from the Absolute is nothing but a divine name. It cannot be an intellect, as Muslim peripatetic philosophers have suggested. The reason is that the First Emanant or divine self-manifestation (*tajallī*) must be a totally and exhaustive representation of one aspect of the Absolute, just as a name is revelatory of a thing. Indeed, Shāh Walī Allāh himself described the First Emanant as the intellect. But he warns that by this intellect he does not mean the entities, which the philosophers invoke as forces that explain the motions of the heavenly spheres. He calls this intellect the "Unitary Intellect" (*al-waḥīd al-ᶜaqlī*) because all the successive world orders and all successive events in a single world order are latent and unfold therefrom just as the infinity of numbers is latent in the number 1. In his Persian work *Saṭaᶜāt* he regularly calls the First Emanant (or the First Determination – *taᶜayyun*) intellect, but in his Arabic *Lamaḥāt*, he calls it by Ibn ᶜArabī's term, *al-wujūd al-munbasiṭ ᶜala hayākil al-mawjūdat*, "the self-unfolding being upon the frames of existents."[5] He says that the First Emanant cannot be characterized by certain qualities to the exclusion of their opposites; on the contrary, it is necessary that its entity is not the opposite of any other entity. Its relationship to all things is like the relationship of the black line to all the characters of a piece of writing. It appears, then, that this entity, which gives being to everything at any level of reality, external or mental, is identical with the intellect since as we have just seen, the intellect, in its unicity, contains everything in a latent or eminent manner. This case

5. Shāh Walī Allāh, *Saṭaᶜāt*, p. 3.

illustrates certain difficulties in Shāh Walī Allāh's terminology and doctrine.

It is this "unitary Intellect" or the self-unfolding being that produces the universe (*shakhṣ akbar*) with all its plenitude of beings, spiritual and physical. With the rise of the universe, we pass from the divine realm of eternity to the created order of the shakhṣ akbar. Before the rise of the *shakhṣ akbar*, however, an infinite series of *tajalliyāt* or epiphanies of divine names occur until we reach the last name, which is the will of God, since all creation is directly under the divine will. The divine will, vis-à-vis the *shakhṣ akbar*, "constitute the external providence" which binds all essences permanently to their properties, such as fire with heat, so that the question of "why" can be asked there, for example: why is fire hot?

The *shakhṣ akbar* is analyzable into two parts or constituents: the universal soul and the material principals, which Walī Allāh calls, after Ibn ᶜArabī, the "breath of the merciful" (*nafs al-raḥmān*). All the essential characteristics of a thing, its generic, specific, and individual qualities, flow from the universal soul as it descends into or is differentiated into genera, species, and individuals. Matter itself has no qualities. For example, when water turns into air (vapor) one specific form changes into another, each having a name, namely water or air. But the subsisting matter has no name because it has no qualities.

The entire *shakhṣ akbar* is pervaded by the power of imagination which is, as is the case with human beings, situated between the perceptual and the intellectual powers. This realm of imagination (*ᶜālam al-mithāl*) is the field of transition between the sensible and intellectual realms. All these spiritual entities and events are clothed in a quasi-physical form before they take on a half-spiritual status. An example is the image of a dollar bill (in my mind) before it is interpreted and transformed it into a meaning. The existence of the *ᶜālam al-mithāl* seems to have been first announced by al-Suhrawardī (d. 587/1191) and then developed into a full-blown doctrine by Ibn ᶜArabī, Mullā Ṣadrā and others, and utilized fully by Walī Allāh in whose thought it plays a central role. All the heavenly and earthly bodies and spiritual (angels) and other living beings possess this faculty of imagination as does the *shakhṣ akbar* as a whole.

Within the *shakhṣ akbar* there is a center, wherein the subtlety of the imagination is focused. It has the greatest ability to function as this imaginary transformer or reflector. It is truly the divine talisman through which God creates, shapes, and directs the universe and its contents. Apart from God and His attributes, this point of the *shakhṣ akbar* manifests God most comprehensively and faithfully. Literally it constitutes the relationship between God and the world. Walī Allāh calls it the "Great Epiphany" (*tajallī-i aᶜzam*) and says: "It is absolutely the highest epiphany and all other epiphanies are its epiphanies or reflections." It is this epiphany that holds the *shakhṣ akbar* together. It is directly related to everything in the *shakhṣ akbar*. If we want to conceive of its relationship to other things, let us immerse a chickpea in water. The water permeates all parts in segments or points of this chickpea uniformly. The proportion of different parts of the chickpea to each other and to the whole remains the same and their interconnections remain unchanged, but the water has pervaded the whole as well as each part. So does the contents of the all (the universe) remain absolutely unchanged despite the permeation of the Great Epiphany. Their mutual relationships remain undisturbed. The external causal relationships are all in their place. Yet the Great Epiphany has, in a deeper sense, supplied the true causation without supporting them. Without this true causality nothing would work. Yet the great epiphany is not a substitute for other (outer) causes. It is the real, intelligible cause of everything. It can be nothing else but cause in the sense of purpose.

This epiphany, which in its existential aspect is part of the *shakhṣ akbar* and hence a part of the world, insofar as it reveals God at a certain level, is purely spiritual.

> [The epiphany is] just like a form appearing in a mirror that has two dimensions. One dimension constitutes the perfection of the mirror, and the other is the instrument for revealing the image of the viewer. Similarly the image of a person also has two dimensions in our mind. One dimension constitutes the perfection of our mind, which is part of our human accidents ... The second aspect is the instrument for revealing the nature or form of a human being and has thus only a mental existence (*mawjūd dhihnī*) and emerges from an absolute non-existence (*ᶜadam muṭlaq*). In the same way the form of the elevated truth, which makes its appearance in the most delicate parts of the *shakhṣ akbar* (universe) also has two dimensions. In one aspect, it constitutes the perfection of the *shakhṣ akbar* and hence it is counted as part of the world. And in terms of

> the other aspect, it reveals God and constitutes a plane of His existence. It is the divine talisman that relates the purely spiritual (non-material) with the sensible world.[6]

In the spiritual root of every human, a spark of the Great Epiphany is ingrained by nature. This, of course, varies immensely from a zero endowment in specimens of distorted constitution (who are relatively few) to a person so gifted they were perfect at birth – in other words, perfect in cognitive, active, and moral–spiritual capacities. The Great Epiphany, insofar as it is concerned with humans and their guidance, radiates a beam of knowledge or light that is called the Holy Precinct (*ḥazīrat al-quds*). All original human knowledge emanates from there. In the case of such an exceptionally gifted person as we have just mentioned, that is, a prophet, a special agency of revelation, Gabriel, opens the conscious mind to the treasure of knowledge and guidance, the *ḥazīrat al-quds*. Shāh Walī Allāh, as we pointed out earlier, speaks of what are generally regarded as supernatural phenomena in quite naturalistic terms simply because in his worldview this age-old distinction between natural and supernatural is inapplicable. Thus he says in his *Saṭaᶜāt* concerning the process of revelation:

> One of the functions performed by the Great Epiphany (*tajallī aᶜzam*) in the world is to provide God's decision [will] to guide mankind; to teach [humans] the meaning of creation and the return to God; as well as elucidating the variety of ways to approach God ... After that, the divine management [of the world] – which is rooted in the choice of the best means followed by the next best – becomes concretized in that a perfect man is made the instrument [or organ] and that purpose is realized through him. Thus, this Divine purpose becomes printed in his tabula rasa (*ḥajar baḥt*), just like the shape of the sun is reflected in a mirror.[7] Then, the faculties of the heart and mind of the person becomes illuminated by the light of his tabula rasa and a multitude of knowledge of different kinds and formations and immensity of volition descend upon him. He develops a unique relationship with the Supernal Plenum (*al-malaʾ al-aᶜlā*)[8]

6. Ibid., pp. 14–15.
7. *Ḥajar baḥt* is a technical term, meaning the original state of a person's mind, which, of course varies in its capacity to reflect the great epiphany and the *ḥazīrat al-quds*.
8. A term we shall meet again, which means the higher constituents, the *shakhṣ akbar*, namely, the higher angels and those humans such as the prophets and other great men who, by contributing palpably towards the development of mankind in different ways, have earned a permanent directive role in the constitution of the universe.

whence wisdom and knowledge of the nature of legislation rains upon his mind torrentially. Those desirable ends [mentioned above] are then realized through him. The name of this great man is "messenger" ... At some point, the divine will becomes attached to the idea that an external guidance be dispensed to the entirety of mankind, so that all mankind and its generations be united with the "indissoluble bond of God" (Q. 3:102). Thus, effulgence from God makes the Messenger's soul subservient [to its cause], and the Book of God is deposited in his tabula rasa in summary form [without concrete details]. The form [of the Book] as it appeared in the *ḥazīrat al-quds* is exactly reproduced in his mind. Because of this relationship [to the *ḥazīrat al-quds*) it becomes indubitably established that it is the word of God ... "The trusted spirit has brought it [revelation] upon your heart (O Muḥammad!) in order that you may be a warner of people" (Q. 26:193). In this state, the Divine outpourings from the treasures of His mercy are showered upon him like tumultuous waters. This entity that had descended is the "Book of God."

"God knew in His primordial providence (*ghayb* or *ᶜināyat-i ulā*) that [at] a given point of time, people will need guidance. The nearest possibility at that time would be to raise up a perfect man [the Prophet Muḥammad] possessing a highly effective tabula rasa. [This person], according to the determination of the higher realm, is destined to enjoy great fortune and decisive ascendancy upon his contemporaries [on the one hand]. And, according to the [context] of the lower world [i.e., his physical constitution], he is characterized by a balanced constitution in terms of his cognitive and practical faculties. [This occurs] in such a manner that he becomes a perfect vehicle for the fulfillment of the requirements of the form of the Human Species ... The descent of the Qurʾān [upon his heart] is at once the function of the [natural] perfection of the soul of this personage as well as the fulfillment of the obligations of the Great Epiphany."[9]

Even more starkly "naturalistic" is the following statement in the historical work *Izālat al-Khafāʾ*:

The first point [to be grasped] is that the immaculate souls of the prophets (peace be upon them) have been created in utter purity and moral exaltation. And, in the Divine Wisdom, they have become worthy of [receiving] Revelation and also the governance of the world has been

9. Shāh Walī Allāh, *Saṭaᶜāt*, quoted selectively from "Saṭᶜa 19 to Saṭᶜa 21," pp. 30–33.

> trusted to them – as God the Exalted has said: "God knows where to put His messengership or message" (Q. 6:124).[10]

Whatever guidance the Messenger (the Prophet) provided for his community or for humankind is related to certain essential properties. In the primordial providence (*ᶜināyāt-i ulā*) which is another name for the divine will and purpose (*irāda maṣlaḥa*), certain essences are necessarily confined with certain properties or effects. Such primordial connections are not liable to the question "why," for example, fire is hot and snow white. These properties are dictated by the nature of specific forms (or forms of species – *ṣuwar nawᶜiyya*) which must work themselves out in the real world unless invincible impediments occur. This primordial conjoining of properties with specific forms is called *qadar* or *taqdīr*, which literally means the "estimation or determination of something or taking its measure." When the manufacturer of a car, for example, estimates that the life of a certain car, given the normal condition of the road, would be for 15,000 miles, then this specification is its *qadar* or *taqdīr* (a measurement of its life expectancy). The concept of *qadar*, therefore, requires that at a certain point in its career the car should be involved in an accident or wear and tear and thus be destroyed.

Now, it is the nature of this *qadar* that gives rise to religious necessity and moral obligations for humanity. Just as it is imperative for fire to burn, so it is imperative for human beings to accept and follow a law that conforms to their higher nature. One cannot, therefore, ask the question why humankind follows a higher nature or a religious law and why they worship a Supreme Being. The only answer is that it is what human nature requires and that is what the specific human form dictates. The universality of religion and its ubiquitous sway is just that:

> Lawgiving (*tashrīᶜ*) is a function or corollary of [divine] determination/measurement (*taqdīr*). As for measurement (*taqdīr*) it means that the physical shape, behavioral traits, and proper activities of every species have been designated. For instance, a human being can be [characterized] as one who is rational, can understand speech, has an exposed skin, upright stature and walks on two feet. A horse [on the other hand] neighs, does not understand speech, has a skin hidden under hair, a bent stature and walks on four feet ... During sexual encounters, every species has

10. Shāh Walī Allāh, *Izālat al-Khafāʾ*, p. 9.

> different movements. So there are also countless differences between them at the time of eating, drinking and raising their young etc. All these traits occur by natural intuition in the souls of volitional beings.
>
> Lawgiving means that since a human being is a composite of two faculties – the angelic and the animal – the specific justice requires that both these faculties remain in equilibrium in order to gain happiness in the hereafter. And in the secular existence [a human being] should not deviate from the upright and firm path in terms of the essentials of socio-economic life such as lawful ways of earning livelihood, the ethics of marital life and the maintenance of political order and conduct. Now, to establish the correct conditions and actions for [members] of the human species is what is called lawgiving (*tashrīᶜ*). The case is something like this. The Great Epiphany undertakes a general and deep examination of the specific human form. Between the Great Epiphany and the human form [i.e., at the point of the *ḥazīrat al-quds*] countless sparks of light are emitted. Now, the purpose of this is that certain performances of actions (*afᶜāl*) are required. Divine pleasure gets attached to these actions. Some of these acts are either obligatory or recommended, while certain others are to be avoided due to divine displeasure, that either makes them prohibited or disapproved. From this arises the wisdom of goodness and sin: "My word does not change" (Q. 50:29). Sometimes this very unchangeable but generic wisdom is outlined in detail to certain individuals and nations. These individuals and nations then implement these universal principles (*umūr kullīyya*) in certain specific ways. An illustration of the first [generic] type is: "He [God] has ordained for you [Muslims] the same religion that He had commended to Noah" (Q. 42:13). An illustration of the second [detailed legislation] is: 'For each one of you [religious communities: Jews, Christians, Muslims] We have appointed a [different] law and form of worship" (Q. 5:48).[11]

The most important and far-reaching characteristics imparted to humankind by their specific form is the power of reason. For Walī Allāh it is this power that creates in us the sense of responsibility whereby we are led to recognize our maker and worship Him and behave responsibly toward our fellow human beings. A great deal of human behavior is instinctive, like that of animals – for instance how a child clings to its mother's breast to feed, how one seeks shelter from excessive heat and cold, how to have sex. This arises from "natural intuitions" (*ilhāmāt jibillīyya*). Despite this

11. Shāh Walī Allāh, *Saṭaᶜāt*, "Saṭᶜa 15."

humans are able to think and work out a superstructure of a sophisticated, elaborate, and beautiful lifestyle, with complicated socio-economic and political institutional networks only through their thinking powers. This process of development, which we shall briefly consider here, is called *irtifāq*, which literally means "planning useful measures." But Walī Allāh uses it to mean "socio-cultural-political development."[12] Then *irtifāq*-development must go along the moral and spiritual development of humankind because without a corresponding solid *irtifāq*-substructure, moral and spiritual development cannot occur.

In humans, the central revolutionary change that takes place and which sets them apart from animals is the nature of the human action. Human volitional action, apart from affecting the extra-human realm, rebounds upon the individual self and penetrates the soul. To sum up Walī Allāh's view on this crucial point: humans are what they do. All the Sharīᶜa has said about the afterlife, the rewards and punishments and the destiny and fate of human beings is, therefore, a natural process determined basically by the deeds of human beings themselves.

"You must know that all actions that humans intend to perform and all the ethical traits that are rooted in them emanate from the rational soul [in the first instance]. Then these effects return to it [the rational soul in the hereafter, in the second instance]. Then these [effects] tenaciously cling to [the rational soul] and, indeed, encompass it."[13] Elsewhere Shāh Walī Allāh says:

> Therefore, you should know that the rules and regulations of revealed laws (*sharāʾiᶜ*) are in accordance with the habits of the common man. In this matter, there is a great and hidden divine wisdom. Therefore, whenever a revealed law (*sharīᶜa*) is in the making, then, at that time God, the Sublime, looks at the habits or customs (*ᶜādāt*) of people. Whatever is harmful among their habits, these are then to be avoided. Whatever good habits are evident, they are to be left in their original condition.[14]

12. [Fazlur Rahman defines Walī Allāh's innovative term *irtifāq* to mean social, cultural, and political development. In translation he uses the shorthand term "culture" to describe this concept. Mercia Hermansen translates *irtifāq* as the "support of civilization" (see Shāh Walī Allāh, *Conclusive Argument*, pp. xviii–xix). Obviously the diference between culture and civilization is not considered here.]
13. Shāh Walī Allāh, *Ḥujjat Allāh*, vol. 1, p. 59.
14. Shāh Walī Allāh, *Fuyūḍ*, p. 89.

We clearly see here that Walī Allāh supported the religious stand of true Islamic orthodoxy, rather than that of Ṣūfism; of the Sharīᶜa (law) rather than that of abstract and inward spirituality; of Ibn Taymiyya rather than that of al-Ghazālī. We have seen while discussing al-Ghazālī that he did return to the recognition of the importance of law in the last years of his life. But al-Ghazālī did not synthesize spirituality into a system, although his thrust was undoubtedly to infuse law with spirituality. Shāh Walī Allāh, on the other hand, integrated spirituality, philosophy, and law into a system. What enabled him to do this is that he considered the universe to be one organism. It develops and is organized under the directive and governing forces of the *ḥazīrat al-quds* and the *malaᵓal-aᶜlā* where its spiritual and material contents are all working together with constant and material interaction. In fact, it is quite true to say that, by selectively taking various elements from Stoicism, neo-Platonism etc., he constructed a system where the cosmology of the Qurᵓān and the *ḥadīth* come alive.

Actions, rather than inner states and dispositions, have become the anchoring points of human behavior. In fact, as we said earlier, actions performed with proper awareness affect the depths of the soul itself. For this reason religious law had to lay down certain quantifications for these acts, for every individual, otherwise, society will end up in stratified class formations. This point is so interesting and far-reaching that I give below a translation of the chapter on the "Distinction Between Salutary Purposes (*maṣāliḥ*) and Laws" in *Ḥujjat Allāh al-Bāligha*:

> Thou should know that the Law-Giver (*Shāriᶜ*) [the Prophet is meant here] has given us two types of knowledge, distinct in their characteristics divergent in their status. One of them is the knowledge of the salutary (*maṣāliḥ*) and unsalutary (*mafāsid*): I mean what he has taught us by way of the acquisition of qualities that would earn us benefits in this world or the next, and how to eliminate the opposite of these qualities. In terms of what he has taught us by way of managing the household, the ethics of earning our livelihood, running the affairs of the states, he did not specify any given quantity of actions. Nor did he tie down its free and indeterminate behavior to any determinate and rigid principle or inflexible rules, nor clarify its ambiguities, with known symbols. Rather, [in this sphere of morals and polity], he simply encouraged praiseworthy conduct and warned against its opposite. He

thus left his speech to be understood by the native speakers of the language themselves. Demand and prohibition should be based on the salutary ends and purposes themselves [which are to be achieved per se], not on anticipated sources [pointing out where they are likely: *mazānn*, sg. *mazanna*]. This he did by setting up quantitative standards and outward symbols which may lead to the realization of these purposes. For example, he lauded the virtues of cleverness and courage, as well as commanded kindness [or gentleness], mutual affection and moderation in earning one's livelihood. But he did not define the required amount of cleverness and the likely quantitative standard by which people should be evaluated.

All salutary purposes to which the *Sharīʿa* has exhorted us and all evils from which it has sought to preserve us can be reduced to three principal types. One is to train and refine our souls by means of four virtues beneficial to the hereafter or all the virtues which are beneficial to this life. The second is to make an effort in order for the "word of truth" (*kalima-t ʾl-ḥaqq*) to prevail [in the world], to establish religious laws and to try to widen their sphere of influence. The third is to organize the affairs of people, to improve their useful cultural and socio-economic pursuits (*irtifāqāt*) and to refine and improve their customs. The meaning of saying [that the pursuit of all salutary purposes and avoidance of all evil] is reducible [to three principal types] is that these activities affect those salutary purposes and their opposites positively or negatively. Thus, some of theses activities may be a segment of a certain quality among those purposes. Or [some] may be its opposite, or may constitute a likelihood (*mazanna*) of its existence or non-existence or a concomitant of that quality or, of its opposite or it may be a means towards [supporting] or avoiding it.

Now [divine] pleasure per se is connected with those salutary purposes and [divine] displeasure per se is connected only with those evil qualities both prior to and after the delegation of prophets. Indeed, if it was not for the fact that divine pleasure and displeasure is attached to those two dimensions [salutary and unsalutary purposes], prophets would have not been sent in the first place. That is why [legally prescribed] punishments (*ḥudūd*) have been imposed only after the delegation of prophets. Hence, God's Grace [for people] did not begin with charging people with obligations and holding them answerable for offenses with regard to these religious laws. [In fact] even before the commissioning of Prophets the very nature of these salutary ends [to be pursued] and evils [to be avoided] had their effects. By themselves these [purposes] required the refinement of the soul and [avoidance of] its pollution with evil as well as pursuit of the establishment of a social order. God's grace brought it about to inform humankind of what is important for them and to oblige them [positively and negatively] with what was necessary for them. This could not be accomplished except by laying down definite quantities (*maqādīr*) and specific laws (*sharāʾiʿ*). Hence Divine Grace comes to require those [quantities] derivatively. Some of those are easily understandable even to an average person. Others are only known to exceptional minds whose intellects are radiated by the light emanating from the hearts of Prophets. Thus they are alerted to the [real meaning] of the revealed law (*sharʿ*) and they became aware of it. The [*Sharīʿa*] merely gestures to them and they understand it. Those conversant with the principal types [of salutary purposes] that we have mentioned would not be hesitant in any of these matters.

The second type of knowledge is that of positive laws, penalties, and legal obligations [i.e., as distinguished from salutary ends and real purposes and their direct quantities]. I mean that which the *Sharīʿa* has clearly explained by way of quantification. In this way, the *Sharīʿa* establishes certain definite and defined anticipated sources (*mazān*) and outward signs (*amārāt*) in order to [attain] the salutary ends and purposes. Now, it is these quantified laws [not the salutary interests for which they stand] that become the immediate rules and constitute the direct obligations. Defining the essential characteristics, conditions, and ethics required for their performance regulates various types of virtues. The Law-Giver appoints for every type [of virtue] a definite amount which is necessarily required of men and also an amount which they are exhorted to peform, but which is not made obligatory ...

Thus, obligation is translated into and directed towards those very anticipated sources (*mazānn*), and judgments are passed on the basis of those very legal signs. This type of obligation, in the last analysis, rests on laws [that] deal with the political management of religious life ... Rather, some salutary purposes are clear in themselves by either being perceptible or otherwise obvious to the mind with all and sundry being aware of them. Sometimes, obligations and prohibitions can have an accidental reason [without a corresponding *maṣlaḥa* (salutary purpose)] and as a result of it the shape (*ṣūra*) of an obligation or prohibition is

> realized in the Supernal Plenum (*al-mala*ʾ *al-a*ᶜ*lā*). For example, someone may ask [a prophet] a question or a number of people may desire it or want to avoid it. This category of legislation has no intelligible reason attached to it. In terms of this we may know the laws of quantification and making of rules, but we do not know whether such a rule has actually been written in the Supernal Plenum. [Nor do we know] that it has taken a definite form of obligation in the Sacred Precinct (*ḥazīrat al-quds*), except through an explicit statement of revelation. This is because it is one of those things for which there is no way [for us] to ascertain except through divine declaration. Just as we know, for example, that ice is formed when coldness reaches water. But we do not know whether the water in the clay jug at the present moment has turned into ice or not, unless we actually see it or someone who has seen it reports to us. Following this analogy, we know that there must definitely be an assessment of wealth-limit beyond which *zakāt* (tax) is payable. And we can also judge that the sum of two hundred dirhams or five camel loads (*awsāq*) is a suitable limit for *zakāt* to be payable. Because with these amounts a person can be regarded as reasonably rich and people generally use these two amounts as a standard. But we still do not know whether God has actually prescribed (*kataba* ᶜ*alaynā*) and charged us to pay *zakāt* on that wealth-limit (*nisāb*) and whether his pleasure and wrath occurs as a result of this, except on the basis of a clear *Sharī*ᶜ*a* declaration ...
>
> A good number of scholars are agreed that in the area of quantities, the procedure of analogical reasoning (*qiyās*) does not apply and that the function of analogy is the transfer of judgement of an original, principal case to [cover] an analogous one on the basis of a common ratio legis (ᶜ*illa*); not to make of the *mazanna* of a salutary purpose (*maṣlaḥa*) a ratio legis.[15]

Immediately after this, Shāh Walī Allāh declares:

> Analogical reasoning is not the proper instrument for locating the *maṣlaḥa* [salutary purpose] but it is useful for finding the ᶜ*illa* [ratio legis] which is the basis for the application of a rule. Thus, the *Sharī*ᶜ*a* has provided certain concessions due to hardship to a traveler in the matter of prayers and fasting (for example, he can shorten the prayer by half) that a non-traveler cannot adopt by analogy. Now, the *maṣlaḥa* [salutary

15. Shāh Walī Allāh, *Ḥujjat Allāh*, vol. 1, pp. 273–275.

> purpose] of this concession is to overcome hardship, neither is the legal cause the shortened prayers and eating [for travellers]. Indeed, the ratio legis is travel ... Perhaps [in cases involving quantification] the purpose (*maṣlaḥa*) is confused as the ratio legis (*ᶜilla*).[16]

This position, which does such palpable violence to the meaning of religion, is nevertheless espoused by a large number of the ᶜulamāᵓ. However, the basis of the concern of these ᶜulamāᵓ is also clear and serious. So serious is it that unless it is duly taken into account, the *Sharīᶜa* as the basis for the life of the community will be jeopardized. A door will be opened where every individual, for his/her own convenience, will do independent interpretation (*ijtihād*) to change the quantities of prescribed rites. But the way to achieve that end is obviously not to forbid thinking about the quantified institutes of religion. For one thing, to include the *zakāt* tax into this category of "imponderables" has obviously proven to be a grave violation of the very purposes of the *Sharīᶜa*. The Qurᵓānic verse (9:60) that lays out the heads of expenditure of *zakāt* covers all the departments and activities of a modern welfare state: (1) the poor and the needy; (2) the civil service (literally, tax-collectors; but then tax collectors were in the Prophet's days the only civil service, since his government was a simple, informal, and undifferentiated form of government); (3) diplomatic expenditure "to win good will" for Islam; (4) to free Muslim war-captives; (5) to relieve the chronic debts of people who cannot free themselves from debt; (6) expenditure "in the path of Allah," a phrase which in the Qurᵓān means both *jihād*, i.e., defense and expenditure on social wealth, for example, health and education etc.; and, finally, (7) "facilitating travel," i.e., communications expenditures.

One can understand the anxiety behind this discussion. The enthusiasm to maintain this loyal position resulted in the emphasis being placed entirely on the "quantified actions" rather than on the "purposes." This is underlined by two concerns: that if the "salutary purpose" is given priority over the "quantified actions" this may affect the sphere of rites of worship, as we said above, and thus jeopardize the cohesiveness of the community. But surely, one can insist that no matter how much one ratiocinates about the quantities of worship rites, these cannot be allowed to change. The reason for this is that besides their inherent salutary effects, they have become anchoring

16. Ibid., vol. 1, p. 275.

points for the cohesive life of the community, which cannot be abandoned merely by the reasoning of individuals. For the Muslim community has, per se, acquired a kind of transcendent cosmic status, to use Walī Allāh's notion, which it is neither possible nor desirable to undo.

Yet, no matter how important the "quantified actions" may be in the "religious" sector proper, in the social sector it is lethal for the individual and even more for the community to substitute these for salutary purposes. In the above-given example of *zakāt* this substitution has wreaked such havoc that it has destroyed the efficacy of this universal institution. The law of *zakāt*, as it came to be elaborated by Muslim jurists, basing themselves on the "quantified actions" performed in the Prophet's days concerning collecting and expending *zakāt*, instead of correctly reading the purpose of the Qur'ān on the subject in terms of all services for the welfare of the communities, tied it down to the rates of *zakāt* (2½ percent of wealth that is in the possession of an owner for a period of one calendar year) appointed by the Prophet apparently in view of the needs of the Islamic society then, and the manner and matter of revenue collection and its expenditure. Despite distortions of the classical legal formulation which are still being perpetuated, "reformers" all over the Muslim world are vociferously demanding that the fiscal system of Muslim countries must be "Islamized." No one has to date dared, or even cared, to reformulate the law.

To return to Shāh Walī Allāh, his teaching on the development of human society and the role of politics and religion therein has something novel despite his debt to al-Fārābī and Ibn Khaldūn. For one thing, his discussion of the human psychological typologies and their roles in the development of the religious–political–cultural complex is definitely a new contribution to "ethics" in Islam. He distinguishes two broad types of people insofar as the acquisition of virtue and happiness is concerned. The first is the type of person whose nature is characterized by "tension" (*tajāzub*, literally, to pull between the angelic forces and the lower self).[17] This type attains virtue by totally negating the lower, animal side and "taking off." Some people are of this type who, despite cultivating harsh and severe disciplinary regimens on themselves, do not share much of the substance of virtue. The second type is that of reconciliation or synthesis (*iṣlāḥ*), and constitutes the bulk of humankind. Because the aim of the

17. Ibid., vol. 1, p. 110.

Sharīʿa is to cater for the majority of humankind and raise its standard, the prophets, under the inspiration and with the support of *al-malaʾ al-aʿlā* (the Supernal Plenum), direct their mission primarily to this second type.

According to Shāh Walī Allāh members of the first type, although they are great persons in their own right, cannot serve as models for humankind, and prophetic revelation only indirectly refers to them. An elaboration of the point is that the first type of achievement comes about at the hands of people in whom there is intense tension between their animal and angelic sides, and this kind is very rare. They are able to achieve their end through strenuous exercises and intense devotion, which are very uncommon. The leaders of this type are people who have abandoned their livelihoods and can provide no guidance for the affairs of this world. In fact, they have to sacrifice a great deal of the spiritual benefits of this world. Because these people have an internal struggle, they have to neglect either the spiritual success of contributing to human development (*irtifāqāt*) in this world or spiritual success in the hereafter. If the majority of people were to follow this path the world would be destroyed, and if this was imposed on all people it would be like obliging someone with an impossibility because human development has become like part of the very nature of the human race.

> As for the second type, its leaders are inspired men (*al-mufahhimūn*) who have synthesized [their animal and angelic natures]. These people supply the leadership of mankind both in religion and in the world simultaneously. It is their mission that is accepted [by people] and it is their example that is followed [by them]. In this type falls the perfection of those who are synthetic figures (*musṭaliḥīn*) and who are the front-runners of virtue (*al-sābiqīn aṣḥāb al-yamīn*). Most people follow this orientation. Both intelligent and unintelligent and those who undertake tasks and those who do not, are able to follow it. It entails no particular hardship. It suffices a person to keep his soul on the straight path, to rectify its crookedness and to safeguard it against the expected afflictions of the next life.[18]

Shāh Walī Allāh goes on to tell us that there are many ways in which the human personality can be developed to cultivate the perfection of the second (synthetic) type of person. But he underlines in particular that the

18. Ibid.

cultivation of four major virtues constitutes such perfection. The first of them is physical purity or cleanliness (*ṭahāra*).[19] Physical cleanliness is no small matter since physical filth and an atmosphere of squalor (*najāsa*) depresses the soul and renders it highly incompatible with itself. Physical purity is the closest condition of the *nasama*, the Arabic equivalent of the Greek *pneuma*, a subtle body inside the coarse material body. It is this element that is the carrier of the "spirit of life" (*rūḥ al-ḥayāt*) and the instrument of sense-perception and imagination. It is in close proximity to the state of the *al-malaʾ al-aʿlā* in its vivid purity and light, at the level of day-to-day practical life.[20] The second virtue is the sense of humility before God (*ikhbāt lillāh*) as a psychological phenomenon, the characteristics of human spirit (*nasama*) closest to the condition of the *al-malaʾ al-aʿlā* in their worship of God and their losing themselves in His majesty. This state is induced in a person when they reflect upon God's great works of creation as reminders of Him. It resembles the state of mind of the person-in-the-street who chances to catch a glimpse of the royal glory of the king and the display of his majesty and awe. The third virtue is magnanimity (*samāḥa*) which is the capacity of a person easily to get over the sense of loss over a precious thing and the ability to transcend the myopic effects of being temporarily immersed in some physical pleasure or anger. Such persons find positive peace and tranquillity soon after mental anguish, whose evil effects they are able to wipe out soon, and thus regain their personal integrity. Because this is a generic virtue, it has many subdivisions in accordance with the object or activity concerned. Finally, the fourth quality is justice (*ʿadāla*) where a person is able to fit into social life with positive results for himself and the social weal. This, as we pointed out earlier, is the central requirement of *al-malaʾ al-aʿlā*. And when a person has fully developed this capacity and accomplished tasks for the improvement of society, he becomes a member of the *al-malaʾ al-aʿlā* itself. These four virtues together constitute the nature (*fiṭra*) upon which God founded the creation of humanity (Q. 30:30).

We underlined earlier the importance of volitional human actions for the building up of the character of the human psyche and the human moral personality. We also pointed out at some length why the *Sharīʿa* made actions, rather than inner dispositions and states, the basis of judgment

19. Ibid., vol. 1, p. 111.
20. Ibid.

(*madār al-ḥukm*). This is because, as we learnt in the first place, actions do create, in varying degrees of perfection, the inner states and disposition, as well as the meanings of these actions in the human personality. Further, and even more importantly, since human beings are essentially social, action must assume the central place in judging human behavior, and not just the inner states. This is what, in fact, gives the *Sharīʿa* its very *raison d'être*. In view of the development of the human species, action is of the essence. Inner states, important as they are, are relevant only to test the individual.

This development of human society from the primitive condition to the most advanced state is described by Shāh Walī Allāh in terms of *irtifāqāt* or cultural development, wherein he distinguishes four stages. The first stage or *irtifāq* is the condition of the primitive person. It must be remembered that in all these stages, all the requirements of the specific human form find expression. The only difference among the different stages is that in the latter, more developed stages, these expressions become more refined and sophisticated, thus transforming the quality of life, but not its very nature. Thus, our thinker does not believe that in the earliest stages of human existence a person had a strictly individual life. The cave-dwellers, for example, who only hunted for themselves, had no idea of any human organization whatsoever. They were also devoid of all religious instinct. For Walī Allāh humankind had a gregarious life, however rudimentary, from the very beginning. If so, then some sort of elemental socio-political organization as well as a kind of instinct-based nature religion should have existed. This is because all these are essential requirements of the specific form of humanity, and none of them can lag behind the others in manifesting themselves.

What happens in the subsequent stages of *irtifāqī* development is that human relationships – social and political – become more refined, organized, and complex. Arts and crafts become more developed; the aesthetic sense becomes more refined and differentiated. Education and communication undergo changes. From the beginnings of human society languages began to develop, along with the use of gesture. Human thought becomes far more *complex,* comprehensive, and capable of capturing truth better, and communicates more effectively. In the second *irtifāq* stage, family life improves in its arrangement. Better shelters are built, more variety of foods is cultivated and consumed, and medical art takes a definite shape. Man becomes the head of the family; marital and other social institutions become well formed.

At the third *irtifāq*, political institutions called "kingdoms" become well organized and fully functioning, although these remain of a local type. For example, kings rule through well-defined and complex administrative structures. By this stage, the human moral and religious senses are also maturing. The natural instinctive guidance (*ilhāmāt ṭabīʿiyya*) never ceases, but in most social, cultural, and technical fields reason takes over, while even the sphere of instinctive religious guidance becomes highly rationalized. Because of the maturity of the moral and religious senses, humankind looks beyond the immediate, the here and the now. Selfish individual and tribal interests gradually disappear, and judgments become more and more universalized or universalizable. This quality of striving towards the universal has always been part of human nature, but has tended to be muted by the strength of the animal impulses. The same is the case with many or most individual human beings in their childhood until they grow up and their senses mature. So, early in human history, human beings were like children, but not like beasts as many biological evolutionists think. Of course the very emergence of humanity requires that the laws of our specific form (*ṣūra nawʿiyya*) express themselves. Nevertheless, there still are and always will be "defective specimens" (*ashkhāṣ mukhdaja*) whose matter disobeys the demands of the laws ingrained in their primordial forms. The vast majority of people, however, respond admirably to these requirements. It is these people who contribute creatively to human progress in all spheres, spiritual, moral and cultural, who are the solid link between living humanity and the Supernal Plenum at all stages of human history.

At the stage of the fourth *irtifāq*, humankind develops simultaneously an international or universal political order and a universal religion with its universal mores and universal or universalizable law. Here the universal sense (*raʾy kullī*) reaches its zenith. Before we go on to discuss this universalism, it is interesting to note that Shāh Walī Allāh does not envisage or recommend that all societies merge to form one colorless humanity and lose their cultural distinctions. He stresses the importance of customs distinctive to every culture and that these customs, unless they become harmful and distorted, must be retained. When customs do become distorted, he says, they ought to be reformed rather than abrogated and replaced.

> You should know that customs in relation to socio-cutural utilities (*irtifāqāt*) are like the heart is in relation to the body of man. [Establishing these customs] were the primary aim of the laws of religions (*sharāʾiʿ*) and the essential subject of discussion of the divinely revealed norms (*nawamīs*) ... These [customs] have primary reasons for their origins stemming, for example, from the formulation of sages and instinctive inspiration by God ... [Secondly], there are reasons for their widespread acceptance among people such as being the adopted practice (*sunna*) of a monarch with a large number of subjects. Or, they can be a conscious elaboration of what people generally and instinctively feel ... [Thirdly] there are reasons why the masses tenaciously cling to them out of fear of being suddenly struck by the unseen [with evil consequences] if these [customs/*sunna*] are abandoned ...[21]
>
> Now, all these customs (*sunan*) are true and right in their origins because they preserve the correct cultural–moral values (*irtifāqāt ṣāliḥa*) and lead individual humans to their perfection in thought and practice. And were it not for these [customs], most people would have been associated with animals ... If a person is asked why he went through a whole set of imposed rules and rituals, he can give no other reply than [to] say: "because everyone else does the same!" And should he profoundly exert himself in thinking he may find some vague inkling in his mind, but he will never be able to express his thoughts clearly, let alone elaborate its moral–cultural bases. This man, if he did not follow such a *sunna*, would most likely have become indistinguishable from a beast.[22]
>
> Sometimes, however, these [customs] become incorporated into error in such a manner that people become confused in knowing the correct custom (*sunna*). This happens, for instance, when leadership falls into the hands of a myopic group that ignores universal salutary ends and interests. This results in: developing bestial characteristics like robbery and plundering; carnal characteristics like homosexuality and effeminate conduct; harmful economic practices such as usury and other commercial malpractice; conspicuous spending in clothing and entertainment which

21. Ibid., vol. 1, p. 103.
22. Ibid.

> force them to ponder new means of generating income; excessive indulgence in amusement and self-gratification; ... imposing exorbitant taxes, as well as destructive taxes on subjects ... [In short, customs that are established under circumstances] when people begin to treat others in ways in which they would not like others to treat them. And, if people do not object to these ways because of the influence and power of the perpetrators, then more wayward people will join them and give them support to expend their energies in popularizing such practices. Things come to a pass when even those in whom there exist no strong inclination towards good or its opposite also come to support such practices because they see influential people indulging in them. Perhaps it may be that good people find constructive ways too demanding.[23]
>
> In the meanwhile, those sound in nature maintain a low profile and do not mix with others. They hide their bitterness and the result is that an undesirable practice (*sunna*) takes root and becomes strong. But in such a situation it becomes incumbent upon those people who think in terms of universal good, to try their utmost in order to spread the truth and make it effective and to extinguish falsehood and contain it. This may often be only possible by after mutual enmities and battles occur. These (corrective moral actions) may be regarded to be among the highest form of virtue.[24]

Much more explicit and elaborate on the subject is the following statement which, in all probability, had been influenced by Ibn Khaldūn as well.

> You must realize that it is not in accordance with God's pleasure that [particularly] the second and the third *irtifāq* [i.e., social and central political organization] be abandoned. Nor has any of the Prophets, peace be upon them, ordered this. The truth is not at all as some people have who fled to the mountains have thought it to be. In so doing they have totally abandoned social intercourse, both in good and in evil, and have joined the ranks of wild animals ... But the Prophets, on whom be peace, have ordered moderation in matters of culture (*irtifāqāt*): neither should people sink into luxury like Persian monarchs [of the Prophet's day], nor should their condition deteriorate to that of the inhabitants of high mountains, becoming like wild beasts. Here we find two mutually

23. Ibid., vol. 1, pp. 103–104.
24. Ibid., vol. 1, p. 103.

contradictory arguments. The one says that [a certain amount of] comfort and luxury are good because it leads to a healthy human temperament and a balanced morality. This comfort allows certain traits to become evident which distinguishes humans from the rest of the animals. [Traits] like stupidity and moral inability arise from a lack of culture (*tadbīr*). The other argument says that comfort and luxury are evil, leading to disputes, inordinate labor and drudgery. [Comfort and luxury] also make people ignore the [higher] unseen (*ghayb*) dimension of their nature and make them disregard those matters related to the hereafter. For this reason, the middle way is desirable: preserve culture that is also accompanied by God's worship and ethical behavior. This is in order [to produce] a spiritually cultivated life and to utilize all opportunities to attend to the Omnipotent.[25]

What each Prophet brought from God, may He be exalted, in this connection is [the following]. [The Prophet] looks at what his people already possess in terms of etiquette of eating and drinking, [customs] of clothing and building, and other forms of cultural amenities; as well as their customs of marriage, the conduct of spouses, their ways of buying and selling; their deterrents against the breaking of laws and their judicial processes etc. If the dictates of universal good are in accord with what people already have, there is no sense in changing anything nor in providing substitutes or altering any part of it in favor of something else. The proper thing to do, rather, is to exhort people to continue implementing what they already have as well as to confirm their beliefs in these practices, and guide them to the salutary purposes (*maṣāliḥ*) they contain.

But if people's practices do not quite tally with these dictates of universal good, there may be a need to alter certain things or eliminate them. [This can] lead to some people being harmed by others, or to be absorbed in worldly pleasures and serve as an impediment to doing good to others. [These latter practices lead] to over-indulgence in amusements which end up in the neglect of both this world and the next. Even under such circumstances it is not proper [for the Prophet] to impose something totally foreign on them [people]. He should, rather, introduce something similar to what they possess, or that which resembles the practices of their model ancestors. In sum, he should introduce something that their rational sensibilities would not reject, but rather find it comfortable as a truth . . . Surely, he [the Prophet] must straighten out the deviant customs

25. Ibid., vol. 1, p. 219.

and restore ailing ones to health. For example, the practice of usury was prevalent among the Arabs, so it was prohibited.[26]

At the time of ᶜAbd al-Muṭṭalib [the Prophet's grandfather], blood-money for murder was ten camels. But when ᶜAbd al-Muṭṭalib saw that this did not deter people, he raised it to one hundred camels and then the Prophet confirmed it ... Indeed, if you have enough perspicacity and knew the wisdom of legislation, you would know that even in the sphere of ritual worship, the Prophets, peace be upon them, did not introduce anything for which some parallel did not exist among their people, even though they wiped out the distortions of the times of barbarity (*jāhiliyya*).

Know that since the Persians and Byzantines continuously governed by hereditary rule for centuries, they became indulgent with the pleasures of life and ignored the hereafter. Satan took control of them, making them enjoy life's comforts to the point that they began to compete with each other in their indulgences. Experts from all over the world would provide them with sophisticated ways of entertainment and luxurious living. Their internecine competitiveness went so far that it is said that if any of their prominent men wore a belt or a hat costing less than a hundred thousand dirhams, they would put him to shame ... What you see today in the behavior of the rulers of your own lands eliminates any need of these [old] stories being repeated ... From this there arose an incurable illness that infected all of the organs of the city-state (*madīna*). The greatest calamity was that the markets and administrators, poor and rich, became a victim of this disease ... unleashing on all endless kinds and various forms of concerns and anxieties. This is because such luxuries could not be afforded except by spending huge sums of money. Such money cannot be gained except by multiplying taxes and levying it upon peasants, traders and people of other professions, while crushing them in the process. If these people refuse to pay taxes, they will be opposed and tortured. And, if they obey [these demands] they are reduced to donkeys and cattle ... which are acquired only to be used for certain needs. Therefore, these people were given respite from hardship until they could not even raise their hopes towards attaining the happiness of the hereafter. In fact they are incapable of doing so.

There would be vast territories wherein no one was concerned with religion and higher values. These luxuries also necessitated that certain people be available whose livelihood only consisted in preparing delicious foods, making luxurious clothes and erecting great buildings

26. Ibid., vol. 1, p. 220.

> and other such things. These would be acquired at the expense of neglecting the basic necessities of production [such as agriculture] upon which human life depends. Even ordinary people felt obliged to imitate these leaders in these matters [of pomp and luxury]. [If they do not conform] they carried no weight, nor gained consideration. Hence everyone became dependent upon the ruler (*khalīfa*). Sometimes they claimed to be soldiers or government administrators, having as a goal not the necessities of life, but following the decadent ways of their ancestors. Others claimed to be poets, it being the practice of kings to reward them. Some people put on the cloaks of the pious and the ascetics, making it difficult for the rulers to ignore them. Thus, these various groups of people made life difficult for each other. Their livelihood depended solely on companionship of rulers in terms of pleasing them, flattering them or providing entertaining conversations. All their thoughts were devoted to these wasteful tasks. When this lifestyle became prevalent, people's mental life became degraded and they became strangers to good human morals.
>
> If you wish to really understand this disease, observe those people who do not have the institution of kingship and who are not indulgent to the pleasures of culinary delight and costly clothing. You would find every individual among them master of his own affairs. He does not carry the burden of heavy taxes on his back. They can, therefore, afford to devote themselves to matters of piety and faith. Then just imagine if they had a monarchy and the aristocratic practices accompanying it that would subjugate the people and oppress them. When this general calamity spread and this sickness intensified [in the Iranian and Byzantine monarchies] God and His angels close to Him became angry with them. God's pleasure was in treating this sickness by cutting off its very root. Thus He raised up an unlettered Prophet who had never mingled with Iranians and the Byzantines nor had he cultivated their [decadent] customs. And He made this Prophet the standard whereby good guidance pleasing to God could be discerned.[27]

When human society reaches the level of the final and fourth *irtifāq*, it simultaneously matures spiritually, morally, and intellectually and is ready to form a human family. As we have seen in the preceding quotation, it is neither possible nor desirable to eliminate cultural differences, which constitute the richness of mankind. The fourth *irtifāq* ushers in an era of

27. Ibid., vol. 1, p. 222.

internationalism where all people, with all their variety, shed their insularity. This requires the simultaneous emergence of political and religious unity so that humanity as a whole – soul, intellect, and body – rises to a new level of universal consciousness. Hence the rise of Islam as a religion, which assumes and subsumes earlier religions and the universal political caliphate (*al-khalīfa al-kubrā*) that includes all local and regional political authorities. Indeed, at this level, religious and political dimensions of human existence became unified in the sense that political life and public institutions are subservient to the moral–spiritual imperatives of religion, and politics ceases to be an autonomous and independent area of human life. All these points are treated in varying degrees of elaboration in the following section by Shāh Walī Allāh, which I quote in full.

> Examine all the religions on the face of the earth. Do thou find any incompatibility therein from what I have informed you [about them] in the preceding chapter? By God, not at all! Every religion believes in the truth of the promulgator of that religion, honors him, and thinks him to be perfect and matchless. This is because they have witnessed him to be steadfast in obedience to God, produce miraculous acts, and that his prayers are answered. [They also witness him] establish laws, including penal laws, and [establish] deterrents from crime, without which no religious community can flourish ... Every people has a custom (*sunna*) and a law (*sharīᶜa*) whereby the practices of the earliest generations are followed, and the conduct of the founders of the religion and its leaders is preferred [to all else]. Thus, its foundations are strengthened and its pillars reinforced so that its followers defend it and champion it and expend of their lives and properties for its sake. And all this is achieved through firm planning as well as solid and purposive observance of the interests of the people. This is what the masses do not understand.
>
> Since every people became mortgaged to a religion and claimed to possess [separate] customs and ways and trumpeted these claims with their mouths and fought over it with their swords, transgression occurred among them. Either, because some undeserving person took charge, or because the laws became imperceptibly mixed up with undesirable innovations. Or, [another reason] was because the leaders ignored their tasks and neglected much of what needed to be carefully preserved.

Thus less than a little remained of the original teaching.[28] Meanwhile, each community vilified the other through repudiation and clashes, resulting in the truth being buried. Therefore, the urgent need arose for a rightly guided leader to arise, who should conduct himself vis a vis religions [as] a righteous ruler (*khalīfa*) deals with unjust monarchs. There is a lesson for you in what the translator of *Kalīla wa Dimna* from Sanskrit to Persian had to say about the confusion and mixing of religion. He wanted to find the truth about this but could attain very little. Historians have also described the conditions of the Age of Barbarity before Islam and the disarray and confusion of their religions.

Now, of course this leader (*imām*) who unites the various communities into one religion requires new principles, different from those we mentioned earlier. One of them is that he would invite one group to the right path, purify and reform them. Thereafter, he would use them as his organs in order to wage a worldwide struggle and spread them out to the four corners of the world. This is the meaning of God's saying: "You are the best community produced for mankind." (Q. 3:110) This is because it is not possible for this leader to personally struggle against an unlimited number of nations. For if this was the case, then it would have required that the content of his law (*sharī*^{c}*a*) be compatible with the natural religion of people of sound and moderate climates, both Arabs and non-Arabs. Then, he must consider what his own people possess by way of knowledge and culture and that he would have to attend to their needs more than that of others. He would have to compel all of humanity to follow that specifc law (*sharī*^{c}*a*). This is because he cannot afford to leave this matter to the discretion of each community or to the discretion of the leaders of each age. For to do so would be to forfeit the original goal of legislation (*tashrī*^{c}). Nor can he [the leader] study the [law] of all the peoples and implement all of it, and therefore legislate for each one of them severally. For it is next to impossible that he can comprehend the customs and cultures of all peoples, given the differences in regions and their mutually opposed religions. The mass of transmitters have been unable to successfully transmit a single law (*sharī*^{c}*a-Islam*). How do you think they will succeed in transmitting different laws? For the most part, the submission and acceptance [of religion] by other peoples occurs only after much effort and long periods of time, not co-extensive to the lifetime of the prophet. This can be demonstrated by the present

28. [Fazlur Rahman translated idiomatically. In the original text a classical Arabic idiomatic expression is used that refers to campsite remains that are so few that there is no trace of Umm Awfa.]

living religions. For example, from among the early contemporary generations of Jews, Christians and Muslims, only a few people believed. But later each group became ascendent. Therefore, nothing is better or easier except for the Prophet to take into account the customs of his own people to whom he was sent [in the first instance] in matters of religious symbols (*shaᶜāʾir*), penal legislation (*ḥudūd*) and in matters of cultural norms (*irtifāqāt*). However, he should not make the field [of thought and legislation] too narrow for others who would succeed him, but leave it flexible.

The earliest generations [of religious tradition] find it easy to accept their Sharīᶜa, with the full consent of their hearts and on the basis of their cultural customs. For later generations this commitment is facilitated by their attachment to the character of their religious leaders and their rulers (*khulafāʾ*). Such is the nature of people in all ages, past and present. Now, the people living in regions of sound climate that is conducive to the production of moderate human temperament were all under the rule of two great kings at that time [i.e., during the rise of Islam]. One was the Khusrau, who ruled ᶜIrāq, the Yemen, Khurasan and other territories in that region. The rulers of Transoxiana and India were under him and paid tribute to him annually. The other was the Caesar who ruled Syria, Egypt, North Africa as well as certain other African countries who paid tribute to him. To destroy the power of these two emperors and to dominate their kingdoms was tantamount to dominating the whole earth. The luxurious life-style of these two had penetrated all the countries under their suzerainty. Thus [there was a necessity] to alter those [indulgent] customs and to prevent people from following them, as a summary warning to all other countries [what to expect], even if their state of affairs changed afterwards. In fact the [Iranian Prince] Hurmazān admitted some of this when ᶜUmar, may God be pleased with him, sought his advice about fighting the non-Arab countries [in the East]. As for the other far-flung regions of the earth, which are not conducive to a balanced temperament, they do not count for much in terms of universal human development. For this reason the Prophet, peace be upon him [is reported to have] said: “Leave the Turks alone as long they leave you alone and keep peace with the Ethiopians as long as they leave you in peace.”

In sum, when God, may He be exalted, wanted to straighten up the religion that had become crooked, and produce for a corrupt humanity a community that would command good and prohibit evil and change their cultural patterns, this depended upon the fall of these two states [Byzantium and Persia]. This could only be facilitated by an intervention in their affairs. For indeed their condition was apt to influence the rest of the temperate world. God therefore decreed the fall of these empires. And the Prophet, peace be upon him, foretold: "The Khusrau has perished and his empire terminated and the Caesar has perished and his empire terminated."

Another principle was that the faith promulgated by [the imām] should contain, as an integral part, the establishment of a universal caliphate. And he should make his successor rulers from among his city-men and co-tribesmen, people who had been brought up in that culture with those customs... Among the co-tribesmen of the Prophet, the sense of religious honor would be corroborated by that of tribal honor, and their greatness and nobility would corroborate the greatness and nobility of the promulgator of the religion himself. This is illustrated by the Prophet's saying: "The rulers shall be from the Quraysh." And he commanded that the Caliphs must undertake the spread and consolidation of the faith, hence the statement of Abū Bakr, may God be pleased with him (to the Muslims): "You will remain on this religion so long as your political leaders remain faithful to it."

Another principle is that he must ensure that this religion is made supreme over all other religions. And none may remain without submitting to the faith no matter who is raised in might and who is laid low in the process. People, thus, would come to be divided in three groups. There are those who accept the faith both externally and with their hearts. And there are those who submit to it only externally, despite themselves, because they have no alternative. And then there are those despicable ones who reject it, but whose labor is used for harvesting, threshing and other crafts and industries, just as animals are employed in agriculture and to haul burdens. And he [the *imām*] would impose upon them the deterrent burden of paying the poll-tax in humiliation.

Now, the factors which make for the supremacy of the faith are several. One of them is the public promulgation of the rites of this faith over those of all other faiths. These rites have to be an open, public affair that will mark out the promulgator of this faith from all others. For example, the practice of circumcision, respect for mosques, giving the daily call to prayer, observing Friday service and the performance of other congregational assemblies. Another [factor] is that other religions be prevented from exalting their rites over those of Islam in public. Another [factor] is that Muslims and non-Muslims not be regarded as equals in retaliation (*qiṣāṣ*), blood money (*diya*), nor in the matter of marriage. Nor may [non-Muslims] be employed as high administrators so that they may decide to accept Islam.

The [fourth] factor is that the common people be obligated to undertake to carry out symbolic acts of virtue and avoid evil acts. He must impose these sternly upon them. But he must not reveal to them much of the real spirit of these symbolic acts. Rather, he must leave them no choice in matters of the *Sharīʿa*. As for the science of inner meanings and spirit of the law, which constitute the source of detailed legislation, he must leave it undisclosed. Those who may attain it will be firmly grounded in knowledge. This is because most people who are the subjects of obligation do not and cannot know the real purposes to be served by these laws. They must be codified concretely so that all can act upon them. If people are given the slightest concession in respect of any of these laws; or if they are told that the real purpose of the law is different from these symbolic acts, then they would employ an undesirable latitude in devising all sorts of pseudo-theories and would deviate widely [from the true path]. The result would be that what God intended [by these laws] would never be fulfilled. And God knows best.

Finally, the [fifth] factor is that mere conquest does not remove the veils of the hearts. For it may be that [conquered people] may relapse into unbelief after some time. Therefore, it is necessary that the truth of the faith be established either by demonstrated rational proofs or by persuasive rhetoric. This is to ensure that in ordinary people's minds it becomes clear not [to] accept these other [non-prophetic] religions. This is to ensure that it becomes clear to ordinary people that they should not accept these [non-prophetic] religions. That is because they do not have origins that are traceable to an infallible source; nor are they compatible with the laws of Islam; and that they had been subject to distortion and misinterpretation. These distortions and misinterpretations should be corrected in the public eye. The strong points of the upright religion [of Islam] should be clarified, so that it becomes clear that this religion is natural and liberal, that its laws are not obscure. Instead, reason can recognize their beauty, that in it night is as clear as day, and that these customs [*sunna*] are the most beneficial for the masses. And it [Islam] comes closest to what they still possess uncorrupted from the legacy of their ancient Prophets, peace be upon them. And God knows best.[29]

Conclusion

Earlier in this chapter we had stated and criticized Shāh Walī Allāh's view that even when no salutary purpose (*maṣlaḥa*) is violated, the quantities (*maqādīr*) prescribed by the *Sharīʿa* may not be altered. We also saw earlier that according to him, the pleasure of the Supernal Plenum (*al-malaʾ al-aʿla*) has become directly connected with the external actions prescribed by the *Sharīʿa*, rather than with the inner meanings or the salutary purposes envisaged by the *Sharīʿa*. Consistent with this, he has also held that the great religious reformers or the prophets have been people who had synthesized their animal and angelic selves. He criticized those spiritual heroes who had negated or destroyed their animal selves and survived only with their angelic selves. The reason for this was that such people cannot serve as models for the common person. Therefore it is only the prophetic model that can promulgate religions, get the masses behind them, and reform the latter. So far, this stand has been remarkably consistent both within itself and with the orthodox view. In our criticism, we had pointed out that that rather than attach the "pleasure" of the Supernal Plenum with the external shell of human actions, it would be better to attach it to the being of the community. It would thus be appropriate to say that since the community has carved out a metaphysical status with the *al-malaʾ al-aʿla*, capricious changes in quantities, depending on the will of an individual, cannot be allowed, no matter how noble and plausible the motivations. This is because this would be disruptive of the very being of the community.

In the last part of the last quote from Walī Allāh, we are faced with a doctrine of intellectual elitism that the orthodox ʿulamāʾ will not accept even in principle. For although the ʿulamāʾ have in practice behaved as an elite beyond the average person, they have never been elitist in theory. They have never held that the inner meanings or salutary purposes of the *Sharīʿa* are exclusively their property. They have always kept the door open to anyone who will learn and understand. The theory of Shāh Walī Allāh expounded above as the "symbolic" rites and laws that should be brutally

29. Shāh Walī Allāh, *Ḥujjat Allāh*, vol. 1, pp. 247–251.

imposed upon the common person, from whom the inner meanings must be guarded and kept a secret, is a travesty of the democratic impulse of the Qurʾān. For indeed, the Qurʾān places the entire responsibility for understanding as well as implementing the Islamic imperatives on the community and not upon any elite. Here, Shāh Walī Allāh has been obviously influenced by the elitist legacy of the Muslim philosophers, and perhaps more directly by certain works of al-Ghazālī. This passage also practically sets to naught the entire drift of his thought outlined earlier and epitomized by us in the preceding passage concerning the importance of action and its quantification and the role of the community.

POSTSCRIPT

As this work and others attest, Fazlur Rahman was a radical intellectual for his time. He tried to open doors. Some of the doors on which he knocked were closed for so long that even their keys were lost. That was the case with his exploration of the encounter of revelation and history through the mind of the Prophet. He also tried to explore the broader thematics of Muslim thought at a time when it could best be characterized by atrophy and excessive fragmentation. Of course, he gave life to the intellectual legacy of medieval Muslim thought and explored its layers, its creases, and opened its contradictions, contingency, ambiguity, and complexity. And yet we must recognize that Fazlur Rahman was uncomfortable with contingency, relativity, and undecidability and for this reason he sought certainty, finality, a conclusion and end to certain moral and intellectual questions. He was very much positioned between the rationality of Arabo-Islamic and Western Enlightenment thought. He was professor of Islamic "thought," with the emphasis on *thought*, ideas, and *cogito*. His belief in modernity, renewal, and progress was not open and undecided, but rather one that contained within it a rational teleology. There is something Hegelian about it, in that he seemed to believe in the necessity of what comes into existence, if only to change it in future in certain instances. What happens, must happen because it "ought" to happen, as if there is a given normativeness to it. This is especially true when one looks at an event in the past such as the normative model of the prophetic society or some other high point of Muslim intellectual achievement during the ᶜAbbāsid period. In such an instance there arises the erroneous belief that if re-created and simulated, the same necessary conditions that existed in the past will reproduce the ideal conditions for the resurrection of the past or something similar, in the present. Distance in time, it has been observed, creates an intellectual illusion just as distance in space provokes a sensory illusion. There is an illusion that the past is a workable model for the present and the future. It is an analogy-based mindset. For this reason the limited metaphorical imagination employed in Muslim legal and ethical thought, which legitimizes only analogical thinking (*qiyās*), may have to be revisited. This form of thinking maps the present and future only in terms of and on the template of the past. The present and future only have legitimacy if they can find a precedent, irrespective of whether it is remote, which acts as their moral vector.[1] This is one reason why Fazlur Rahman could not endorse contemporary Islamic fundamentalism – it remained attached to a past utopia, without having a *telos*.

Like that of many modernists, Fazlur Rahman's thought is rooted in a metaphysics, a worldview that privileges the abstract and rational over the real. He tried to wed logic to existence; thought to movement; and necessity to freedom. This means that thought can flourish only in the element of necessity and essence, while *becoming* can only be appropriated at the expense of what is self-evidently definitive for such unfolding, namely contingency. Thought can construct a system at a high price by saying no to reality. Fazlur Rahman had to do battle with reality and the existential flux. His concern was to create a world in the flux and change of internal time consciousness; he wanted both intentional life and genesis.

This is a postscript, not a conclusion. This book can only come to an end, but cannot conclude. For indeed an ending is also an opening. It is the perpetual openness of the issues that Fazlur Rahman raised that will occupy us in future. His responses to historical issues, as well as his interpretation of events, are provisional just as the counter-claims will also be conditional and incomplete. What gives it this openness is the shimmer or ray of a radical in the work of Fazlur Rahman. He for instance recognizes the radical nature of Qurʾān hermeneutics that will be required if Muslim thought is to be effective. It will cause disruptions and displace the inherited notions of exegesis and revelation. In the intellectual portraits of radical figures such as al-Ghazālī, Ibn Taymiyya, and Shāh Walī Allāh he sought inspiration in order to provide Muslim intellectual thinking with

1. See Laroui, *Crisis of the Arab Intellectual.*

models of hope. It is a hope that does not see the utopian moment in the past but in the future. It is a hope that is derived from the prophetic spirit in the figure of the prophet Ibrāhīm (Abraham), whom the poet-philosopher Muḥammad Iqbāl held out as a paradigm of hope. "This age is in search of its Abraham," Iqbāl said. It will be a generation that is inspired and emboldened by the ardor, courage, love and excessive devotion of Ibrāhīm that becomes the symbol of supreme obedience to God, even if it means breaking the normal and agreed rules of the time. For it was Ibrāhīm who against the law of the sanctity of life was prepared to sacrifice his son, the "idol" in the heart or ego of the father. This he did to obey only God, irrespective of the rules of history, in order to make new history or to change the course of humankind. Fazlur Rahman provided us with one road map of that path of hope and for that we are in all his debt.

GLOSSARY

ahl al-kalām	proponents of dialectical theology
ahl al-nuṣūṣ	jurists who rely on Sharīʿa texts
ʿālim, pl. *ʿulamāʾ*	lit."learned," scholar
al-amr waʾl-nahy	commands and prohibitions
al-malaʾ al-aʿlā	the Supernal Plenum
ʿaql	reason
baqāʾ	survival
baqāʾ fī ʾl-fanāʾ	"survival-in-annihilation"
dīn	religion
falsafa	philosophy
fanāʾ	annihilation
fanāʾ fī ʾl-baqāʾ	"annihilation-in-survival"
faqīh, pl. *fuqahāʾ*	jurist
fāsiq	sinner, heretic
fāsiq millī	grave sinner who remains within the pale of Islam
fatwā, pl. *fatāwā*	authoritative legal opinion, legal response/responsa
fiqh	law, jurisprudence
fitna, pl. *fitan*	strife, civil war
ghayb	unknown
ḥadīth, pl. *aḥādīth*	prophetic report or tradition
ḥadīth qudsī	holy tradition or non-Qurʾānic prophetic report
ḥazīrat al-quds	the holy precinct or enclosure
ijmāʿ	consensus
ijtihād	independent thinking by a master jurist
ikhtilāf	dispute

ᶜilm, pl. *ᶜulūm*	knowledge
ᶜilm al-kalām	dialectical theology
ᶜilm al-khilāf	science of legal disagreement
ᶜilm uṣūl al-dīn	science of the principles of faith or religion
ᶜilm uṣūl al-fiqh	science of the principles of law, legal theory
imām, pl. *aʾimma*	religious leader
īmān	faith
irjāʾ	postponement; suspension of judgment; predestination; political quietism
irtifāq, pl. *irtifāqāt*	development
jabr	predestination
jamāᶜa	community
jamāᶜat al-muslimīn	the community of Muslims
kāfir	unbeliever
kāfir millī	grave sinner who remains within the pale of Islam
kalām	dialectical theology; speech
khilāfiyāt	science of legal differences
kufr	unbelief
madrasa	school, center of orthodox learning
maṣlaḥa, pl. *maṣāliḥ*	good, salutary, public interest, common weal
muḥaddith, pl. *muḥaddithūn*	traditionalist, *ḥadīth* scholar
mujaddid	renewer of faith
mujtahid	master jurist
muʾmin	believer
murjiʾa	one who postpones ethical judgment
mushrik, pl. *mushrikūn*	polytheist
mutakallim, pl. *mutakallimūn*	theologian
muwaḥḥid	monotheist
naṣṣ, pl. *nuṣuṣ*	clear text, designation
qadar	free will
qadarīyya	doctrine of free will
qaṭᶜī	certainty; apodictic
qaṭᶜiyya	decisive, certain
qiyās	analogical reasoning

ṣaḥīḥ	legitimate, sound
salaf	early fathers of the religion
shakhṣ akbar	the universe: lit.,“the greatest person”
sharʿ	revelation
sharīʿa, pl. *sharāʾiʿ*	revealed law
sunna, pl. *sunan*	custom, practice
tafsīr	Qurʾāniʿ exegesis
tajallī, pl. *tajalliyāt*	self-manifestation
taṣawwuf	mysticism
tawḥīd	monotheism, oneness of God
taʾwīl	interpretation
umma	community
ʿumūm khalqihi	universal creative will
umūr kullīyya	universal principles
uṣūl	lit.“roots”; foundations; legal principles
uṣūl al-dīn	principles of faith
uṣūliyyūn	legal theorists
waḥdat ʾl-wujūd	unity of being
waḥy	revelation; intuitive knowledge
zakāt	annual tax

BIBLIOGRAPHY

Works by Fazlur Rahman

BOOKS

Avicenna's De Anima. New York, Oxford University Press, 1959

Avicenna's Psychology. New York, Oxford University Press, 1952; repr. Westport, Conn., Hyperion Press, 1981

Health and Medicine in the Islamic Tradition. New York, The Crossroad Publishing Company, 1987

Intikhābāt-i Maktūbāt-i Shaykh Aḥmad Sirhindī; Selected Letters of Shaykh Aḥmad Sirhindī. Karachi, lqbal Academy, 1968

Islam. 2nd ed., Chicago, University of Chicago Press, 1979

Islam and Modernity: Transformation of an Intellectual Tradition. Chicago, University of Chicago Press, 1982

Islamic Methodology in History. Karachi, Iqbal Academy, 1965

Major Themes of the Qur'ān. Chicago, Bibliotheca Islamica, 1980

The Philosophy of Mulla Ṣadrā – Ṣadr al-Dīn al-Shirāzī. Albany, State University of New York Press, 1975

Prophecy in Islam: Philosophy and Orthodoxy. 2nd ed., Chicago, University of Chicago Press, 1979

ARTICLES

"Approaches to Islam in Religious Studies: A Review," in *Approaches to Islam in Religious Studies*, ed. Richard C. Martin. Tucson, University of Arizona Press, 1985

"Avicenna and Orthodox Islam: An Interpretive Note on the Composition of his System," in *Harry Austryn Wolfson, Jubilee Volume on the Occasion of his Seventy-Fifth Birthday*, vol. 2. Jerusalem, American Academy for Jewish Research, 1965

"Challenge of Modern Ideas and Social Values to Muslim Society," *International Islamic Colloquium, University of Punjab, 1957–1958, Papers.* Lahore, Punjab University Press, 1960

"The Concept of Ḥadd in Islamic Law," *Islamic Studies*, 4:3 (September 1965), pp. 237–251

"Concepts of Sunnah, Ijtihād and Ijmā^c in the Early Period," *Islamic Studies*, 1:1 (March 1962), pp. 5–21

"Controversy Over the Muslim Family Laws Ordinance," *South Asian Politics and Religion*, ed. Donald Smith. Princeton, N. J., Princeton University Press, 1966

"Currents of Religious Thought in Pakistan," *Islamic Studies*, 7:1 (March 1968), pp. 1–7

"Divine Revelation and the Prophet," *Hamdard Islamicus*, 1:2 (Fall 1978), pp. 66–72

"Dream, Imagination and ^cĀlam al-Mithāl," *Islamic Studies*, 3:2 (June 1964), pp. 167–180; repr. in *The Dream and Human Societies*, ed. G. E. von Grunebaum and R. Caillois. Berkeley, University of California Press, 1966

"Economic Principles of Islam," *Islamic Studies*, 8:1 (March 1969), pp. 1–8

"Essence and Existence in Avicenna," *Mediaeval and Renaissance Studies*, 4 (1958), pp. 1–16

"Essence and Existence in Ibn Sina: The Myth and Reality," *Hamdard Islamicus*, 4:1 (Spring 1981), pp. 3–14

"The Eternity of the World and the Heavenly Bodies," in *Essays on Islamic Philosophy and Science*, ed. George F. Hourani. Albany, State University of New York Press, 1975

"Evolution of Soviet Policy Toward Muslims in Russia: 1917–1965," *Journal of the Institute for Muslim Minority Affairs*, 1:2 (1979–1980), pp. 28–46

"Fazlur Rahman: My Belief-in-Action," in *The Courage of Conviction*, ed. Phillip L. Berman. Santa Barbara, Dodd, Mead & Company, 1985

"Functional Interdependence of Law and Theology," in *Theology and Law: Second Giorgio Levi Della Vida Conference, 1969*, ed. G. E. von Grunebaum. Wiesbaden, Otto Harrassowitz, 1971

"The God–World Relationship in Mulla Sadra," in *Essays on Islamic Philosophy and Science*, ed. George F. Hourani. Albany, State University of New York Press, 1975

"Ibn Sina," in *A History of Muslim Philosophy*, vol. 1, ed. M. M. Sharif. Wiesbaden, Otto Harrassowitz, 1963

"The Ideological Experience of Pakistan," *Islam and the Modern Age*, 2:4 (November 1970), pp. 1–20

"The Impact of Modernity on Islam," *Islamic Studies*, 5:2 (June 1966), pp. 113–128; also in *Religious Plurality and World Community*, ed. Edward J. Jurji. Leiden, E. J. Brill, 1969

"Implementation of the Islamic Concept of State in the Pakistani Milieu," *Islamic Studies*, 6:3 (September 1967), pp. 205–224; Reprinted as "Islamic Concept of State," in *Islam in Transition: Muslim Perspectives*, ed. John J. Donahue and John L. Esposito. New York, Oxford University Press, 1982

"L'Intellectus Acquistus in Alfarabi," *Giornale critico della Filosofia Italiana*, 3:7 (1953), pp. 351–357

"Internal Religious Developments in the Present Century Islam," *Journal of World History*, 2 (1954–1955), pp. 862–879

"Iqbal, the Visionary; Jinnah, the Technician; and Pakistan, the Reality," in *Iqbal, Jinnah and Pakistan: The Vision and the Reality*, ed. C. M. Naim. Syracuse, Syracuse University, 1979

"Iqbal's Idea of the Muslim," *Islamic Studies*, 2:4 (December 1963), pp. 439–445

"Islam: Challenges and Opportunities," in *Islam: Past Influence and Present Challenge, in Honor of W. M. Watt*, ed. Alford T. Welch and Pierre Cachia. Albany, State University of New York Press, 1979

"Islam and the Constitutional Problem of Pakistan," *Studia Islamica*, 32 (1970), pp. 275–287

"Islam and Health: Some Theological, Historical and Sociological Perspectives," *Hamdard Islamicus*, 5:4 (Winter 1982), pp. 75–88

"Islam: Legacy and Contemporary Challenge," *Islamic Studies*, 19:4 (Winter 1980), pp. 235–246; repr. in *Islam in the Contemporary World*, ed. Cyriac Pullapilly. Notre Dame, Ind., Cross Roads Books, 1980

"Islam and Medicine – A General Overview," *Perspectives in Biology and Medicine*, 27:4 (Summer 1984), pp. 585–597

"Islam in Pakistan," *Journal of South Asian and Middle Eastern Studies*, 3:4 (1985), pp. 34–61

"Islam and Political Action: Politics in the Service of Religion," in *Cities of God: Faith, Politics and Pluralism in Judaism, Christianity and Islam*, ed. Nigel Biggar, Jamie S. Scott, and William Schweiker. New York, Greenwood Press, 1986

"Islam and the Problem of Economic Justice," *The Pakistan Economist*, 24 (August 1974), pp. 14–39
"Islam and the New Constitution of Pakistan," *Journal of Asian and African Studies*, 8 (1973), pp. 190–204; repr. in *Contemporary Problems of Pakistan*, ed. J. Henry Korson. Leiden, E. J. Brill, 1974
"Islamic Modernism: Its Scope, Method and Alternative," *International Journal of Middle Eastern Studies*, 1 (1970), pp. 317–333
"Islamic Studies and the Future of Islam," in *Islamic Studies: A Tradition and its Problems. Seventh Giorgio Della Vida Conference*, 1979, ed. Malcolm H. Kerr. Malibu, Undena Publications, 1980
"Islamic Thought in the India–Pakistan Subcontinent and the Middle East," *Journal of Near Eastern Studies*, 32 (1973), pp. 194–200
"Islamization of Knowledge: A Response."*American Journal of Islamic Social Sciences*, 5 (1988), pp. 3–11
"Islam's Attitude Toward Judaism," *The Muslim World*, 72 (1982), pp. 1–13
"Law and Ethics in Islam," in *Ethics in Islam: Ninth Giorgio Levi Della Vida Conference, 1983, in Honor of Fazlur Rahman*, ed. R. Hovannisian. Malibu, Undena Publications, 1985
"Law of Rebellion in Islam," in *Islam in the Modern World: 1983 Paine Lectures in Religion*, eighth series, ed. Jill Raitt. Columbia, University of Missouri-Columbia, 1983
"Letter to the Editor," *The Pakistan Times*. Lahore, December 25, 1967
"The Message and the Messenger," in *Islam: The Religious and Political Life of a World Comnunity*, ed. Marjorie Kelly. New York, Praeger Publications, 1984
"Mīr Dāmād's Concept of Ḥudūth Dahrī: A Contribution to the Study of the God–World Relationship Theories in Safavid Iran," *Journal of Near Eastern Studies*, 39 (1980), pp. 139–150
"Modern Muslim Thought," *Muslim World*, 45 (1955), pp. 16–25
"Modern Thought in Islam," in *Colloquium on Islamic Culture in its Relation to the Contemporary World, September, 1953*. Princeton, Princeton University Press, c. 1954
"Muhammad Iqbal and Ataturk's Reform," *Journal of Near Eastern Studies*, 43 (1984), pp. 157–162
"Mulla Sadra's Theory of Knowledge," *Philosophical Forum*, 4 (1972), pp. 141–152
"Muslim Attitudes Toward Family Planning," paper presented at Lahore seminar in March 1964

"Muslim Modernism in the Indo-Pakistan Sub-Continent," *Bulletin of the School of Oriental and African Studies*, 21 (1958), pp. 82–99

"A Muslim Response to Christian Particularity and the Faith of Islam," in *Christian Faith in a Religiously Plural World*, ed. Donald G. Dawe and John B. Carman. Maryknoll, N. Y., Orbis Books, 1978

"Notification of the Government of Pakistan," *Pakistan Gazette*. July, 1961

"Pre-foundations of the Muslim Community in Mecca," *Studia Islamica*, 43 (1976), pp. 5–24

"The Principle of Shūra and the Role of the Ummah in Islam," *Journal of the University of Baluchistan*, 1982; repr. in *American Journal of Islamic Studies*, 1 (1984), pp. 1–9 and in *State Politics and Islam*, ed. Mumtaz Ahmad. Indianapolis, American Trust Publications, 1986

"The Post-Formative Developments in Islam," *Islamic Studies*, 1:4 (December 1962), pp. 1–23 and 2:3 (September 1963), pp. 297–316

"The Qurʾānic Concept of God, the Universe and Man," *Islamic Studies*, 6:1 (March 1967), pp. 1–19

"The Qurʾanic Solution of Pakistan's Educational Problem," *Islamic Studies* 6:4 (December 1967), pp. 315–326

"The Religious Situation of Mecca from the Eve of Islam up to the Hijra," *Islamic Studies* 16:4 (Winter 1977), pp. 289–301

"Revival and Reform in Islam," in *Cambridge History of Islam.* ed. P. M. Holt et al., vol. 2. Cambridge, Cambridge University Press, 1970

"Riba and Interest," *Islamic Studies*, 3:1 (March 1964), pp. 1–43

"Roots of Islamic Neo-Fundamentalism," in *Change in the Muslim World*, ed. Philip H. Stoddard, David C. Cuthell and Margaret V. Sullivan. Syracuse, Syracuse University Press, 1981

"Social Change and the Early Sunnah," *Islamic Studies*, 2:2 (June 1963), pp. 159–203

"Some Islamic Issues in the Ayyūb Khān Era," *Essays on Islamic Civilization, Presented to Niyazi Berkes*, ed. Donald P. Little. Leiden, E. J. Brill, 1976

"Some Key Ethical Concepts of the Qurʾān," *Journal of Religious Ethics*, 2 (1983), pp. 170–185

"Some Recent Books on the Qurʾān by Western Authors," *Journal of Religion*, 64:1 (1984), pp. 157–162

"Some Reflections on the Reconstruction of Muslim Society in Pakistan," *Islamic Studies*, 6:2 (June 1967), pp. 103–120

"Sources of Dynamism in Islam,"*Al-Ijtihād*, 15:1 (January 1978), pp. 53–64

"The Status of the Individual in Islam," *Islamic Studies*, 5:4 (December 1966), pp. 319–330

"The Prophet's Society as the Ideal for Contemporary Muslims," *Journal for Islamic Studies*, 6 (1986), pp. 40–51

"Towards Reformulating the Methodology of Islamic Law: Sheikh Yamani on 'Public Interest' in Islamic Law," *New York University Journal of International Law and Politics*, 12:2 (Fall 1979), pp. 219–224

"Translating the Qur'ān," *Religion and Literature*, 20:1, (Spring 1988), pp. 23–30

ENCYCLOPEDIA ARTICLES

Encyclopedia of Philosophy, ed. Paul Edwards. New York, The Macmillan Company and the Free Press, 1967. S.v. "Islamic philosophy"

Encyclopaedia Britannica, 15th edn., ed. Philip W. Goetz. Chicago: Encyclopaedia Brtiannica, Inc., 1974. S.v. "The Legacy of Muhammad"; "Sources of Doctrine and Social Views"; "Doctrines of the Qur'ān"; "Fundamental Practices and Institutions of Islam"; "Theology and Sectarianism"; "Religion and the Arts"

Encyclopaedia of Islam, new ed., ed. H. A. R. Gibb et al. Leiden, E. J. Brill, 1979, S.v. "ᶜAkl"; "Andjuman"; "ᶜAraḍ"; "Bahmanyār"; "Bakā wa Fanā"; "Barāhima"; "Basīṭ wa Murakkab"; "Dhāt"; "Dhawk"

Encyclopedia of Religion, ed. Mircea Eliade. New York, MacMillan Publishing Company, 1987. S.v. "Islām"; "Iqbāl"; "Muḥammad"; "Mulla Ṣadrā"

WORKS TRANSLATED INTO OTHER LANGUAGES

ARABIC

al-Islām wa Ḍarūra-t 'l-Taḥdīth: Naḥw Iḥdāth Taghyīr fī 'l-Taqālīd al-Thaqāfiyya [Islam and Modernity], trans. Ibrāhīm al-ᶜArīs. Beirut, Dār al-Sāqī, 1993

INDONESIAN

Tema Pokok al-Qur'ān [Major Themes of the Qur'ān], ed. Ammar Haryono, trans. Anas Mahyuddin. Bandung, Penerbit Pustaka, 1983

Membuka Pinto Ijtihād [Islamic Methodology in History], ed. Ammar Haryono, trans. Anas Mahyuddin. Bandung, Penerbit Pustaka, 1984

Islam Dan Modernistas, Tentang Transformasi Inteletual [Islam and Modernity], ed. Ammar Haryono, trans. Ahsin Mohammad. Bandung, Penerbit Pustaka, 1985

SERBO-CROAT

Duh Islam [Islam] trans. Andrija Grosberger. Biblioteka Zenit Velike Avanture Coveka Series. Belgrade, Yugoslavia, 1983

TURKISH

Islam, trans. Mehmet Dağ and Mehmet Adyin. Hicri 15, Asir Kullyāt Series no. 2. Ankara, Selçuk Yayinlari, 1981

Ana konulartyla Kuran [Major Themes of the Qur'ān], trans. Alparsalan Açikgenç. Ankara, Feer Yayinlari, 1987

Islāmiyet ve Iktisadi Adalet Meselesi [Islamic Methodology in History], trans. Yusuf Ziya Kavakçi. Islām Ilimer Fakültesis series, no. 4; Tercüme Serisi, no. 1. Ankara, Islāmi Ilimer Fakültesi, 1976

General Bibliography

Adkins, Arthur W. H. *Moral Values and Political Behaviour in Ancient Greece*. London, Chatto & Windus, 1972

al-Anṣārī, Abū Yūsuf Yaᶜqūb b. Ibrāhīm. *Kitāb al-Āthār*, ed. Abū ᵓl-Wafā. Beirut, Dār al-Kutub al-ᶜIlmiyya, n.d

al-Ashᶜarī, Abū l-Ḥasan ᶜAlī b. Ismāᶜīl. *Kitāb al-Lumaᶜ fī l-Radd ᶜalā ahl al-Zaygh wa ᵓl-Bidaᶜ*, ed. ᶜAbd al-ᶜAzīz ᶜIzz al-Dīn Sayrawān. Beirut, Dār Lubnān li ᵓl-Ṭibāᶜa wa ᵓl-Nashr, 1408/1987

Maqālāt al-Islāmiyyīn wa Ikhtilāf al-Muṣallīn, ed. Muḥammad Muḥyī al-Dīn ᶜAbd al-Ḥamīd, 2 vols. Cairo, Maktaba al-Nahḍa al-Miṣriyya, 1369/1950

Berman, Phillip L. (ed). *The Courage of Conviction*. New York, Dodd, Mean & Company, 1985

Betti, Emilio. "Die Hermeneutik als allgemeine Methodik der Geisteswissenschaften [Hermeneutics as the General Methodology of the *Geisteswissenschaften*]," in *Contemporary Hermeneutics: Hermeneutics as Method, Philosophy and Critique*, ed. Josef Bleicher. London, Routledge & Kegan Paul, 1980

Bleicher, Josef (ed.). *Contemporary Hermeneutics: Hermeneutics as Method, Philosophy and Critique*. London, Routledge & Kegan Paul, 1980

al-Dhahabī, Shams al-Dīn Abū ᶜAbd Allāh Muḥammad b. Aḥmad b. ᶜUthmān. *Mīzān al-Iᶜtidāl fī Naqd al-Rijāl*, ed.ᶜAlī Muḥammad al-Bajāwī and Fatḥiyya ᶜAlī al-Bajāwī, 6 vols. Beirut, Dār al-Fikr, n.d

Siyar Aᶜlām al-Nubalāᵓ, ed. Shuᶜayb al-Arnaᵓūṭ, 25 vols. Beirut, Muᵓassasa al-Risāla, 1990/1410

al-Dihlāwī, Shāh Walī Allāh b. ᶜAbd al-Raḥīm. *Fuyūḍ al-Ḥaramayn*: Mushāhadāt wa Maᶜārif (Urdu), trans. Muḥammad Surūr. Karachi, Dār al-Ishāᶜat, 1414 A.H.

Ḥujjat Allāh al-Bāligha, ed. Al-Sayyid Sābiq, 2 vols. Cairo, Dār al-Kutub al-Ḥadītha, n.d.; trans. as *The Conclusive Argument from God: Shāh Walī Allāh of Delhi's Ḥujjat Allāh al-Bāligha*, trans. Mercia K. Hermansen. Leiden, E. J. Brill, 1996

Izālat al-Khafāʾ ᶜan Khilāfa-t al-Khulafāʾ. Lahore, Suhayl Academy, 1396/1976

"al-Juzʾ al-Laṭīf fī Tarjama al-ᶜAbd al-Ḍaᶜīf," *Journal and Proceedings of the Asiatic Society of Bengal*, 8 (1912), pp. 161–175, English trans. by Mawlawi M. Hidayat Husain with original Persian text

Saṭaᶜāt, ed. Ghulām Muṣṭafā al-Qāsimī. Hyderabad, Sind, Shāh Walī Allāh Academy, 1964

Gadamer, Hans-Georg. *Truth and Method*. New York, Cross Road, 1975

al-Ghazālī, Abū Ḥāmid Muḥammad b. Muḥammad. *Iḥyā ᶜUlūm al-Dīn*, 5 vols. Cairo, Muʾassasa al-Ḥalabī wa Shurakāʾahu, 1967/1387

Jawāhir al-Qurʾān, 2nd ed. Beirut, Dār al-Āfāq al-Jadīda, 1977

al-Mustaṣfā fī ᶜIlm al-Uṣūl, ed. Muḥammad ᶜAbd al-Salām ᶜAbd al-Thānī. Beirut, Dār al-Kutub al-ᶜIlmiyya, 1413/1993

al-Munqidh min al-Ḍalāl, in *Majmūᶜ Rasāʾil al-Imām al-Ghazālī*, ed. Aḥmad Shams al-Dīn. Beirut, Dār al-Kutub al-ᶜIlmiyya, 1409/1988

Hodgson, Marshall G. S. "How Did the Early Shīᶜa Become Sectarian?" *Journal of the American Oriental Society*, 75 (1955)

The Venture of Islam, 3 vols. Chicago, University of Chicago Press, 1974

Homerin, Th. Emil, *From Arab Poet to Muslim Saint*. Columbia, S.C., University of South Carolina Press, 1994

Hourani, George F. *Islamic Rationalism: The Ethics of ᶜAbd al-Jabbār*. Oxford, Clarendon Press, 1971

Ibn ᶜArabī, Muḥyī al-Dīn. *Fuṣūs al-Ḥikam*, ed. Abū ʾl-ᶜAlā ᶜAfīfī. Beirut, Dār al-Kitāb al-ᶜArabī, n.d

Ibn Bābwayh, Abū Jaᶜfar Muḥammad b. ᶜAlī b. al-Ḥusayn al-Qummī. *Kitāb al-Tawḥīd*, ed. al-Sayyid Hāshim al-Ḥusaynī al-Ṭahrānī. Beirut, Dār al-Maᶜrifa, n.d.

Ibn Taymiyya, Abū ʾl-ᶜAbbās Taqī al-Dīn Aḥmad b. ᶜAbd al-Ḥalīm. *Kitāb al-Istiqāma*, ed. Muḥammad Rashād Sālim, 2nd ed., 2 vols. Cairo, Maktabat al-Sunna, 1409

Majmūᶜ Fatāwā, ed. ᶜAbd al-Raḥmān b. Muḥammad b. Qāsim al-ᶜĀṣimiyyi al-Najdī al-Ḥanbalī, 36 vols. no place, n.p., 1418/1997

Jesse, Mary Catherine. "A Modern Muslim Intellectual: The Thought of Fazlur Rahman with Special Reference to Reason," unpublished MA diss., University of Regina, Saskatchewan, Canada, 1991

al-Junayd, Abū ᵓl-Qāsim b. Muḥammad, *Rasāᵓil al-Junayd – The Life, Personality and Writings of al-Junayd: A Study of a Third/Ninth Century Mystic*, ed. and trans. Ali Hassan Abdel-Kader. London, Luzac & Co, 1962

al-Kulaynī, Abū Jaᶜfar Muḥammad b. Yaᶜqūb b. Isḥāq al-Rāzī, *al-Uṣūl min al-Kāfī*, ed. ᶜAli Akbar al-Ghifārī, 8 vols., 3rd ed. Tehran, Dār al-Kutub al-Islāmiyya, 1388 A.H.

Laroui, Abdallah. *The Crisis of the Arab Intellectual: Traditionalism or Historicism*, trans. Diarmid Cammell. Berkeley, University of California Press, 1976

MacIntyre, Alasdair C. *After Virtue*. Notre Dame, Ind., University of Notre Dame Press, 1981

Massignon, Louis. *Essai sur les origines du lexique technique de la mystique mussulmane*, trans. as *Essay on the Origins of the Technical Language of Islamic Mysticism*, trans. and intro. Benjamin Clark. Notre Dame, Ind., University of Notre Dame Press, 1997

The Passion of al-Hallāj: Mystic and Martyr, trans. Herbert Mason. Princeton, Princeton University Press, 1982

Metcalf, Barbara Daly. *Islamic Revival in British India: Deoband, 1860–1900*. Princeton, Princeton University Press, 1982

Moosa, Ebrahim. "Law as Simulacrum," *History of Religions*, 38:1 (August 1998)

Mūsā, Ibrāhīm (Ebrahim Moosa), "al-Ḥadātha wa ᵓl-Tajdīd: Dirāsa Muqārana fi Mawqif Faḍl ᵓl-Raḥmān wa Ḥasan Ḥanafī," in *Jadal ᵓl-Ana wa ᵓl-Ākhar: Qirāᵓāt Naqdiyya fī Fikr Ḥasan Ḥanafī fī ᶜĪd Mīlādihī al-Sittīn*, ed. Aḥmad ᶜAbd al-Ḥalīm ᶜAṭiyya. Cairo: Maktaba Madbū lī al-Ṣaghīr, 1997

Muslim b. al-Ḥajjāj al-Qushayrī al-Nīsābūrī. *Jāmiᶜ al-Ṣaḥīḥ*, ed. Ayman Ibrāhīm al-Zamīlī, Muḥammad Mahdī al-Sayyid, and Maḥmūd Khalīl, 5 vols. Beirut, Ālam al-Kutub, 1998

al-Qummī: see Ibn Bābwayh

Rizvi, S. Athar Abbas. *Muslim Revivalist Movements in Northern India in the Sixteenth and Seventeenth Centuries*. Agra, Agra University, Lucknow, 1965

St. John of the Cross. *Dark Night of the Soul*, ed., trans., and intro. E. Allison Peers from the critical ed. of P. Silverio de Santa Teresa, 3rd rev. ed. Garden City, N.Y., Image Books, 1959 al-Ṣarīfīnī, Ibrāhīm b. Muḥammad b. al-Azhar. "al-Muntakhab min Kitāb al-Siyāq li Taʾrīkh Nīsabūr of Abū ʾl-Ḥasan ʿAbd al-Ghāfir al-Fārisī," in *The Histories of Nishapur*, ed. Richard N. Frye. Cambridge, Mass., Harvard University Press, 1965

Shāh Walī Allāh: see al-Dihlāwī

al-Sharastānī, Abū ʾl-Fatḥ Muḥammad ʿAbd al-Karīm b. Abī Bakr Aḥmad. *Kitāb al-Milal wa ʾl-Niḥal*, ed. ʿAbd al-ʿAzīz Muḥammad al-Wakīl, 3 vols. Cairo, Muʾassasa al-Ḥalabī, 1387/1968

Sivan, E. *Radical Islam: Medieval Theology and Modern Politics*. New Haven, Yale University Press, 1985

al-Subkī, Tāj al-Dīn. *Ṭabaqāt al-Shārfiʿiyya al-Kubrā*, ed. Maḥmūd Muḥammad Tanāḥī and ʿAbd al-Fattāḥ al-Ḥilw, 10 vols. Cairo, Dār Iḥyāʾ al-Kutub al ʿArabiyya, 1396/1976.

al-Ṭūṣī, Abū Naṣr ʿAbd Allāh b. ʿAli al-Sarrāj, *Kitāb al- Lumaʿ fi ʾl-Taṣawwuf*, ed. Reynold Alleyne Nicholson. London, Luzac & Co., 1963

Underhill, Evelyn. *Mysticism: A Study in the Nature and Development of Man's Spiritual Consciousness*. New York, Meridian Books, 1911

al-ʿUqaylī, Abu Jaʿfar Muḥammad b. ʿAmr b. Mūsā b. Ḥammād al-Makkī. *Kitāb al-Ḍuʿafāʾ al-Kabīr*, ed. ʿAbd al-Muʿṭī Amīn Qalʿajī, 4 vols. Beirut, Dār al-Kutub al-ʿIlmiyya, n.d

van Ess, Josef. *Anfänge muslimischer Theologie: Zwei antiqadaritische Trakate aus dem ersten Jahrhundert der Hiğra*. Beirut, Orient-Institut der Deutschen Morgenländischen Gessellschaft, 1977

Wan Daud, Wan Mohammed Nor. "Islamization of Contemporary Knowledge: A Brief Comparison Between al-Attas and Fazlur Rahman," *al-Shajarah*, 2:1 (1997)

Wasserstrom, Steve. "The Moving Finger Writes: Mughīra b. Saʿīd's Islamic Gnosis and the Myths of its Rejection," *History of Religions*, 25:1 (August 1985)

INDEX